NONE DARE CALL IT TREASON

By
John A. Stormer

D1570001

LIBERTY BELL PRESS
P. O. Box 32   Florissant, Missouri

NONE DARE CALL IT TREASON
A LIBERTY BELL BOOK

To Holly,
May her future be as bright
as mine was at age 5.

© 1964 by John A. Stormer

First Printing, February, 1964—100,000
Second Printing, April, 1964—100,000
Third Printing, April, 1964—100,000
Fourth Printing, May, 1964—100,000
Fifth Printing, May, 1964—100,000
Sixth Printing, June, 1964—100,000
Seventh Printing, June, 1964—100,000
Eighth Printing, June, 1964—100,000
Ninth Printing, July, 1964—100,000
Tenth Printing, July, 1964—100,000
Eleventh Printing, July, 1964—400,000
Twelfth Printing, July, 1964—400,000
Hardcover Edition, July, 1964
Thirteenth Printing, August, 1964—400,000
Fourteenth Printing, August, 1964—400,000
Fifteenth Printing, August, 1964—800,000

Liberty Bell Books are published by
THE LIBERTY BELL PRESS

P. O. Box 32   Florissant, Missouri

Printed in The United States of America

ABOUT THE AUTHOR

John Stormer is, like most young Americans who grew up during the Depression, the product of a conservative home and a liberal education. In the late 1950's he gradually came to realize that the political candidates and philosophies he was asked to support in the voting booth did not reflect the standards and principles he tried to apply in his business and personal life.

He started an intensive study of communism about four years ago, and since then has lectured on college campuses, addressed hundreds of church, civic, political and service organizations, and appeared frequently on radio and television programs.

A frequent visitor to Washington, D. C., he has been a regular participant in conferences and meetings on the inroads made by communism and socialism in America.

In 1962, he left a successful career as editor and general manager of a leading electrical magazine to devote full time to conservative anti-communist activities. He is chairman of the Missouri Federation of Young Republicans and a member of the Republican State Committee of Missouri.

A native of Altoona, Pennsylvania, he attended the Pennsylvania State University and graduated from California's San Jose State College in 1954 after Korean War service as an Air Force historian.

He is a member of Sigma Delta Chi, the professional journalism society, attends a fundamental Christian Church, and has received awards for anti-communism educational activities from Rotary, the Knights of Columbus, and other civic groups.

CONTENTS

Treason doth never prosper, what's the reason?
For if it prosper, none dare call it treason.

— Sir John Harrington, 1561-1612

Chapter 1

Have We Gone Crazy?

> *As long as capitalism and socialism exist we can-
> not live in peace; in the end, one or the other will
> triumph — a funeral dirge will be sung over
> either the Soviet Republics or over world cap-
> italism.* — *V. I. Lenin*[1]

THE COLD WAR is real war. It has already claimed more lives, enslaved more people, and cost more money than any "hot" war in history. Yet, most Americans refuse to admit that we are at war. That is why we are rapidly losing — why America has yet to win its first real victory in 18 years of "cold" war.

Within the framework of the "cold" war there have been "hot" wars in China, Malaya, Indonesia, Algeria, the Congo, Cuba, Iraq, the Gaza Strip, Hungary, Korea, Angola, Burma, Tibet, and Egypt. In 1963, there was fighting in Laos, Viet Nam, and on the Indian-Chinese border, renewed skirmishing along the 38th parallel in Korea, and terrorist activity in Africa. The forces of freedom have lost or will lose them all.

There has been no "big" war because the communists are winning without one.

In 1945, the communists held 160-million Russians in slavery. They controlled a land area smaller than the Russia of the Czars. Soviet industry had been largely destroyed by the Nazi war machine. Communism was a third rate power, militarily, industrially, and economically.

Today, after the United States has spent $600-billion to fight communism and sacrificed the lives of 50,000 of its youth to thwart Red aggression, the Kremlin has grown to become the absolute slavemasters of one-billion human beings. The communists openly control 25% of the earth's land mass. Their puppet, Fidel Castro, has been installed in Cuba, just 90 miles from our shores. The hidden tentacles of the communist conspiracy exert unmeasured influence over the rest of the world.

Where have we failed?

Almost unnoticed by most Americans, Congress while appropriating billions for defense *against* communism, has at the same time given over $6-billion in direct military and economic aid *to the communists*.[2] Here are examples:

> Radar-equipped F-86 jet fighter planes worth over $300,000 each have been sold to the communist dictator of Yugoslavia for $10,000. This "sale" to Tito has been defended because both the Eisenhower and Kennedy Administrations approved it. The planes were said to be "obsolete." Yet, during the Berlin crisis, reactivated U. S. Air National Guard units flew to possible battle against communists in Europe *in even more obsolete* F-84 jets.[3]

Nikita Khrushchev has said that peaceful coexistence involves peaceful economic competition. Our leaders agree, and place great emphasis on this aspect of the cold war in urging disarmament. Why then has the United States . . .

> . . . supplied nuclear reactors to the communist government of Czechoslovakia, railway equipment to Bulgaria, chemical plants to Yugoslavia, and synthetic rubber plants to Soviet Russia? Why has America given Russia the machinery to produce the precision ball bearings used in the guided missiles they "rattle" during every international crisis?[4]

> Why has America built the world's most modern, most highly automated steel finishing plant for the communist government of Poland? Constructed in Warren, Ohio, the plant was dedicated as the *Lenin Steel Works* by the U. S. Ambassador to Poland in July 1961. The American people "lent" the communists $2.5-million to pay for it.[5]

The examples are endless. The failure of Russian agriculture has historically been communism's weakest "link." So, in 1961 . . .

> . . . officials in the U. S. Department of Agriculture and the Commerce Department agreed to sell surplus wheat to the Soviet Union for $.62 per bushel less than the baker who bakes your bread pays for it. Only quick action by an awakening public stopped this folly which would have supplied wheat to ease food shortages and the resultant unrest against the communists in the Soviet Union. The officials who initiated the program are still holding responsible government positions.[6]

Much American aid to communists is hidden in U. S. grants to the United Nations and its specialized agencies. For example, the United Nations Special Fund is giving Castro, the communist dictator of Cuba, funds to bolster his agricultural programs. The American who heads the fund, Paul Hoffman, approved the grant, and the U. S. taxpayer is paying

40% of the total bill of $1.6-million.[7] The grant was made just after the attempted invasion of Cuba failed in April 1961.

Is it any wonder that Nikita Khrushchev predicted confidently in a speech in Bucharest, Rumania on June 19, 1962 that:

> The United States will eventually fly the Communist Red Flag . . . the American people will hoist it themselves.

The communists have sworn to bury us. We are digging our own graves.

Does aid to communism make sense? If, during World War II, anyone had suggested sending food or industrial materials to Nazi Germany, they would have been tried for treason, or carted off to a mental institution. Today, favoring aid to communism is, to some, evidence of good *mental health*.

After years of such folly, where do we stand today in the battle from which, Lenin, first head of communist Russia, said there could be no coexistence, that either capitalism or socialism would emerge triumphant?

Senator Thomas Dodd (D-Conn) is a former FBI man. He's vice chairman of the Senate Internal Security Subcommittee, and a member of the Senate Foreign Relations Committee. Speaking in Los Angeles, California on August 28, 1961, just eight months after President Kennedy was inaugurated, Senator Dodd said:

> There is a developing mood of anger and frustration in this country and there ought to be for we are losing round after round in the Cold War and our people do not like it.
>
> At the close of World War II, our forces stood triumphant on the land and sea and in the air. We had at our command the mightiest array of military power in all history. Yet, the last 16 years have witnessed a calamitous retreat from victory. During all these years we have suffered defeat after defeat at the hands of international communism. We have retreated from position after position and committed folly after folly.[8]

Senator Dodd explained that because such defeats and retreats took place in faraway lands such as Latvia, Poland, Hungary, Czechoslovakia, China, Korea, and Indo-China, Americans were inclined to feel smug and secure. Then, he continued:

> But in December 1958, what many people had considered impossible came to pass. While we stood by in confusion and disarray and apparent helplessness a communist dictator was installed on the island of Cuba, only 90 miles off our own shores. In 1959, Tibet was brutally annexed by the Chinese

communists despite again, the anguished protests of free men throughout the world.

Since the beginning of this year (1961) alone there has been the sealing-off of East Berlin, the disaster in Laos, the fiasco in Cuba, and only last week, the victory of Cheddi Jagan and his communist-dominated Peoples Progressive Party in British Guiana elections.

Everywhere we are on the defensive. Everywhere we find ourselves being pushed back. We have retreated so far that we now stand perilously close to the brink of total disaster.[9]

How close are we to this disaster, the total enslavement of the world? Senator Dodd gave this evaluation:

Last December, I was privileged to speak in the City of Paris and at that time I said if there were another 15 years like the last 15 years there would be no more free world left to defend. In the light of what has happened over the intra-vening eight months since I made that observation in Paris, I feel compelled to revise that timetable.

I do not believe we have 15 years left. The next five years will contain a series of decisive battles which will determine for centuries to come whether mankind is to live in freedom or live in slavery. We stand now, my friends, with our backs to the precipice. We have no more ground to give, no time to lose, no margin for error.[10]

Since Senator Dodd issued that warning in August 1961, America has yielded further ground. The Congo, Algeria, Dutch New Guinea, Laos, Viet Nam, Cuba, Brazil, and the Dominican Republic have had the tentacles of communism drawn more tightly about their throats.

Senator Dodd was not the first to speak out. The warning has been issued many times. Several years ago, General Albert C. Wedemeyer, chief of strategic planners during World War II, appeared before the House Committee on Un-American Activities for a consultation. Wedemeyer was asked:

Based on your background and experience, and current studies of the operation of this conspiracy, how late is it on the communist timetable for world domination?[11]

Richard C. Arens, staff director of the Congressional com-mittee, reported that Wedemeyer dropped his eyes to the floor, looked up, and said:

Sir, my humble, honest judgment is, that it is too late.[12]

Before it was printed, Wedemeyer edited his testimony. He struck out those words and wrote:

I am not completely a pessimist, but it is very, very late. If I were the senior planner in the Soviet hierarchy, I would advise Khrushchev, "Continue to do exactly what you are doing now. Do not involve the Soviet Union in major war, but employ the satellites in brush fires or limited wars against our enemies, the capitalist countries.[13]

That is just what has happened. Khrushchev has threatened nuclear war to get his way. He has employed the satellites in brush fires in Tibet, Laos, Viet Nam, Algeria, the Congo, and most recently, on the Indian-Chinese border.

Consider the sobering implications of Cuba in the perspective of the following words. Written in 1951, they were based on a study of communist sources:

> Communist strategy teaches that there can be no successful revolution followed by the creation of Soviets in any Latin American country unless an internal revolution has been effected within the United States. The Comintern views the Western hemisphere as an integral unit in which the United States must first be *rendered helpless* before a Soviet-type government can be established in any other of the 20 republics in the hemisphere.[14]

Part of a study on Latin American communist activities, this analysis was published by the House Committee on Un-American Activities in a volume entitled, *Soviet Total War*. It was issued on September 30, 1956, *almost two-and-a-half years before Fidel Castro established the first Soviet-type government in the western hemisphere.*

Could the American government possibly have been rendered helpless in the struggle against world communism or is this official analysis wrong?

In 1961, the Senate Internal Security Subcommittee issued a 12-volume study entitled, *Communist Threat to the U. S. Through the Caribbean.* It showed conclusively that Castro could not have brought communism to Cuba *except for the continual aid and assistance of the U. S. State Department.*[15]

Even so, the State Department personnel implicated by the Senate study as being directly involved in Castro's rise to power still held important State Department jobs two years later. William Wieland, a man branded as "either a damn fool or a communist," before the Senate committee has been promoted to the highest foreign service rank and pay.[16]

As head of the State Department Caribbean desk, Wieland received and "buried" continuing intelligence reports which indicated that Castro was a communist.[17] After the U. S. Senate revealed this and other derogatory information, Wieland was promoted and named to the State Department committee studying a revision of *security practices.*[18] He was still employed in the State Department as of February 23, 1963.

Wieland is not an isolated case. John Stewart Service, a career diplomat, was arrested by the FBI on June 7, 1945 for passing secret documents to Soviet espionage agents. He was deeply involved in the communist-influenced web in the State Department which lost China to communism. In the early 1950's, Service was dismissed, but the Supreme Court, without questioning his guilt ordered him reinstated in 1956. The Court's decision was based on the technicality that proper procedures had not been used in firing him.[19] At first assigned to the menial task of handling baggage for diplomats, Service started working his way back up the State Department ladder. By 1961, he occupied a key diplomatic post in Liverpool, England.[20] In 1962, he retired, and is now drawing a pension from the American taxpayers.

Owen Lattimore was deeply involved in the betrayal of China to the communists in the late 1940's. In 1952, the Senate Internal Security Subcommittee found him to have been "a conscious articulate instrument of the Soviet conspiracy"[21] for 15 years. In May 1961, he was granted a passport to go to Outer Mongolia, a communist satellite.

When questioned by newsmen, the State Department said, "He's not there as an official representative, of course, but we are anxious to get his impressions."[22] Four months after Lattimore's return to America, the U. S. agreed to admit Outer Mongolia to the United Nations.

No one *denies* these facts. They are just *ignored*.

Is it possible in view of these facts that the United States government has been rendered helpless in the struggle with communism? It did happen once. The grave question which few appear willing to face today is, "Could it happen again?"

Twenty years ago, similar warning signs were uncovered by the FBI and Congressional investigating committees. In the eight years which passed before the alarms were finally heeded, Alger Hiss had reached a high State Department post and sat at FDR's side. He was there at Yalta when decisions were made which ultimately committed 700-million human beings to communist enslavement.[23] Harry Dexter White, as assistant secretary of the U. S. Treasury, controlled all fiscal matters in which foreign policy was involved.[24] Nathan Witt, as secretary of the National Labor Relations Board, was the Board's top executive officer.[25] He controlled board proceedings and all hiring and firing of NLRB employees. Board actions, under Witt's direction, were the deciding factor in many labor-management negotiations across the country. Lee Pressman was General Counsel of the WPA.[26] John J. Abt was special assistant to the Attorney General.[27] Lauchlin Currie was executive assistant to President Roosevelt.[28] All were identified before Congressional committees as communist agents.

High government officials ignored authoritative reports that these men, and others in equally high places, were Soviet agents. Some warnings came as long as eight years before the conspirators were publicly exposed.[29]

Could such infiltration of American government happen again? Has it happened? We can't know.

In 1954, an order by the President who had pledged to "clean up the mess in Washington" reiterated earlier "gag" rules which placed security files of executive department employees (about 98% of all federal employees) firmly "off-limits" to Congressional investigating committees.[30] The job of uncovering future security risks was thus made nearly impossible.

In a nutshell, America as a nation, and you as an individual, are in trouble. A look at the shrinking map of the free world confirms the warnings of responsible leaders. The future of Americans as a free people is threatened. The continued refusal of elected officials to rid the government service of the Wielands, the Services, the Lattimores, for whatever reason, tells why.

What can we do?

A responsible person must first gather information on which to base his judgments and actions. Motivation without knowledge produces fanaticism. J. Edgar Hoover, director of the Federal Bureau of Investigation has told us:

> Attributing every adversity to communism is not only irrational, but contributes to hysteria and fosters groundless fears. Communism is, indeed, our paramount adversary, and it leans on its credo of invincibility to accomplish its ends. The way to fight it is to study it, understand it, and discover what can be done about it. This cannot be achieved by dawdling at the spring of knowledge; it can only be accomplished by dipping into thoughtful, reliable, and authoritative sources of information.[31]

The study of communism must be approached objectively. For too long Americans have been "paralyzed by politics." They have seen only the mistakes, errors, and omissions of the opposition political party. Leaders of both parties have been at fault. Members of both political parties have blindly supported their own party leadership — and nothing has been done about the very real menace which threatens America.

It is not enough to assess blame or point an accusing finger at past or present political leaders. The guilt also belongs to those apathetic Americans who have ignored warning after warning and let this chain of events continue. The past mistakes, and they are many, must be spotlighted so similar errors can be avoided in the future.

Chapter II

The Origin of Communism

> *Communists everywhere support every revolu-*
> *tionary movement against the existing political*
> *and social order of things. The communists*
> *disdain to conceal their aims. Let the ruling*
> *classes tremble at a communist revolution. The*
> *proletarians have nothing to lose but their*
> *chains. They have a world to win. Working*
> *men of all countries, unite!*
> — *Karl Marx, The Communist Manifesto*

THE STORY OF COMMUNISM is a story of contradictions. Despite Marx's call for the workers of the world to
unite, communism has never been a working class movement.
Its strength is in the intellectual and thought centers of the
world.

Communism is commonly believed to rise out of poverty.
Yet, Fidel Castro was a product, not of the cane fields of
Cuba, but of the halls of Havana University.[1]

Joseph Stalin was not a simple peasant rebelling at the
oppression of the Czar. He became a communist while studying for the priesthood in a Russian Orthodox seminary.[2]

Dr. Cheddi Jagan, communist premier of British Guiana,
became a communist, not as an "exploited" worker on a
plantation of a British colonial colony, but as a dental student
at Chicago's Northwestern University.[3]

The membership of the first Communist spy ring uncovered
in the U. S. Government was not spawned in the sweat shops
of New York's lower east side or the tenant farms of the
South. Alger Hiss, Nathan Witt, Harry Dexter White, Lee
Pressman, John Abt, Lauchlin Currie and their comrades
came to high government posts from Harvard Law School.[4]

The Senate Internal Security Subcommittee's *Handbook for
Americans* delves into why people become Communists. It
says:

> A trite explanation offered by the ill-informed is that com-
> munism is a product of inequalities under our social system.

Hence, these people argue, if we will alleviate these conditions, we will never have to worry about communism . . . The misery theory of communism runs contrary to actual facts in our country. New York State, for example, has approximately 50% of the total Communist Party membership. Yet it is second in terms of per capita income and per capita school expenditures . . . Conversely, Mississippi is lowest in the scale of Communist Party membership but is also lowest in per capita income.

The Senate committee comments on these facts, saying:

The misery theory of communism does not jibe with these figures nor with the fact that such wealthy persons as Frederick Vanderbilt Field, and prominent members of the Hollywood film colony, have been found to be members of the Communist Party. Indeed the misery theory of communism is exactly what the Communists would have us believe, in order to mislead us.[5]

According to John Williamson, then organizational secretary of the Communist Party, USA, writing in the Party's top theoretical journal, *Political Affairs*, for February 1946, "71% of the Party in New York City consists of white collar workers, professionals and housewives."[6]

Communism is a disease of the intellect. It promises universal brotherhood, peace and prosperity to lure humanitarians and idealists into participating in a conspiracy which gains power through deceit and deception and stays in power with brute force.

Communism promises Utopia. It has delivered mass starvation, poverty, and police state terror to its own people and promoted world-wide strife and hatred by pitting race against race, class against class, and religion against religion. Treason, terror, torture, and Moscow-directed wars of "national liberation" spread communist "brotherhood, peace and social justice" around the world.

Communism is frequently described as a philosophy — but it is not a philosophy in which intellectually honest men can believe for long. It is a conspiracy in which hate-driven men participate.

Lenin confirmed this. In his important and authoritative work, *What Is to Be Done,* written in 1902, he set forth his views on the structure of the Communist Party, and said:

Conspiracy is so essential a condition of an organization of this kind that all other conditions . . . must be made to conform with it.[7]

In other words, the philosophy of communism must be

bent and twisted as needed to fit the conspiratorial needs of the situation.

There is much first-hand evidence that Communists quickly see through the fallacies of Marxism-Leninism but continue in the Party as blind believers, as conspirators against the established order, or for the personal power and privilege Party membership gives the select few.

Colonel Frantisek Tisler, former military and air attache in the Czechoslovakian Embassy in Washington, D. C., defected from communism in 1959 and sought permanent asylum in America. A few months later he told his story to the House Committee on Un-American Activities. Tisler said:

> I have not been a believer in communism for a long period of time, although in the early days of my association with the Communist Party of Czechoslovakia I was an ideological believer.
>
> My initial disillusionment with communism in practice began to take place while I was attending Military Staff School in Prague. It was at this school that I witnessed many incidents which proved to me that communism in practice was greatly different from theoretical communism. I was exposed to numerous incidents where members of the Communist Party who were high-ranking officers in the Army took advantage of their position in order to obtain personal advantages and job security. The disillusionment which set in as a result of the excesses . . . began to shatter my faith in Marxism-Leninism.[8]

This realization that communism was not an idealistic philosophy came while Tisler was still a relatively young student officer. He continued as a conspirator for ten years before he defected, rising in that time to a high ranking position in the Party and its international intelligence network.

What is the "philosophy" which traps the student intellectual and transforms him into a conspiring, conforming, never-questioning tool of the Communist Party? How are brilliant young minds twisted to swear that "slavery" is "freedom," "dictatorship" is "democracy" or that "war" is "peace" — *and actually believe that it is so?*

Karl Marx compounded the theories which "explain" all the contradictions. He called it dialectical materialism. Marx, the 19th Century father of communism, was not a worker but a university-trained intellectual with a doctorate in philosophy. Although his ideas have had a deep impact and lasting effect on the intellectual world, he was not an original thinker.

Marx concocted dialectical materialism by blending Feuerbach's atheistic materialism with Hegel's theory that everything in nature is in a state of constant conflict. In its simplest form, dialectic materialism teaches:

All people and things in the universe and the universe itself are simply matter in motion. As matter moves, opposites attract. When the opposites come together, conflict results and from the conflict comes change.

With this theory, Marx explains the origin and development of the universe, everything in it, and all life. Man, plants, animals, and their world are all products of "accumulated accidents." Ignored is the creative force which produced the first "matter" and made it "move" and develop in an orderly way. This First Mover and Great Planner, we know as our Creator, God.

Marx applied his theories of conflict and change to society. Human beings were arbitrarily divided into two classes (opposites). The bourgeoisie (propertied classes) were considered the degenerate class. The proletariat (unpropertied wage earners) was the progressive class.[9]

Communism teaches that a state of continual conflict or class warfare exists between the two groups. In this conflict, according to dialectical materialism, the bourgeoisie will be destroyed. This *change* is "inevitable" and is defined by Marx as *progress*.

SCIENTIFIC SOCIALISM

Marx was a self-proclaimed scientist. His "scientific" theories explained the entire history of man and determined his future. They are to be used to transform man's nature. Being "scientists," communists have certain basic "scientific" laws which underly their beliefs and teaching. They include:

There is no God. When communists deny God, they simultaneously deny every virtue and every value which originates with God. There are no moral absolutes, no right and wrong. The Ten Commandments and the Sermon On The Mount are invalid.[10]

Accepting this concept of "morality," the communists teach that all is right which advances the cause of socialism. All is wrong which impedes its progress. For the communist, to lie, cheat, steal or even murder, is perfectly moral if it advances communism. Conversely, a communist who would refuse to lie, cheat, steal or murder to aid the socialist movement is immoral. In the words of Lenin:

We do not believe in eternal morality — our morality is entirely subordinated to the interests of the class struggle.[11]

The second "scientific" law of communism follows the first logically. It is:

Man is simply matter in motion. As such, he is without soul, spirit, or free will and is not responsible for his own acts.[12]

Marx taught that man was entirely an evolutionary animal, the highest animal form, without significant individual value or eternal life. Man is a body completely describable in terms of the laws of chemistry and physics.

The third "scientific" law, economic determinism, is to be the means for *transforming* man. It states:

Man is an economically determined animal. Qualities of human intelligence, personality, emotional and religious life merely reflect man's economic environment. The evil a man does is just a reflection of his environment.[13]

After coming to this conclusion, Marx taught that the only way man could be improved or changed would be to change or eliminate the evil-producing elements in man's environment. He reasoned that the one common influence in man's life was the economic environment. Mid-19th Century Europe's predominant economic system was a rough-and-tumble combination of feudalism, mercantilism, and free enterprise. Marx called it *capitalism* and blamed it for all the evil in man and the world. He concluded that the only way to eliminate evil and improve man was to destroy capitalism. Marx taught that this was both desirable and historically inevitable because the continued conflict between the classes had to produce *change*.

The inevitable outcome of the class war, according to Marx, was the triumph of the proletariat in a revolution which would destroy a decaying capitalism and replace it with socialism. Under socialism, the dictatorship of the proletariat (Communist Party) would work towards the establishment of communism.

Marx taught that once the material needs of man were satisfied, greed, profit-taking, avarice, and hate would disappear. The State would wither away. There would be no laws or need for a police force. A heaven on earth would result. Man's nature would be magically transformed. Each would work according to his ability. Each would desire to receive only according to his needs.

To reach this goal, the proletariat must achieve control of the entire earth, Marx taught. All poisoning traces of capitalism must be eliminated. In practice, as the communists conquer a country, and if they conquer the world, they are left with those people raised in a capitalist environment. It has formed their character and personality. They will transmit the "illness" to their children.[14]

Being materialist "scientists" the communists do not hesitate. All the "animals" infected with the "disease" of capitalism and freedom must be exterminated. To the communists, this is not murder. Murder means killing for bad reasons. They will kill the bourgeoisie class for a "good" reason, the establishment of world communism. This "end" justifies the "means."[15]

The communists, therefore, are not interested in converting you, the reader, to communism, particularly if you are over 30 years of age. *If you can be lulled into doing nothing to oppose the triumph of world communism, that is enough.* Once the takeover comes, you, like millions of others, who believe in God and man's responsibility for his own life and actions, can be slaughtered like diseased animals or worked to death in slave labor camps or brothels for the Red Army.

The communists are after your children or grandchildren who can still be molded into obedient slaves of the State.

Gus Hall, General Secretary of the Communist Party, USA, told Americans what to expect when the communists take over. Speaking at the funeral of Eugene Dennis in February 1961, Hall said:

> I dream of the hour when the last Congressman is strangled to death on the guts of the last preacher — and since the Christians love to sing about the blood, why not give them a little of it.[16]

WHO WAS MARX?

What sort of man could dream of Utopia, and yet advise, even command his followers to lie, cheat, steal, and commit individual or mass murder to achieve it?[17]

Marx was born in 1818 of scholarly Jewish parents in a Germany which was just becoming a nation. His early life was torn as his family left the Jewish faith and adopted a more "accepted" Protestantism.

His radical ideas, even as a student, caused his ejection from several universities, and he toured the intellectual and political capitals of Europe associating with a varied assortment of revolutionaries and "free thinkers."

The Communist Manifesto, written in conjunction with his friend, Engels, was published before Marx was 30. His major work, the first volume of *Das Kapital,* was completed before Marx was 50.

His marriage resulted in six children. Marx, however, was so engaged in formulating theories to "uplift" the downtrodden masses that he never bothered to accept a job to support his family. Three of his six children died of starvation in infancy. Two others committed suicide. Only one lived to maturity.

Marx, at one point, was so taken up with his concern for "humanity" that when a gift of 160 pounds (about $500) arrived from a rich uncle in Germany, he used the money for a two-month drinking spree with continental intellectuals. His wife, left penniless in London, was evicted from their apartment with the infant children.

During these years, Marx's ideas and philosophy were accepted only by the radical fringe groups which comprised the First International, and his friend and collaborator, Friedrich Engels. Engels, a rich man's son, was Marx's chief source of income. When Marx died, his funeral was attended by only six persons.

THE FABIANS AND THE COMMUNISTS

Following Marx's death in 1883, his theories were made a world force by two developments. They were the rise of the Fabian Society in England and Lenin's Bolshevik movement.

In 1884, a small group of English intellectuals formed the Fabian Society. It was their goal to establish the same classless, godless, socialistic one-world society envisioned by Marx.[18] Leadership of the group was assumed by Beatrice and Sidney Webb and the Irish author and playwright, George Bernard Shaw. Shaw described himself as a "communist"[19] but differed with Marx over how the revolution would be accomplished and by whom. He spelled out these differences in 1901 in his, *Who I Am, What I Think,* when he wrote:

> Marx's *Capital* is not a treatise on Socialism; it is a jeremiad against the bourgeoisie . . . it was supposed to be written for the working class; but the working man respects the bourgeoisie and wants to be a bourgeoisie; Marx never got hold of him for a moment. It was the revolting sons of the bourgeoisie itself, like myself, that painted the flag Red. The middle and upper classes are the revolutionary element in society; the proletariat is the conservative element.[20]

On this basis, Shaw and the Fabians worked for world revolution not through an uprising of the workers but through indoctrination of young scholars. The Fabians believed that eventually these *intellectual* revolutionaries would acquire power and influence in the official and unofficial opinion-making and power-wielding agencies of the world. Then, they could quietly establish a socialistic, one-world order.

Webb formulated the highly successful method these future

rulers would use to change the world. He called it the "doctrine of the inevitability of gradualness." In practice, it has
meant slow, piecemeal changes in existing concepts of law,
morality, government, economics, and education. Each change
is so gradual that the masses never awaken in time to stop
the "inevitable."

Shaw, in the preface to the 1908 edition of *Fabian Essays*,
stated the goal, which was . . .

> . . . to make it as easy and matter-of-course for the ordi-
> nary Englishman to be a Socialist as to be a Liberal or
> Conservative.[21]

Shaw, in his *Intelligent Woman's Guide to Socialism*, explained what life would be like once the new order was
established:

> I also made it clear that Socialism means equality of income
> or nothing, and that under Socialism you would not be allowed
> to be poor. You would be forcibly fed, clothed, lodged, taught,
> and employed whether you liked it or not. If it were dis-
> covered that you had not the character and industry enough to
> be worth all this trouble, you might possibly be executed in a
> kindly manner; but whilst you were permitted to live you
> would have to live well.[22]

The Fabian Socialists rejected all suggestions that they form
a political movement of their own. They planned to spread
their influence by penetrating existing educational institutions,
political parties, the civil service, etc.

As a starting point, the Webbs established the London
School of Economics on the first floor of 10 Adelphi Street in
London. The upper floors were occupied by Shaw and his
wife, Charlotte, who financed the venture. It was from this
humble beginning that the intellectual center of the Fabian
Socialist movement has grown. Today, it has world renown
as a branch of the University of London. Its influence has
been spread around the world by such faculty, students, and
supporters as Harold Laski, Bertrand Russell, Joseph Shum-
peter, John Maynard Keynes, H. G. Wells, and Nehru of
India.

Down through the years, the Fabians, while masquerading
under all sorts of "respected" labels have achieved power
and influence far out of proportion to their numbers, which
have never exceeded about 3,000. By 1889, when the Society
was only six years old and had fewer than 300 members,
two of the group were elected to the London School Board.[23]

When the British Labour Party came to power in 1924,
Fabian leader Ramsey MacDonald was Prime Minister.

Fabian founder, Sidney Webb was Minister of Labour. When the party regained power in 1929, MacDonald was again Prime Minister and 20 Fabians held high positions. Eight served in the Cabinet.[24]

FABIANISM IN AMERICA

The seeds of Fabianism were planted in the United States before the start of the 20th Century. Leading English universities exchanged professors, scholars and writings with top American colleges. Sidney Webb himself came to America in 1888. The following year, his *Socialism in England* was circulated at Harvard and other schools by the American Economic Association.[25] By 1905, American Fabians had formed the Rand School of Social Science in New York and incorporated the Intercollegiate Socialist Society.[26] Within three years, chapters were formed at Harvard, Princeton, Columbia, New York University, and the University of Pennsylvania.[27]

Early adherents of this socialist movement in America included such later day leaders as John Dewey (education), Walter Rauschenbusch (theology), Walter Lippmann (government and press) and Supreme Court Justice Felix Frankfurter. Other equally skilled but lesser known theorists and conspirators operated in other fields. Their beliefs, their careers, their methods, and the influence they have exerted on American life will be explored later.

THE COMMUNISTS

Meanwhile, the other movement which was to make Marxism a potent, dynamic world force developed on the Continent in 1903. Nicolai Lenin, a Russian revolutionary and an ardent student of Marx, came to believe, like George Bernard Shaw, that it was neither possible nor desirable to sell Marx's theories to the masses.

Lenin and about seven followers split away during a meeting of socialist radicals in London, forming the Bolshevik "splinter group."

Lenin's major contribution to the world struggle, and the development which made Marx's theories a potent force, was his plan for organizing the Communist Party along conspiratorial lines. Lenin said:

> The only serious organizational principle the active workers of our movement can accept is strict secrecy, strict selection of members, and the training of professional revolutionaries.[28]

Lenin's plan called for a small, highly disciplined, well-schooled, and fanatically dedicated core of revolutionaries. They would "combine illegal forms of struggle with every form of legal struggle."[29] Their power would be multiplied through infiltration and penetration of existing governments, organizations and groups. Thus, they would redirect the influence, prestige, and power of capitalistic institutions for the benefit of world communism. In the labor field, for example, Lenin advised his followers:

> . . . to agree to any and every sacrifice, and even — if need be — to resort to all sorts of devices, maneuvers, and illegal methods, to evasion and subterfuge, in order to penetrate the trade unions, to remain in them, and to carry on Communist work in them at all costs.[30]

Another of Lenin's strategies for "multiplying" the power and strength of the small, dedicated group of revolutionaries was to exploit the differences between non-communist groups so as to "incite one against another."[31] Stalin later spelled out Lenin's theory in detail in the book, *Stalin on China*. He said:

> The most powerful enemy can be conquered only by exerting the utmost effort, and by *necessarily*, thoroughly, carefully, attentively and skillfully taking advantage of every, even the smallest "rift" among enemies, of every antagonism of interest among the bourgeoisie of the various countries and among the various groups or types of bourgeoisie within the various countries, and also by taking advantage of every, even the smallest opportunity of gaining a mass ally, even though this ally be temporary, vacillating, unstable, unreliable, and conditional. Those who do not understand this do not understand even a particle of Marxism, or of scientific, modern Socialism.[32]

A classic example of such modern socialism in practice was Fidel Castro's takeover of Cuba. Of Castro's followers, about 98% were non-communists. The Cuban people would not have tolerated the bearded fanatic had they known he was a communist. Yet, by exploiting their differences with another anti-communist, Batista, Castro was able to get the temporary support he needed to establish a communist regime in Cuba.

In America, communists inspired the student riots against the House Committee on Un-American Activities in San Francisco on May 12-14, 1960 using the same tactics. A small group of trained, dedicated communist agents fanned the differences between the students and a committee of Congress. Several thousand non-communist students were stirred, first to demonstrate, and then to riot against lawful authority.[33]

An excellent example has been the implementation of a special Moscow Manifesto issued December 5, 1960 which ordered the destruction of the growing free world anti-communist movement.[34] American communists alone could not neutralize the fast-growing grass roots anti-communist movement in the the United States with a frontal attack.

Instead, the comparatively few communist agents in America and their more numerous fellow-travellers in liberal movements, the press, and other opinion-making positions have worked to pit sizeable segments of the American people against other Americans dedicated to fighting communists. The methods and tactics used are documented in a fascinating study by the Senate Internal Security Subcommittee[35] which is discussed at length in Chapter IV.

Teaching these and equally devious methods, and by restricting their recruits to only the most fanatical and dedicated, Lenin and the seven followers who formed the Bolshevik movement, swelled their ranks to 17 in the first four years. They returned to London in 1907 and searched for a suitable meeting place.

The Fabians came to their assistance. Ramsey MacDonald, later a three-time prime minister of Great Britain arranged for Lenin's Bolsheviks to use the Brotherhood Church in London's east end.[36] The conference was financed by a grant of 3,000 pounds from Joseph Fels, a wealthy American soap manufacturer and a leader of the Fabian movement.[37]

Just ten years later, Lenin's 17 followers had become 40,000. They subverted and seized the Democratic Socialist Republic established by Kerensky in Russia after the fall of the Czar in 1917.

The early cooperation between the communists and the Fabians, without which Lenin might have faded into oblivion, has continued as a united "anti-capitalistic front" down through the years. The Fabians abhor the "aggressive nature of communism" but cannot attack communism's godless, classless, socialistic one-world concepts because the Fabian creed is based on the same goals and beliefs.

Fabians flock to the defense of the accused communist, as did Eleanor Roosevelt, Dean Rusk, Adlai Stevenson, and Felix Frankfurter when a top State Department official, Alger Hiss, was exposed as a communist agent.

"He can't be a communist," the Fabian reasons, "he believes the same as I do." When Hiss and Lauchlin Currie, executive assistant to President Roosevelt, were exposed, Mrs.

Roosevelt's outburst was typical. In her syndicated column, *My Day,* for August 16, 1948, she said:

> Smearing good people like Alger Hiss and Lauchlin Currie, is, I think, unforgiveable.

Currie later fled the country rather than answer questions about his activities. Hiss served five years in the Federal Penitentiary for perjury after denying his participation in a Soviet spy ring.

Fabians are frequently found working in the communist camp under the mistaken belief that *they* are "using the communists." To a degree this accounts for the long lists of communist-front affiliations accumulated by many leading "liberals." The mutual goals of the communists and socialist "liberals" often lead to false accusations against "liberals" by those who assume "if he waddles like a duck, quacks like a duck, and is found in a flock of ducks, he must be a duck."

Indeed the loudest praise for the Russian communist "experiment" has come, not from Moscow-directed communists, but from Fabians. Fabian founder George Bernard Shaw, on a trip to Russia in 1931, stated in a speech in Moscow:

> It is a real comfort to me, an old man, to be able to step into my grave with the knowledge that the civilization of the world will be saved . . . It is here in Russia that I have actually been convinced that the new Communist system is capable of leading mankind out of its present crisis, and saving it from complete anarchy and ruin.[38]

Shaw, after an earlier trip to Russia, had praised Lenin as the "greatest Fabian of them all." Shaw helped formulate the Fabian concept of eventual control through infiltration, permeation, penetration, and piecemeal acquisition of power. He strongly admired Lenin and Stalin. He said they publicly championed Marx and his principles of world revolution while quietly working to communize one country after another. They used, Shaw said, *the Fabian methods of stealth, intrigue, subversion, and the deception of never calling socialism by its right name.*[39]

THE PLAN

After only seven years at the head of the world's first communist state, Lenin died in 1924. Before he died, he formulated a plan for world domination. Summarized and paraphrased, Lenin's plan stated:

> First, we will take eastern Europe, then the masses of Asia, then we will encircle the United States which will be the last bastian of capitalism. We will not have to attack. It will fall like an overripe fruit into our hands.

Chapter III

The Growth of World Communism

> *I do not believe in communism any more than you do but there is nothing wrong with the communists in this country; several of the best friends I have got are communists.*
> — *Franklin D. Roosevelt*[1]

USING LENIN'S PLAN, the communist followers of Marx and Lenin have moved "step-by-step" until today they hold 40% of the world's population in absolute slavery. With the capture of Cuba in 1959, the Kremlin bosses started on the last phase of Lenin's plan, the encirclement of the United States.

How has this been done by a nation which has never completed one of its highly publicized *Five Year Plans?* The Soviets have had police state control of their people, 44 years of centralized economic planning, and some of the world's richest natural resources. They have produced nothing but economic failure.

How has a nation which cannot feed its own people while employing 55% of its total working force on the farms come so close to conquering the world?[2]

The communist world revolution has been largely financed from its start in 1903 until the present day by American wealth, public and private. Lenin and his heirs have had the sometimes knowing, sometimes unknowing, cooperation of the United States State Department every step of the way.

Every communist country in the world literally has a "Made in USA" stamp on it.

Look at true history and prove for yourself what has happened.

The part an American soap manufacturer played in financing Lenin's early career has been detailed.[3] In 1916-17, Leon Trotsky was in exile in America.[4] In New York, he recruited, financed, and trained a cadre of gangsters and hoodlums.

Transported to Russia, this hard core of cutthroat shock troops was used by Lenin and Trotsky to sieze control of the shaky Kerensky Republic.

Immediately following World War I, economic chaos developed in Russia. Lenin's attempt to make the big leap into communism had failed. The toppling of the socialist experiment was imminent.

Millions were starving when American relief, food, medicine, and other supplies, eased the pressure. Lenin had time to consolidate his strength.[5] This well-meaning, humanitarian gesture of the United States solidified the power of tyrants whose heirs in the succeeding 40 years have murdered at least 60-million human beings and enslaved one-billion others.

During the 1920's, American oilmen, technicians, and their machinery opened Russian petroleum fields. Other American engineers, scientists, and production experts assisted the communists in building steel plants, assembly lines for tractors, trucks, and autos.[6]

Even so, by 1933 the communist state was again faltering. Then, the USSR was recognized by the United States. With U. S. diplomatic recognition came world-wide prestige, and access to the credit and money markets of the world. In return for recognition, the communists promised, in writing, that Russia would not interfere in the internal affairs of the United States.[7]

While the agreements were being signed, Alger Hiss, and other agents were infiltrating the New Deal. Soviet intelligence officers were busy in Washington setting up elaborate spy networks in government agencies.[8]

Six years later, Stalin made another agreement which was to have an equal impact on the course of history. In 1939, he and Hitler entered into a non-aggression pact. Together they carved up Poland in a blitzkrieg "war" which set records for its lightning speed, and the savage butchering of the Polish people. The attack on little Poland started World War II.

The Hitler-Stalin pact was shortlived and in 1941 Russia came under Nazi attack. The Kremlin, now an ally, received more than $11-billion in American lend lease aid. It was all supposedly war materiel to bolster the USSR in the fight against Germany. Actually, Russia received non-military supplies and materials worth billions. Stockpiled until the war's end, they were the foundation on which the Communist industrial machine of today was built.

Deluded U. S. officials and actual traitors, exposed later,

arranged these shipments, in knowing defiance of laws passed by Congress prohibiting such non-military aid.[9]

In 1943, Congressional investigations later revealed, before the United States had itself assembled the first atomic bomb, half of all American uranium and the technical information needed to construct a bomb were sent to Russia.[10] Is it any wonder that the communists became a nuclear power years ahead of "expectations?"

At the same time, a communist agent, Harry Dexter White, became Assistant Secretary of the U. S. Treasury.[11] He sent the Soviet Union engraving plates, paper, and ink to print occupation currency which was redeemable by the U. S. Treasury.[12]

In actual conduct of the war, military decisions were made, not according to the tactical needs of the day or to capitalize on the weaknesses of the enemy, but for the long-range political advantage of the communist conspiracy.[13]

For instance, at the wartime conferences, Roosevelt agreed to Stalin's demands for a "cross-channel" invasion of Europe, over Churchill's objections. Churchill urged an attack on Europe's soft "underbelly." Such an offensive, aimed at the Balkans, through Yugoslavia, would have defeated Hitler, *and* prevented communist occupation of eastern Europe.[14]

At Yalta, Roosevelt, with Alger Hiss at his side, gave Stalin the eastern half of Poland, and the Baltic states of Estonia, Latvia, and Lithuania. He agreed to coalition governments for Yugoslavia and Poland, with communists holding all the key posts. Stalin's occupation of the 11 eastern European countries was approved. Stalin promised to permit free elections in these communist-occupied countries.[15] The U. S. government has never demanded that the agreements be fulfilled as a condition for further negotiations.

Thus, at Yalta, the first step of Lenin's master plan was accomplished. In addition, the foundation was laid for the completion of the second phase. Our Chinese ally, Chiang Kai-shek, was excluded from the Yalta Conference. Roosevelt and Churchill acceded to Stalin's demands for increased influence in postwar Asia.[16]

When the war ended, the United States demanded that Chiang Kai-shek give the communists representation in the government of China. He refused. On orders of General George C. Marshall, all American aid was withheld from Chiang.[17]

With Marshall's embargo enforced, Chiang had tanks and planes, but no gasoline. His troops had guns, but no ammunition. By 1949, the communists, supplied by Russia, were overrunning China. Chiang evacuated the remnants of his army and his government to Formosa.

In 1951 and 1952, the Senate Internal Security Subcommittee under the late Senator Pat McCarran (D-Nev) unraveled the sordid story of China's betrayal.

A quasi-official agency, the Institute of Pacific Relations, was found to have held a near controlling influence over American far eastern policies for 15 years. The IPR, as an unofficial State Department recruiting and training agency, had planted communists and pro-communists in sensitive diplomatic posts in Washington and China.[18]

IPR-oriented State Department officials in China deliberately falsified reports to Washington on the status of Chiang's government. Chinese communists were depicted as "agrarian reformers."[19]

The Chinese people's confidence in Chiang's government was shaken by runaway inflation. It was planned in Washington by IPR officials in conjunction with Assistant Secretary of the Treasury Harry Dexter White, a communist agent. White's plan to destroy China's currency was implemented by the U. S. Treasury Department's representative in Chungking, Solomon Adler. He was also a communist.[20]

In its report, the Senate Internal Security Subcommittee concluded that . . .

> . . . the Institute of Pacific Relations was a vehicle used by the communists to orientate American far eastern policy toward communist objectives.[21]

Owen Lattimore, an influential member of the IPR and sometime government official and State Department adviser, was found to have been "a conscious articulate instrument of the Soviet conspiracy" for 15 years.[22] Two years earlier, a young Senator from Wisconsin, Joseph McCarthy, had warned that Lattimore and the IPR were serving the communist conspiracy. McCarthy's charges were regarded by some as "red herrings" and "unfounded smears."

Lattimore's activities were not limited to influencing State Department policies and placing his proteges in key diplomatic posts. As a best-selling author and book reviewer for the New York Times, Lattimore and a handful of pro-communist and pro-Soviet writers flooded the book channels with anti-Chiang, pro-communist books. Objective, anti-communist books on the Far East were "killed" when Lattimore and his pro-Soviet colleagues in the book review trade "panned" them.[23]

The *Saturday Evening Post, Colliers* and other influential magazines were flooded with articles glorifying the Chinese communists as "agrarian reformers" and other Soviet-inspired materials. During the 1943-49 period, the *Saturday Evening Post* published over 60 articles which promoted the communist line.[24]

The American people were misled. About 600-million Chinese were betrayed into communist slavery. It was all done by a handful of American traitors and their liberal dupes.

With the fall of China, the second step in Lenin's plan for world conquest was nearly accomplished.

Dean Acheson, one of the diplomats who participated in the series of decisions and actions which ultimately led to the fall of China in 1949, announced to the world in a speech on January 12, 1950 that Korea was "outside our defense perimeter."[25] Within six months, the North Korean communists accepted the invitation and attacked South Korea on June 25, 1950. President Truman responded by committing the meager American forces in the Far East to the defense of South Korea. Once action was started the United Nations was asked to assume the responsibility for the "police action."

General Douglas MacArthur, in fighting the delaying action down the Korean peninsula, showed the same brilliance he displayed in playing for time against overwhelming odds in the Bataan Campaign at the start of World War II. Within two months, the communists controlled all of Korea except for the small perimeter around Pusan. Meanwhile, MacArthur received minimum reinforcements.

In one of the greatest displays of military genius in history, MacArthur attacked the enemy's rear with an "impossible" amphibious assault at Inchon, far up the Korean peninsula.[26] Within eight weeks, the communists had been driven pell-mell north to the Manchurian border. Six days later on November 26, 1950, hordes of Chinese communist "volunteers" swarmed across the border and entered the fight. Even while under savage attack, MacArthur was forbidden to bomb the Red supply bases and lines of communication north of the border. The Yalu River bridges across which communist supplies and re-inforcements flowed were also "off-limits."[27]

With the enemy operating from this sanctuary, the war was thrown into a stalemate. American casualties mounted in the hopeless effort. MacArthur protested the restrictions placed on his military operations by the diplomats and the United Nations.

He was "muzzled" by Presidential order on December 5, 1950.[28]

MacArthur maintained a discrete silence until April 1951. Then, in answer to a written inquiry from Congressman Joseph W. Martin (R-Mass)[29] MacArthur alluded to how military efforts in Korea were handcuffed on orders from Washington. His letter indicated agreement with Martin's suggestions for using Chinese nationalist troops. He expressed the view that the battle against communism around the world would be won or lost in Asia. It was read to Congress on April 5, 1951. Five days later, Truman fired MacArthur.

The significance of MacArthur's dismissal was not understood by most Americans. Ostensibly, he was replaced for violating the "gag" imposed by President Truman on December 5, 1950. Much of the world understood, however, that future U. S. policy was to be one of "containment" of communism and not victory. Wanting victory, not stalemate or defeat, was the real crime for which MacArthur was punished.

When it was too late to correct the tragedy, Congress investigated. Top commanders in Korea, MacArthur and his successors, testified.[30] General Mark Clark, one of MacArthur's several successors said:

> I was not allowed to bomb the numerous bridges across the Yalu River over which the enemy constantly poured his trucks, and his munitions, and his killers.

General James Van Fleet, another Korean commander, told Congress:

> My own conviction is that there must have been information to the enemy from high diplomatic authorities that we would not attack his home bases across the Yalu.

General George Stratemyer, Air Force commander in the Far East, said:

> You get in war to win it. You do not get in war to stand still and lose it and we were required to lose it. We were not permitted to win.

General MacArthur told the Congressional committee:

> Such a limitation upon the utilization of available military force to repel an enemy attack has no precedent, either in our own history, or so far as I know, in the history of the world.

The American plum, which Lenin predicted would one day drop into communist hands without a fight was beginning to ripen.

AMERICA REBELS

America, however, was learning of some of the treachery in high places. There was an awakening. The story of Yalta and Alger Hiss unfolded. Harry Dexter White, John Abt, Nathan Witt, and other agents who reached top spots in at least six cabinet departments before, during and after World War II were exposed. The role of the Institute of Pacific Relations in the betrayal of China was disclosed. The web of subversion which reached into dozens of executive agencies unraveled. The White House Staff itself had been infiltrated as Lauchlin Currie became executive assistant to President Roosevelt.

As the communist agents were exposed by Congressional committees, aroused Americans demanded action. They were in a fighting mood, ready to root out the conspirators. They'd had enough and were ready to stop the international cancer of communism.

Dwight Eisenhower appeared on the scene.

Eisenhower campaigned on his victorious war record, a winning smile, and the slogan "Let's Clean Up the Mess in Washington." He promised "peace with honor" in Korea. He piled up a landslide victory in the 1952 Presidential elections. Most Americans, whether they voted for him or not, believed and hoped that Eisenhower would clean up the mess.

The hero was elected. The Korean War ended. A public tired of conflict and controversy settled down to approve $40-billion annual military budgets. More billions were appropriated for foreign aid to keep the world "safe." Disturbing thoughts that communism might be more than a vague threat which required higher taxes were carefully ignored.

In short, the mess in Washington wasn't cleaned up. The public never noticed.

The first disturbing signs came with the signing of the truce agreement in Korea on July 26, 1953.

Eisenhower's "peace with honor" abandoned at least 400 American soldiers to rot, forgotten in Chinese communist prison camps. Few people at home, except for the mothers, wives, and children of the forgotten few even noticed. Today, after 100 "polite" requests in negotiations with the Chinese Reds at Warsaw, Poland, these Americans are still in communist captivity.

Even the "official" and sympathetic biographer of Eisenhower's first years[31] in the White House, Robert Donovan, admitted in *Eisenhower, The Inside Story,* that the Eisenhower truce made even more concessions than Truman had offered. The 1952 Republican platform had labelled the Truman plan "ignominious bartering with our enemies."[32] Few Americans noticed, but some Republicans were themselves critical.

Senator William Knowland (R-Cal) was asked in a radio interview, "Is this a truce with honor that we are about to get?" Knowland replied, "I don't think so."[33] On the Senate floor, Senators William Jenner (R-Ind) and George Malone (R-Nev) traded these remarks:[34]

> MALONE: Does the distinguished Senator remember any change in State Department policy — by Mr. Dulles since he has taken office?
>
> JENNER: I have noticed no change.

The venerable Senator Robert A. Taft (R-Ohio) said prophetically that Eisenhower's acceptance of a divided Korea would spark further wars by freeing the Chinese to attack anywhere in Southeast Asia. Within a year, the communists had moved into Indo-China.[35] Using the Korean precedent, John Foster Dulles negotiated a settlement which split Indo-China into North and South Viet Nam along the 17th parallel. Today, American boys are paying for that appeasement with their blood in Southeast Asia's undeclared war.

Senator Joseph McCarthy (R-Wis) called attention to the "mess which remained." On a nationwide radio and TV broadcast on November 23, 1953, he charged Eisenhower with failing to liquidate the "foulest bankruptcy" of the Truman Administration. He asked that foreign aid to Great Britain be withheld as long as the English traded with Red China, "the jailers of American soldiers captured in the Korean War." McCarthy said:

> Are we going to continue to send perfumed notes? It is time that we, the Republican Party, liquidate this blood-stained blunder. We promised the American people something different. Let us deliver — not next year or next month — let us deliver now. We can do this by merely saying to our allies and alleged allies, "If you continue to ship to Red China . . . you will not get one cent of American money."[36]

Seven days later, the Administration said that McCarthy's proposal "attacks the very heart of U. S. foreign policy."[37] It was sometime before even astute Americans fully understood this cryptic statement. Then it became obvious that it would be ridiculous to cut off aid to the British for *trading* with Red China when Eisenhower was readying a program of expanded trade with and foreign aid direct to the communist nations![38] British trade with the enemy and their aid continued.

Criticism of Eisenhower soon grew weaker. Eisenhower planned it that way. The American people elected Eisenhower in 1952 to "clean up the mess in Washington." He did not see this as his primary goal. According to both Sherman Adams, assistant president under Eisenhower, and the "official biographer" of his first term, Robert J. Donovan, Eisenhower saw his mission this way:

> When Eisenhower took office in 1953 he had hoped that in four years the Republican Party could be reformed from its role of an opposition party and invigorated with more progressive leaders. He had hoped for the rise of what he called "positive" Republicans as opposed to "negative" Republicans.[39]

The "negative" Republicans were the "hard" anti-communists in the Senate who pointed out that Eisenhower's foreign policy differed little from the appeasing actions of Roosevelt and Truman. They had been outspoken critics of subversion in government under Roosevelt and Truman and continued their warnings with Eisenhower in the White House. Before Eisenhower left office they were all gone. Taft and McCarthy died. Bricker, Malone, Welker, Potter, and others were beaten at the polls. Knowland and Jenner left Washington disgusted and discouraged. In all, Republicans lost 80 Congressional seats and 15 Senatorial positions in Eisenhower's eight years.

AID TO COMMUNISTS

With the critics gone, Eisenhower initiated foreign aid programs for the communist enemy in Poland and Yugoslavia. Before he left office in 1961, Poland and Yugoslavia were to receive nearly $3-billion[40] in American food, industrial machinery, jet fighter planes, and other military equipment. The aid continued even after Tito, Yugoslavia's dictator, repeatedly pledged his allegiance to Moscow.

For example, in June 1956, Tito went to Russia for a state visit and said:

> The spirit of Lenin's principles of collective leadership are such that I am sure there never again will be misunderstanding among the nations of the socialist camp . . . In peace as in war, Yugoslavia must march shoulder to shoulder with the Soviet Union.[41]

Two weeks later, John Foster Dulles warned that if Congress stopped aid to Tito, we would drive Yugoslavia back into the Soviet camp. The few skeptics asked, "When did they leave?" but no one listened.

By the fall of 1956, Khrushchev and Tito had exchanged two more warm visits. Eisenhower then announced that Yugoslavian aid would continue because Tito had *clearly demonstrated his friendship for the west.* When a month later, in November 1956, the Soviets raped Hungary and butchered Budapest, Tito publicly branded the Hungarian patriots as "bandits" for rebelling against Moscow.[42] His American aid continued. In December 1956, President Eisenhower invited Tito to the U. S. for an official visit. After public opposition developed to the visit in America, Tito refused to come.

In 1957, Tito and Khrushchev met in Rumania on August 1 and 2 and pledged mutual cooperation.[43] On August 15, President Eisenhower announced that U. S. aid had "broken Tito away from Moscow." On September 17, Tito announced full support for Soviet foreign policy.[44] On December 9, 1957, Tito announced rejection of further U. S. military aid.[45] On December 23, American diplomats went to Belgrade and asked that he reconsider. He did, and military and economic aid has continued.

Since 1956, American aid has provided about half of communist Yugoslavia's national income. In 1961, they instituted their own foreign aid program to spread communism to under-developed nations of the world.[46]

Poland and Yugoslavia were not the only communists to benefit from Eisenhower's generosity. Achmed Sukarno received the planes, tanks, and guns he used to crush the last anti-communist resistance in Indonesia from Eisenhower's mutual security program.[47] Since 1955, Sukarno's Indonesian government has received $479-million from the United States.[48]

Patrice Lumumba was widely known as a communist terrorist in 1960 when he became Premier of the newly independent Congo in Africa. Eisenhower and the U. S. State Department gave Lumumba's prestige and his treasury a big boost with a Washington welcome and $20-million in American foreign aid.[49] Even so, he was deposed and later killed by the anti-communist forces in the Congolese government.

By the time Eisenhower's two terms ended, direct economic and military aid to communist and "neutralist" nations totaled over $7-billion.

CULTURAL EXCHANGES

Eisenhower's Administration developed the "cultural exchange" idea jointly with the communists. Under this experiment, Americans go to Russia and return to tell other Americans about the "progress" they see and the friendly Russians they meet. In return, the communists are supposed to come to America and learn about our superior system.

Congressman Walter Judd (R-Minn) told how it worked in practice:

> Who goes over from our side? Anybody who wants to go. He may be the most ignorant and naive person . . . totally unequipped to deal with them.
>
> Who comes over from their side? Any Russian who wants to? No; only those who are "reliable," which means so thoroughly indoctrinated and tested that their bosses are sure they can trust them. And further, they are skilled in presenting Communist ideas, trained in the dialectic — that is agents.
>
> Who goes from our side? Farmers. Whom do they send? Agents. Who goes over from our side? Journalists — to get information. Who is sent from their side? Agents — to sell their ideas. Who goes from our side? Professors. Who comes from their side? Agents.
>
> From our side, clergymen. Their side, agents. From our side, students. Their side, agents. From our side, businessmen. Their side, agents.[50]

What effect will this Eisenhower-conceived "people-to-people" program have? Congressman Judd tells us:

> We will lose, not win, in this exchange of persons if the Americans who go over and see that the ordinary Russian people are friendly and conclude that therefore we can relax and trust the communist rulers.[51]

In April 1960, the House Committee on Un-American Activities became so concerned about the misinformation tourists were bringing back from Russia and Red China that two special hearings were held.[52] Witnesses told how tourists are shown "model" showplace prisons — not slave labor camps. Visitors to China are shown special "show" cities, housed in special hotels with excellent food and service at very low prices. Churches are refurbished to impress important visitors. Visitors who return and report their experiences help to further break down the anti-communist attitudes of the American people.

THE CLEANUP IS BLOCKED

In the 1952 campaign, Republicans had promised to uncover security risks in government who escaped detection in the hectic 1948-52 period when Hiss, Lattimore, White and others were exposed.

Three Eisenhower actions in his first term vetoed fulfillment of that promise.

The appointment of Earl Warren as Chief Justice of the United States was to have an impact in destroying the security laws of the United States not fully felt for several years. In the meantime, two Eisenhower executive orders effectively closed the door on congressional investigation of communists in government.

After Warren's appointment to the Supreme Court, in the first eight cases involving communism in which he participated, he supported the communist position five times, the government's case on three occasions. *After that, Warren supported the communist position in 62 cases without deviation.*[53]

In the three year, 1956-58 period, the Supreme Court decided 52 cases involving communism and subversion in government. The decisions supported the communist position 41 times, the anti-communist position only 11 times. Warren's consistent pro-communist votes were the deciding factor in the many narrow 5 to 4 decisions.[54]

By contrast, in the ten years before Warren's appointment by Eisenhower, the court decided 37 cases involving communism and subversion. Of these, 23 were decided *against* the communists.[55] The communist position was upheld 14 times.

Under Warren's leadership, the Court voided the long-standing sedition laws of 42 states. Communists convicted under them were freed.[56] The government was denied the right to fire federal employees who were proved to have contributed money and services to communist organizations.[57] Schools and colleges were denied the right to fire teachers who refused to answer questions about their communist activities.[58] In the Watkins decision, later modified, the Court questioned the right of Congress to inquire into and publicize communism and subversion suggesting that this "involved a broad scale intrusion into the lives and affairs of private citizens."[59]

Apologists for the Supreme Court's decisions justify them as "leaning over backwards to protect the rights of the individual." However, when the *individual* was a Yugoslavian *anti-communist* refugee, the Court denied his right to political asylum. Andrew Artukovic, who lived with his wife and children in California, was forced to submit to an extradition hearing based on political charges made by the communist government of Yugoslavia.[60]

The Court set aside the discharge of John Stewart Service by the State Department. As was noted in the opening chapter, Service, a career diplomat, had been deeply involved in the loss of China but held his job. He was finally fired, eight years after an FBI arrest for violation of the Espionage Act.

Without disputing his guilt, the Supreme Court ordered Service reinstated in 1956 with back pay of over $30,000. The Court's action was based on the technicality that proper procedures had not been used in firing him.[61]

The decisions of the Warren Court stirred thoughtful, earnest criticism from highly reputable authorities. In August 1958, the Conference of State Chief Justices, the highest judicial officials of the then 49 states, adopted a scorching appraisal of the Supreme Court and its actions by a 36 to 8 vote.[62]

The same month, the American Bar Association Committee on Communist Strategy, Tactics, and Objectives prepared a special report on communism and the Supreme Court decisions.[63]

J. Edgar Hoover testified before a Congressional committee that 49 top communists convicted of advocating the overthrow of the U. S. government had been freed by the Supreme Court. Hoover said that a top communist had described the Court's decision in the Smith Act case as the greatest victory the Communist Party had ever received.[64]

The New York *Daily News*, largest circulation newspaper in America, suggested impeachment of Justices whose decisions consistently favored the communists.[65]

EISENHOWER'S ROLE

Actually, effective Congressional investigations of subversion in government has been quietly stymied by executive order before the full impact of Warren's appointment to the Supreme Court was felt. On March 5, 1954, President Eisenhower in a "Personal and Confidential" letter ordered his cabinet to "shield" executive department employees from Congressional investigations into their loyalty, actions, and background.[66]

In practice, Eisenhower's order has meant that when Congress questions the loyalty or conduct of a government employee, the department head, and not the person under investigation, answers the committee's questions. Had this principle, known as the "executive fifth amendment," been used in 1948, Alger Hiss could not have been exposed, convicted and jailed.

The Eisenhower-ordered "executive fifth amendment" stymied congressional investigations but left one embarrassing loophole. In screening security files, Congress turned up employees who were "cleared" by department heads despite unfavorable or derogatory FBI reports. When the department heads were subpoenaed and asked "Why?" in open hearings, a public clamor for corrective action resulted.

This last "loophole" through which subversives in government might be detected was plugged nine months after Eisenhower's original order. On December 29, 1954, all security files of executive department employees were placed "off-limits" to congressional committees *by Presidential Order*. Congress then couldn't learn if an employee was cleared despite FBI warnings.[67]

Was there a real threat and danger from communists hidden in government in 1954? Was there still a "mess" to be cleaned up in Washington? Or were Senators McCarthy and Jenner, Congressman Harold Velde and others simply "witch-hunting" in search of headlines?

Elizabeth Bentley, a former communist, exposed the two Soviet spy rings in which Harry Dexter White, Lauchlin Currie, and about 80 others had participated. On May 29, 1952, she testified that at least two other Soviet espionage rings were operating in government. She had learned of their existence from her Soviet superiors, but never knew who was in them, or in what branches of government they operated.[68] Whittaker Chambers, the man who exposed Alger Hiss, gave collaborating testimony.[69]

Neither of these groups has been exposed to this day!

There are other proven threats which the Eisenhower Administration refused to correct.

On May 26, 1953, Senator William Jenner, Chairman of the Senate Internal Security Subcommittee, notified key officials *including President Eisenhower* that the American Communications Association, a union so heavily dominated by communists that it was expelled from the CIO, was servicing communications lines to and from key defense installations in the United States and the cable facilities to overseas defense installations.[70] The warning was ignored.

Four years later, the Senate Internal Security Subcommittee conducted a study on the *Scope of Soviet Activity in the U. S.* Eisenhower's Secretary of the Army, Wilbur Brucker, testified.

Committee counsel Richard Arens asked Secretary Brucker about the serious security situation:

ARENS: Are you conversant with the fact that the North Atlantic Cable which carries important messages vital to the security of our nation is now serviced by the American Communications Association, a communist-controlled labor organization.

SEC. BRUCKER: I am aware of that.[71]

Neither Congress, nor Secretary Brucker, nor President Eisenhower acted to correct the situation. It still exists today.

It was in trying to uncover trails leading to the unexposed spy rings about which Elizabeth Bentley testified that Senators Jenner and McCarthy ran afoul of the Eisenhower Administration. The first major scrape came in August 1953, just seven months after Eisenhower took office.

McCarthy's subcommittee learned that a Government Printing Office employee was given a security clearance even though 40 FBI sources had reported on his communist activities. This was before Eisenhower placed security files off-limits to Congressional committees. Administration officials did not deny the employee's communist affiliations. Instead, they attacked McCarthy, saying that the security file contained *nothing like 40 derogatory FBI reports*.[72] This was a typical tactic. McCarthy's charges were rarely denied. Instead, the critics would engage in a "numbers game." In the resultant controversy, a smokescreen would be created around the uncontested fact that derogatory information did exist.

McCarthy investigated the Voice of America and the U. S. Information Agency. His finding that communist literature and authors were being used to "sell America" were not denied. Instead, McCarthy was denounced by Eisenhower as a "bookburner." Attacks were directed not at the facts uncovered, but at McCarthy's investigators and their alleged activities in Europe.

McCarthy finally met his doom when he tried to find out how and why a man *known* to be a communist, Irving Peress, could be promoted to the rank of Major in the Army Dental Corps. Before his promotion, Peress had refused to answer questions about his Communist Party membership on Army Security Forms. He attempted to set up a communist cell on the Army base at Camp Kilmer, N. J. and tried to recruit military personnel into the Communist Party. The Korean War was underway at the time. The Army knew these things and promoted Peress.[73] McCarthy wanted to know why.

It was that simple, in the beginning.

McCarthy wrote to Army Secretary Robert Stevens requesting that the Army court-martial Peress *and* make an investigation to find out *who* promoted him and *why*. Was it a simple case of bureaucratic bungling, or were subversive influences at work? With foresight, McCarthy said in his letter to Stevens:

> I realize that this letter will be interpreted by the left wing elements of press, radio, and television as a "fight with Army Secretary Stevens." Therefore, let me try again to make it clear that I have great respect for you both as an individual and as Secretary of the Army. I feel that you have served tremendously well in a most thankless job.[74]

In reply, the Army gave Peress an honorable discharge three days later.

McCarthy summoned Brigadier General Ralph Zwicker, the commanding officer of Camp Kilmer, N. J. Zwicker had issued the formal orders promoting, and then honorably discharging the communist, Peress.

On the witness stand, Zwicker was evasive. He first said that when he promoted Peress and then discharged him he didn't know Peress was under investigation. Then he admitted that he had known. Under questioning, his answers became contradictory. He agreed that he *could* have stopped both actions but then said he *couldn't*. Finally, he said that he *couldn't* stop Peress' promotion and discharge because of *orders*.

McCarthy tried to clarify the cloudy situation with a hypothetical question. McCarthy was more smeared over the result than over any other incident in his stormy career.

Read the actual hearing transcript, reproduced here. Then check newspaper accounts of the incident:

> McCARTHY: Let us assume that John Jones is a major in the United States Army. Let us assume that there is sworn testimony to the effect that he is part of the Communist conspiracy, has attended Communist leadership schools. Let us assume that Maj. John Jones is under oath before a committee and says, "I cannot tell you the truth about these charges because, if I did, I fear that might tend to incriminate me." Then let us say that General Smith was responsible for this man receiving an honorable discharge, knowing these facts. Do you think that General Smith should be removed from the military, or do you think he should be kept on in it?
>
> ZWICKER: He should by all means be kept if he were acting under *competent orders* to separate the man.
>
> McCARTHY: Let us say General Smith is the man who *originated* the order . . . directing his honorable discharge.

ZWICKER: I do not think he should be removed from the military.

MCCARTHY: Then, General, you should be removed from any command. Any man who has been given the honor of being promoted to general and who says, "I will protect another General who protected communists is not fit to wear that uniform."[75]

Lionel Lokos, author of *Who Promoted Peress?*, the authoritative and comprehensive book-length study of the Peress-Zwicker-McCarthy case, said of those few words:

Those words were to haunt McCarthy to the end of his life. Completely lost sight of was Zwicker's shocking answer to McCarthy's question. All that the public could, or would remember was that McCarthy had said Zwicker was "not fit to wear that uniform" — not why he said it or what provoked it.[76]

Why did the public lose sight of McCarthy's question and Zwicker's answer? From the *New York Times* here are a series of four typical news stories showing the distortion and falsehoods in the reporting of the event:

On that occasion, the Senator told the Camp Kilmer commander, who has been decorated 13 times during his Army career, that he was "shielding communist conspirators" and was a "disgrace to the uniform." (NY Times, Aug. 2, 1954, pg. 7)

The *New York Times* use of quotation marks denotes, falsely, that they were reproducing McCarthy's exact words. Note the "hero" buildup for Zwicker. Three months later when the Senate was considering the resolution censuring McCarthy, the *New York Times* said:

Called to testify in the case, General Zwicker declined to answer some security questions about Dr. Peress because he said he was prohibited by Presidential order. *Thereupon,* Senator McCarthy denounced the General as unfit to wear the uniform. (NY Times, Nov. 8, 1954, pg. 13)

Note how two completely unrelated incidents are tied together. The real provocation for McCarthy's outburst is deleted. Who, upon reading this in the "reputable" *New York Times* could conclude that McCarthy was other than a complete cad? Who wouldn't look upon Zwicker as a poor, persecuted victim of McCarthyism? Two months later, the *New York Times* repeated the lie:

Senator McCarthy denounced General Zwicker, commanding officer at Camp Kilmer, N. J. as unfit to wear his uniform because he said he would not answer questions on the Peress case before a hearing of Senator McCarthy's subcommittee. (NY Times, Jan. 6, 1955, pg. 14)

Two years later, the *New York Times* was still painting the image of the "monster" McCarthy brow-beating a dedicated soldier:

> Senator Joseph R. McCarthy, Republican of Wisconsin, charged during the hearings that General Zwicker was "not fit to wear that uniform." General Zwicker had refused to tell Senator McCarthy who ordered an honorable discharge for former Army Major Irving Peress, an Army dentist. (NY Times, Jan. 15, 1957, pg. 20)

The much distorted Zwicker episode, more than any other, crystallized public opinion on McCarthy.

In succeeding years, several Senate committees restudied the issue. Subsequent testimony showed that General Zwicker had committed perjury during the several hearings. The Justice Department, however, refused to prosecute.[77] To have done so would have vindicated McCarthy.

McCarthy's "trial," the harrowing eight weeks of televised Army-McCarthy hearings, was staged in an atmosphere of untrue, twisted, and slanted news coverage. In addition, McCarthy's gruff, cold, business-like manner, his deep, booming voice, and heavy bushy eye-brows were not made for TV.

His mistakes were magnified. His staff, if the reports were true, abused the committee's prestige and power, not an uncommon practice in Washington. McCarthy stood by them. His booming, "Point of order, Mr. Chairman," was ridiculed. The conflicting testimony and procedural violations McCarthy tried to question were ignored. Later study showed that Army Secretary Stevens was regularly guilty of conflicting statements which bordered on perjury,[78] but in the planned confusion they were ignored.

The basic issue "Who Promoted Peress?" was also ignored. The magnitude of the furor the question provoked leaves a lingering suspicion that more than bureaucratic bungling had to be hidden. Even Defense Secretary Charles Wilson admitted this possibility.[79]

However, by the end of 1954, McCarthy was censured and silenced. By 1957, he was dead. The liberals cheered. The communists breathed a sigh of relief. Dwight Eisenhower's delight at the destruction of McCarthy is chronicled in Donovan's book, *Eisenhower, The Inside Story,*[80] and the memoirs of Eisenhower's assistant, Sherman Adams.[81]

The tragedy of the McCarthy story is that McCarthy was essentially right. What he said and tried to prove was rarely denied. It was simply buried in the controversy his charges provoked.

His targets were unsuitable for government service, if not by reason of treason, then because of gross negligence and complete naivete about the communist conspiracy. That is all McCarthy tried to prove. His critics discredited him by disputing, not that guilt existed, but his presentations of the facts. The communist-conceived slogan, "I like what Mc-Carthy is trying to do, but I can't stand his methods," was parroted by millions. The inherent unfairness of such criti cism is underlined by the fact that after McCarthy was destroyed those who "liked what he was trying to do" never completed the job by more acceptable "methods," or at all.

What were McCarthy's "methods?"

He drew unprovable, although logical conclusions from accumulations of damning and uncontested facts. In the resulting controversies, the facts were ignored or brushed aside and forgotten. It would do an injustice to Dwight Eisenhower, the communists, and the fellow travellers in our society, the liberals, and the press to say McCarthy was his own worst enemy. He only provided the weapons they used against him. The case of Philip C. Jessup was typical.

Jessup was the State Department's influential ambassador-at-large and chief troubleshooter in the Dean Acheson period following World War II. In a Senate speech on March 30, 1950, McCarthy charged Jessup with . . .

> . . . having pioneered the smear campaign against China and Chiang Kai-shek, and with being the originator of the myth of the democratic Chinese communists.[82]

For liberals, this attack on Jessup was to become both the symbol and proof of the evils of McCarthyism. McCarthy could not prove that Jessup had *pioneered* the smear against Chiang, or that he *originated* the myth of the "democratic" Chinese communists. His conclusions were based on a damning collection of provable and largely uncontested facts.

For 13 years Jessup was an influential member of the Board of Trustees of the infamous Institute of Pacific Relations, which was later to be cited by the Senate Internal Security Subcommittee as "a vehicle used by the communists to orientate American far eastern policy toward communist objectives."[83] Jessup headed the IPR's American Council for two years, and was chairman of the Pacific Council for another three years.[84]

In 1944, when the anti-Chiang drive started, Jessup headed the IPR's policy-making Research Advisory Council. If this

group did not *originate* the anti-Chiang smears, it at least
implemented their dissemination.[85] The same year, Jessup
helped block the investigation requested by several IPR members who charged that the organization was becoming com-
munist-oriented.[86]

Jessup associated with 46 communists and eight others in
the IPR, including Owen Lattimore, who were cooperating
with Soviet intelligence. He knowingly worked closely with
an open communist, Frederick Vanderbilt Field. Field was
secretary of the IPR's American Council in 1939 and 1940
when Jessup was its head.[87]

McCarthy charged that Jessup accepted $7,000 of Field's
"communist money" to finance IPR projects. It was later
proved that the total actually exceeded $60,000.[88] McCarthy
charged that Jessup belonged to and/or sponsored five communist front organizations.[89] Four such affiliations were
finally proved.[90]

Finally, Jessup appeared as a character witness for Alger
Hiss. After Hiss was convicted, Jessup said:

> I see no reason to alter the statements which I made under
> oath as a witness in that case.[91]

The Tydings Committee, formed to investigate McCarthy's
"unfounded smears" called Jessup to testify. He denied
Communist Party membership.[92] Of this, he had never been
accused. He also denied communist sympathies. The committee accepted the statements as true. Senator Tydings
refused to permit McCarthy to cross-examine Jessup. All the
provable evidence was ignored, and the committee "cleared"
Jessup with this statement:

> The subcommittee feels that the accusations made against
> Philip C. Jessup are completely unfounded and unjustified and
> have done irreparable harm to the prestige of the United
> States.[93]

To many, the whitewash of Jessup and similar "clearances"
of others by the Tydings committee *proved* that McCarthy
was a sadistic, irresponsible, headline-seeking smear artist.
The public retains this impression even though the U. S.
Senate vindicated McCarthy to a degree 18 months later by
refusing to confirm President Truman's appointment of Jessup
as the U. S. Ambassador to the United Nations.[94]

Today, McCarthy is dead. Jessup is the United States
representative on the International Court of Justice (World
Court). His election by the United Nations General Assembly
in the closing days of the Eisenhower Administration pro-

voked little or no public dissent. Editorially, the *New York Times* on November 16, 1950 said about Jessup's selection:

> It is hard to conceive of a better selection than that of Philip C. Jessup for the International Court of Justice at the Hague, made by vote of the United Nations General Assembly on Wednesday.

The McCarthy story plays up the striking double standard and inconsistency in our society. A murder suspect can be convicted and executed on the strength of circumstantial evidence. It is extremely difficult or impossible, however, to remove an alleged communist, fellow traveller, or incompetent from a government post using the same rules of evidence.

THE IRON CURTAIN CRACKS

By the end of President Eisenhower's first term, concern about communism was almost non-existent. Then, suddenly, Americans warmed again. The first possible break appeared in the Iron Curtain.

Aroused by American campaign oratory and Voice of America broadcasts about "rolling back the Iron Curtain" and "freeing the captive peoples," the Hungarians revolted and drove out their Russian captors.

During their five days of freedom, Imre Nagy's Freedom Fighter government appealed in vain for help. U. S. diplomatic recognition was requested. It was never given. The U. S. announced that it couldn't get involved.

The Hungarian affair was referred to the United Nations. Americans sat up through the nights in early November 1956 listening to the stirring oratory of Ambassador Henry Cabot Lodge in the UN. They didn't know that it had no real meaning. When President Eisenhower sent the Hungarian affair to the United Nations, he was, in effect, telling the Soviet Union to do as it pleased. The communists had the veto in the UN Security Council and could stop any action.

Finally, on November 4, 1956, the Hungarian Freedom Fighter Radio Station broadcast these last words:

> People of the world, listen to our call. Help us not with words, but with action, with soldiers and arms. Please do not forget that this wild attack of Bolshevism will not stop. You may be the next victim. Save us . . . Our ship is sinking. The light vanishes. The shadows grow darker from hour to hour. Listen to our cry. Start moving. Extend to us your brotherly hands . . . God be with you and us.[95]

The Hungarian Freedom Fighters conducted their rooftop

...ain, watching and waiting for American planes
...r came.

...ericans didn't understand what it meant when the
United States referred the Hungarian affair to the UN. Is it
possible that President Eisenhower and his State Department
didn't know what they were doing?

They did know. They meant for the Hungarian revolt to
fail. After four years of silence, Congressman Michael
Feighan (D-Ohio) released the text of a State Department
cablegram to Tito, the communist dictator of Yugoslavia.
Dispatched on November 2, 1956, the telegram to Tito read:

> The Government of the United States does not look with
> favor upon governments unfriendly to the Soviet Union on the
> borders of the Soviet Union.[96]

It was no accident, Congressman Feighan charged, that
just 36 hours later Soviet tanks re-invaded Hungary. The
Kremlin butchered Budapest, secure in the knowledge that
America would not oppose them. The U. S. State Department had given its approval.

Would aid to Hungary have provoked war? It is unlikely.
Khrushchev and the Kremlin have one overriding fear, the
simultaneous revolt of the enslaved peoples. In November
1956, the satellites were restless. Localizing rioting had
erupted even in Russia. The Red troops in Budapest deserted
their officers and joined the Freedom Fighters.[97] For this
reason, Khrushchev could not risk war.

He hesitated five days in Hungary. Finally, savage Mon-
golian troops were imported from Asia to crush the uprising.
Even these forces were not committed until Khrushchev had
tacit U. S. approval.

Three years later in a speech in Budapest, Khrushchev
himself admitted the Kremlin's indecision on using force in
Hungary.[98] Had the United States made a show of force,
or even granted diplomatic recognition, the Kremlin would
have abandoned Hungary. The United Nations, if the U. S.
feared to intervene, could have sent observers into Hungary
the instant the Russians were driven out.

When the Hungarians were condemned to die alone, the
hopes and faith of millions of the world's most dedicated anti-
communists died with them. Our staunchest allies, the enslaved people behind the Iron Curtain now believe they cannot expect help from America. If Americans lose their freedom, the beginning of the end came in Hungary.

Any hope remaining behind the Iron Curtain was erased

forever in July 1959 when President Eisenhower invited the Butcher of Budapest, Nikita Khrushchev, to America.

To protest Eisenhower's action, the House Committee on Un-American Activities scheduled hearings on the "Crimes of Khrushchev." The distinguished editor of the *Reader's Digest*, Eugene Lyons, testified. Lyons, a longtime student of international communism, said of Eisenhower's invitation to Khrushchev:

> It amounts to a body blow to the morale of the resistance forces in the Communist world. It's a betrayal of the hopes of the enemies of communism . . . The announcement of the invitation was a day of gloom and despair for nearly the whole population of every satellite country and for tens of millions inside Russia itself. What has been underway in the Red orbit, ever since 1917, is a permanent civil war between the rulers and the ruled . . . we have not merely been neutral in that civil war, but we have constantly by our policies sided with the Kremlin against its victims.[99]

Khrushchev accepted Eisenhower's invitation and toured American cities. Proper "precautions" were taken so that irate friends and relatives of the dead of Budapest, the refugees from Poland, and patriotic Americans could not get near enough to the communist dictator to cause "tensions." It was to the credit of most Americans that, outside of government circles, Khrushchev was greeted with stony silence.

Before Khrushchev arrived, the House Committee on Un-American Activities completed its documentation of Khrushchev's bloody record as Stalin's most trusted killer. In seven volumes, it showed:

> Khrushchev personally conceived and executed the mass starvation and liquidation of six to eight million Ukrainians in the early 1930's.[100]
>
> Khrushchev was the chief executioner for the bloody Moscow purge trials in 1936. He supervised the killing of thousands.[101]
>
> Khrushchev, during a second two-year reign of terror in the Ukraine in 1937-38, slaughtered another 400,000 people.[102]
>
> Khrushchev's post war Ukrainian purge liquidated or exiled hundreds of thousands to slave labor camps.[103]

Even after that bloody record had been starkly documented, Eisenhower entertained Khrushchev at Gettysburg, had his grandchildren photographed on the killer's knee, and announced to the world:

> This was the kind of heart-warming scene that any American would like to see taking place between his grandchildren and a stranger.[104]

This was the statement of the man elected six years before to "clean up the mess in Washington." Pictures of the event and Khrushchev's triumphant tour of 20 American cities were published in every Iron Curtain country. They carried the unwritten message, "Forget your hopes that America will rescue you. The Kremlin bosses and the American president are allied against you."

Of the entire visit, the Catholic prelate, Richard Cardinal Cushing of Boston said:

> For the past 25 years the United States has by and large been pursuing a policy of appeasement before Soviet Russia . . . if we are to save our country, it is clear we must halt this process which came to a new high point with the invitation to Nikita Khrushchev to visit the United States in 1959.[105]

CUBA

By the time Khrushchev came to America, the Kremlin puppet, Fidel Castro, had already been installed as the communist dictator of Cuba. His rise to power was largely the work of the U. S. State Department.

Castro was supported by but a few dozen bandits and a handful of communists in May 1957, when a career diplomat with a questionable record was named to head the Caribbean Desk in the U. S. State Department. His name was William Arthur Wieland. Nineteen months later, Castro was Cuba's communist dictator.

Castro's rise to power is documented in a series of reports issued by the Senate Internal Security Subcommittee in 1960-61. William Wieland's actions are prominent in the story. Here is a digest of Wieland's record:[106]

> Before joining the Foreign Service during World War II Wieland lived in Cuba under the alias "Arturo Montenegro" (pg. 746). Wieland entered the Foreign Service when its Latin American Department was headed by a Soviet agent, Laurence Duggan. As a reported "protege" of Summer Welles, Wieland "earned" four promotions in nine months and was assigned to Brazil in 1947 as press attache. The American ambassador to Brazil, William Pawley, filed reports on Wieland's "leftist" ideas and activities with Washington (pg. 736), after which Wieland was promoted again and transferred to Bogota, Columbia as vice consul. (pg. 756)

While in Bogota in 1948, Wieland engaged in strange activities. The Senate report disclosed:

> While the American vice consul in Bogota, Wieland knew a young Cuban revolutionary, Fidel Castro (pg. 806). Castro was a leader of the communist-inspired riots at the time of

the Foreign Ministers Conference in Bogota in 1948. During the riots, Castro captured a radio station and U. S. officials heard him broadcast, "This is Fidel Castro. This is a communist revolution." (pg. 725) Both Wieland and Roy Rubottom, Assistant Secretary of State and Wieland's superior during the Castro era were in Bogota during the riots.

Former Ambassador Pawley testified that he was shocked when Wieland was appointed to head the State Department's Caribbean Desk. Pawley contacted high State Department officials and President Eisenhower to tell his story, but no action was taken. The Senate committee disclosed that *after* the State Department and President Eisenhower were warned of Wieland's background, the career diplomat's activities included:

> From the time of his appointment to the key State Department post in May 1957, Wieland regularly disregarded, sidetracked or denounced FBI, State Department, and Military Intelligence sources which branded Castro as a communist and showed that his associates were Moscow-trained (pg. 793, 797-800). In August 1959, Wieland "wrecked" an intelligence briefing given to Dr. Milton Eisenhower by the American Embassy staff in Mexico City when it became obvious they were going to prove that Castro was a communist (pg. 798). For this action, Wieland was denounced to his face, with Eisenhower present, as "either a damn fool or a communist" (pg. 798). Milton Eisenhower chose to ignore the incident (pg. 798).

Despite all the warnings from reliable sources, Wieland was continued in control of American policy toward Cuba. The Senate study concluded:

> Wieland is considered author of the fatal arms embargo which cut off munitions shipments to the anti-communist Batista while Castro was being liberally supplied by sources in Florida and by Russian submarines surfacing off the Cuban coast (pg. 738). Similar State Department action ten years earlier had crippled Chiang Kai-shek's Army and permitted the communists to come to power in China.

Wieland managed to remove all anti-Castro diplomats from influential positions. The American ambassador to Cuba, Arthur Gardner, who forwarded continual reports to the State Department which exposed Castro as a communist, was replaced. He was prevented from briefing his replacement, Earl T. Smith. Instead, Wieland sent Smith to Herbert Matthews, a *New York Times* reporter and Castro's principal "press agent" in the United States.[107]

Ambassador Smith did not fall for Matthews' pro-Castro

"briefing" and was also replaced as the U. S. representative in Cuba. Smith in testifying before the Senate committee exposed the role Matthews played in Castro's rise to power:

> Three front page articles in the *New York Times* early in 1957, written by the editorialist Herbert Matthews, served to inflate Castro to world stature and world recognition. Until that time, Castro had been just another bandit in the Oriente mountains of Cuba, with a handful of followers who had terrorized the campesinos, that is the peasants, throughout the countryside.[108]

Matthews articles likened Castro to Abraham Lincoln. At the time, Castro's small force of trained terrorists were committing horrible atrocities against the peasants to force their "support" in the characteristic communist tactic used by the FLN in Algeria, the Mau Mau in South Africa, and the Chinese "agrarian reformers." However, typical of Matthews "reporting" at this time was a front-page story in the February 24, 1957 *New York Times,* which described Castro as . . .

> . . . the most remarkable and romantic figure to arise in Cuba since Jose Marti, hero of Cuba's wars of independence.

Even though Matthews had used similar praise in describing the communists in the Spanish Civil War in 1936,[109] a majority of the American press fell into line after his articles appeared, just as they had in depicting the Chinese communists as "agrarian reformers" ten years before. The usually reliable Jules Dubois of the *Chicago Tribune* said in his friendly biography of Castro:

> . . . Castro was to become the Robin Hood of the Sierra Maestra and was to pursue the same policy of taking from the rich to give to the poor.[110]

Edward R. Murrow of CBS-TV staged a highly complimentary "documentary" on Castro. Ed Sullivan made a brief, but spectacular trip to Cuba and returned with a filmed interview. Thirty million TV viewers saw Sullivan ask Castro such leading questions as:

> You are not a communist are you, Fidel? You are a devout Catholic, aren't you.[111]

Sullivan capped off the whitewash with this statement to the bearded Castro:

> The people of the United States have great admiration for you and your men because you are in the real American spirit of George Washington.

Eighteen months later, Sullivan retracted his statement, but by then it was too late. Religious magazines, the book publishers, all communications media pictured Castro as a romantic rebel, a Robin Hood leading a fight for social justice. Even with all the press buildup, however, if President Eisenhower and his State Department officials had heeded the warnings of reliable intelligence sources, Castro could not have come to power.

Castro did come to power. He proceeded, in classic communist fashion, to execute thousands of Cubans in bloody firing squad marathons. Even so, he continued to receive the praise of liberals in press and government.

In April 1959, Castro was brought to America and given a hero's welcome. He had well-publicized audiences with Secretary of State Christian Herter and Vice President Nixon. Nixon, to his credit, tried without success after the interview to convince Eisenhower that Castro was a communist.[112] Assistant Secretary of State Roy Rubottom arranged the prestige-building appearance Castro made before the American Society of Newspaper Editors. The State Department announced that Castro was being welcomed as "a distinguished leader."[113]

The rise of Castro was as inexcusable as it was tragic. The State Department was warned that Castro had a long communist background, that his supporters were Moscow-trained, that he was promoting a communist revolution.

Eisenhower and high State Department officials were warned in 1957 — 18 months before Castro came to power that William Wieland was "leftist" oriented, and unsuitable for his high post.[114]

All the warnings were ignored.

Thus ended the eight years as President of the man who promised to "clean up the mess in Washington."

Chapter IV

Words vs. Action

> *Look at the means which a man employs;*
> *consider his motives; observe his pleasures.*
> *A man simply cannot conceal himself.*
>
> — *Confucius*[1]

UNLIKE THE ELECTION CAMPAIGN OF 1952 when Communist infiltration of government and appeasement of world communism were key issues, these crucial topics were largely ignored in the 1960 presidential campaign.

Tragic handling of the Hungarian revolt was given passing mention by the Democrats, but only in areas with high concentrations of immigrants from Eastern Europe. Castro's rise to power was discussed in a partisan way. The sordid story of the State Department's direct responsibility for hiding the bearded dictator's communist affiliations, as disclosed by a Senate committee, was not mentioned.

Why?

Richard Nixon was not likely to dredge up the record of failure and appeasement of the Administration of which he was part. Under pressures for "party unity" anti-communist Republicans remained silent.

The few knowledgable anti-communists in the Democratic Party were paralyzed by politics also. They knew that any loud voice raised against the dismal record of Modern Republicanism would have provoked only partisan replies, such as, "Well, we don't have an Alger Hiss in our party."

Candidate John F. Kennedy didn't turn the spotlight on the tragic actions of the William Wielands in government. Instead, when Kennedy became President, William Wieland was promoted to the State Department committee charged with revising security procedures. As was noted in the opening chapter, President Kennedy denounced the woman reporter who described Wieland as a "security risk" during a televised press conference and questioned his appointment. Kennedy stated that Wieland's record, cleared by the State Department, qualified him for the highly sensitive post.[2]

The party in power in Washington changed on January 20, 1961. The basic direction of American foreign policy remained the same.

JUDGMENT

John F. Kennedy himself set the standard by which his administration must be judged. On November 8, 1961, he wrote the foreword for *To Turn the Tide,* a published collection of the speeches and statements he made in his first ten months as President. He said:

> Strong words alone, of course, do not make meaningful policy; they must, in foreign affairs, in particular, be backed both by a will and by weapons that are equally strong. Thus a collection of Presidential statements cannot convey their true perspective unless it is realized or recalled precisely what they signified in committing the power and majesty of the American people.[3]

To evaluate President Kennedy's Administration using the standard he suggested requires a careful analysis of his words and actions in crisis after crisis.

LAOS

In a widely publicized talk with Congressional leaders on March 26, 1961, President Kennedy promised that Laos, then under attack from Red China and North Viet Nam, would not be permitted to fall.[4]

After Kennedy's strong words, U. S. and Soviet diplomats agreed on a "peaceful" solution in Laos. The "coalition government" they proposed was the same "peaceful solution" which led to the communization of Poland, Czechoslovakia, and China. Prince Boun Oum, legal head of the anti-communist government of Laos, was ordered to give communists key positions in his cabinet.[5]

When Boun Oum refused, his monthly allotment of $4-million in American foreign aid was stopped on February 16, 1962.[6] Without money to pay his army, which was under communist attack, Boun Oum was helpless. Within four months he bowed to joint American-Soviet pressures and a coalition government was formed. The communists and the "neutralists" named 13 of the 15 cabinet ministers.[7] The pro-western, anti-communist, Boun Oum, was out.

President Kennedy and Nikita Khrushchev praised the "peaceful" settlement in Laos.[8] Once the communists were firmly established in the coalition government, American foreign aid payments were resumed.[9] U. S. military forces were withdrawn. The 10,000 North Vietnamese communists and Red Chinese troops stayed in Laos in violation of Khrushchev's pledge.

President Kennedy's actions directly contradicted his promise to keep Laos from going communist. They repudiated the sharp condemnation of "coalition government" he expressed on January 30, 1949, when as a young Congressman from Massachusetts, he said:

> Our policy in China has reaped the whirlwind. The continued insistence that aid would not be forthcoming unless a coalition government with the Communists was formed, was a crippling blow to the Nationalist government. So concerned were our diplomats and their advisers, the Lattimores, and the Fairbanks, with the imperfections of the diplomatic system in China after 20 years of war, and the tales of corruption in high places, that they lost sight of our tremendous stake in a non-communist China.
>
> There were those who claimed, and still claim, that Chinese communism was not really communism at all but an advanced agrarian reform movement which did not take directions from Moscow.
>
> This is the tragic story of China whose freedom we once fought to preserve. What our young men have saved, our diplomats and our President have frittered away.[10]

In 1961, the diplomats whom Kennedy condemned in 1949 were named to run his State Department. They used the same methods in destroying the anti-communist Laotian government as had been used against Chiang Kai-shek and China 15 years before.

Dean Rusk, who served in the State Department's Far Eastern Section during the tragic China period, became Kennedy's Secretary of State.

Rusk was a longtime affiliate of the Institute of Pacific Relations.[11] In 1952 while the IPR was being branded "a vehicle used by the communists to orientate American far eastern policy toward communist objectives," Dean Rusk, as head of the Rockefeller Foundation, was recommending a $2-million grant to the communist-influenced organization. Two years later, Rusk defended Rockefeller support of the IPR to a Congressional committee.[12]

In 1949, Congressman Kennedy voiced scorn for "those who claimed, and still claim, that Chinese communism was not really communism at all but merely an advanced agrarian movement."

Dean Rusk was one of them. A full 18 months after Kennedy made his speech in 1949, and after Chinese communists had murdered millions, Dean Rusk, speaking at the University of Pennsylvania, compared Mao Tse-tung to George Washington and indicated that the Chinese revolution did not aim at dictatorship.[13]

Even so, in 1961, President Kennedy appointed Rusk as Secretary of State.

To the post of Assistant Secretary of State for Far Eastern Affairs, Kennedy named W. Averell Harriman. It was Harriman who conceived and executed the policy of cutting off aid to Laos when the Laotians refused to put communists into their government.[14] While President Kennedy was pledging support for Laos, Harriman at a critical point in the negotiations told members of Congress:

> It doesn't matter much to us, one way or the other, what happens in Laos.[15]

Instead of being fired for his handling of the Laotian situation, Harriman was promoted to the number two post in the State Department. In July 1963, he was sent to Moscow to negotiate the nuclear test ban treaty on which the survival of America may depend.

Harriman is a longtime Soviet apologist. He was ambassador to Moscow during World War II. He was one of FDR's top advisers during the tragic Teheran-Yalta period when the groundwork was laid for the betrayal of China. As late as July 1951, after the communists had completed their conquest of Eastern Europe and China, Harriman still defended the Yalta agreements.[16]

CUBA

As a candidate, John F. Kennedy's criticism of the Eisenhower Administration's Cuban policy led many Americans to hope that under his leadership, the United States would topple Castro. On October 20, 1960, for example, Kennedy said:

> We must attempt to strengthen the non-Batista democratic anti-Castro forces in exile, and in Cuba itself who offer eventual hope of overthrowing Castro . . . thus far, these fighters for freedom have had virtually no support from our government.[17]

On the morning of April 17, 1961, three months after Kennedy's inauguration, a task force of 1,400 anti-Castro Cubans invaded communist Cuba at Cochinos Bay — the Bay of Pigs.

The invasion was planned, financed, and controlled by the U. S. State Department and the Central Intelligence Agency.[18]

President Kennedy approved the plan and promised air cover to the invaders. Two U. S. carriers, including the Boxer, were in the task force of five World War II Liberty ships and other supporting vessels. The carriers stood by, within easy striking distance during the invasion. Their decks were loaded with fighting planes. *U. S. News and World Report* in its September 17, 1962 issue summed up what happened. It said in part:

> Secure in this assurance of air support, the invaders went ashore . . . 1,400 armed men reached the beaches . . . In the battle that followed Castro's troops suffered heavy casualties . . . Castro's tanks, coming up to the battle were sitting ducks for attack by air. Confidently, the little invading force waited for its air support to arrive. Its leaders had assurance of that support. It was provided in the pre-invasion planning.
>
> Hours before, on Sunday evening, a small but potent force of B-26's was sitting in readiness on an airstrip 500 miles away, waiting to take off for the Bay of Pigs. Those were planes of the invasion force with Cuban pilots.
>
> But those planes didn't take off. The reason: President Kennedy forbade their use.
>
> That was the fateful decision President Kennedy made on that Sunday evening. He decided that the anti-Castro Cubans could not have the support of their own air force during the invasion. Without that support, the invasion failed.

Absence of air cover was not the sole factor in the failure of the invasion. Many other fatal "blunders" doomed the attempt to topple Castro. For example:

> A near impossible supply problem was created when the CIA armed the 1,400 man invasion force with weapons requiring over 30 different types of ammunition. The guns were purchased in second hand stores "to avoid identifying the invading force with the U. S."[19]

Weapons and ammunition were supplied to the underground in Cuba by the CIA in such a way as to insure that they could never be used:

> Some guerilla groups were supplied with 30.06-cal. ammunition and "grease guns" which fired .45-cal. bullets. In other areas the CIA supplied .45-cal. ammunition to accompany BAR's (Browning Automatic Rifles) which shoot 30.06-cal. bullets.[20]

Planned coordination of an underground uprising with the Bay of Pigs invasion was so mismanaged as to indicate deliberate sabotage. To be successful, even with air cover, such a small invasion force had to be supported almost immediately by uprisings all over Cuba. Some of the reasons why the uprisings did not occur were uncovered later. They included:

The underground was never advised of the landing date and did not know whether the Bay of Pigs operation was a real or diversionary invasion. Radio SWAN, the CIA's mysterious short wave broadcast station which blankets the Caribbean, failed to broadcast the pre-arranged signals to trigger the underground into action. Instead, the station broadcast one conflicting and false report after another of uprisings in Cuba.[21]

U. S.-based coordinators of the nearly 100 underground organizations in Cuba were rounded up several days before the invasion by CIA agents and were held incommunicado by U. S. authorities at a secluded spot in Florida. They were not advised that the invasion had started — until it had already failed. By then, it was too late to alert their contacts in Cuba.[22]

Some details on why the invasion failed became clouded in official accusations, admissions, denials, and contradictions. The controversy over whether or not air cover was planned — and then withdrawn from the invasion — raged for 18 months. Then, the Senate Internal Security Subcommittee released testimony given by Whiting Willauer three months after the invasion attempt failed.[23]

Willauer, former ambassador to Honduras and associate of Flying Tiger chief, General Claire Chennault, had directed the *only* successful overthrow of a communist dictatorship anywhere in the world, the Guatamalan revolution in 1954.

On December 10, 1960, after President Kennedy's election but before his inauguration, Willauer was recalled from Honduras and placed in charge of plans for an invasion of Cuba. Working with the CIA, Joint Chiefs of Staff, etc. he formulated the overall blueprint for the invasion. He planned air cover, both low-level close support to be provided by Cuban-flown B-26 bombers and high level cover for the B-26's to be provided by carrier-based Navy jets.[24]

Willauer held the title, Special Assistant to Secretary of State Christian Herter. After Kennedy's inauguration, Dean Rusk asked him to continue in this capacity. Within two weeks, however, he was "frozen out." His CIA contacts were ordered not to talk with him. He was ignored in the State Department. For 30 days, Willauer's immediate superior, Chester Bowles, refused to see him. He was never consulted or "debriefed" by a successor for the background information, suggestions, etc. that Willauer could have passed on.[25]

Finally, on April 16, 1961, the day before the Bay of Pigs invasion, Willauer received an informal telephone call dismissing him from the State Department. He had been in "isolation" for nearly two months.[26]

Because the monstrous story has unfolded bit by bit, much of it largely ignored by the press, the American people have never faced the full implications of the first Cuban fiasco. Was the Bay of Pigs invasion planned to fail? Were young Cubans deliberately sent onto the beaches to die, with no hope of success?

The father of two of the boys who were missing in the invasion attempt wrote a letter to the Superintendent of Culver Military Academy in Indiana where they had gone to school. He said:

> This letter is to inform you that my two sons, Jorge (Culver '59) and Mario (ex-Culver '61) together with other Cuban men, were in the U. S.-endorsed invasion attempt in Cuba during the past week. Jorge is a captive and Mario is missing. I want you to know and the world to know that all of us who once believed in the greatness of the United States feel that they and all of us have been the victims of gross, high official treason.
>
> I allowed them to go because they had an ideal . . . and we were told that they would be backed to the end by the United States government and its armed forces if necessary. We believed this because we know that this fight is not for Cuba or the Cubans. It is a fight for the very life of all Americans.[27]

Just weeks after the disastrous Bay of Pigs invasion failed, the United Nations Special Fund, headed by an American Paul Hoffman, voted to give Castro, the communist dictator of Cuba, a $1.6-million grant to improve his agriculture.[28] The U. S. taxpayer is paying over 40% of the bill. The grant was one of 10 the United States is helping to finance in Cuba.

Within four weeks after the failure of the Cuban invasion, the Kennedy-Johnson Administration asked Congress for authority to give economic aid to the communist nations of Hungary and Czechoslovakia — and broaden aid given to Yugoslavia and Poland under programs started by President Eisenhower.

Even though Czechoslovakian arms had been used to repel the attempted invasion of Cuba less than 30 days before, the U. S. Senate voted 43 to 36 to give the aid to the communist enemy.[29] Of the 36 Senators who voted against the bill, 18 were Democrats and 18 were Republicans. A few months later, the Senate killed by a 45-43 vote another measure which would have barred foreign aid to countries selling arms and strategic goods to communist countries.[30]

MISSILES IN CUBA

In the aftermath of the Bay of Pigs fiasco, recurring reports from Cuban underground sources indicated that Russian communist troops, missiles, and jet bombers were being moved into Cuba.

After nearly a year of official denials, evidence of the buildup in Cuba became so overwhelming it could not be ignored. President Kennedy acknowledged the presence of Soviet troops and missiles in Cuba in September 1962 — but assured Congressional leaders that they were "defensive types."[31]

Concerned Americans and Congressional leaders refused to be appeased. "Weapons are weapons," they answered, "and troops can be used offensively as well as defensively." As President Kennedy campaigned for Democratic congressional candidates in Cincinnati, Chicago and Detroit, he was greeted with signs, placards, and posters asking, "What about Cuba?" and demanding "Less Profile, More Courage."

Senators Kenneth Keating (R-NY), Homer Capehart (R-Ind) and Barry Goldwater (R-Ari), Charles Bacon, national commander of the American Legion, and others called for a naval blockade or military invasion of Cuba to remove the missiles and Russian troops.[32]

Such demands were labelled "irresponsible warmongering." President Kennedy applied this term to Senator Capehart on October 16, 1962 in Indiana. In a speech in Albuquerque, New Mexico, Vice President Lyndon Johnson said that Americans who advocated a blockade of Cuba have "more guts than brains . . . stopping a Russian ship is an act of war."[33]

Five days later, as public pressure continued to build up, President Kennedy admitted that Castro did have offensive missiles and jet bombers. He ordered a naval blockade.[34] The American people rallied to his support. Khrushchev quickly agreed to remove his troops and missiles. Democrat losses in the Congressional election were held to a handful of seats.

To win the election, President Kennedy paid an appalling price. In the pre-election excitement and tension, few Americans read the full text of Khrushchev's agreement. The communist dictator in his message to Kennedy, which the *New York Times* published, said:

I regard with respect and trust the statement you made in your message on October 27, 1962, that there would be no attack, no invasion of Cuba, and not only on the part of the

United States, but also on the part of other nations of the Western Hemisphere as you have said in the same message of yours.[35]

President Kennedy had given Khrushchev a personal guarantee that the U. S. would not attempt to liberate Cuba — and would not allow other forces to do so.

This part of the agreement was later denied by the Administration — even as it moved to uphold its guarantee to protect Castro.

Anti-Castro refugee groups in Florida were subjected to harassment and weapons were confiscated from groups training for raids on Cuba. Exile groups were refused time on radio stations in Florida for anti-communist broadcasts to Cuba. Remarks derogatory to Castro were deleted from Spanish language newscasts on Miami radio stations WGBS, WCKR, and WMIE.[36]

American naval forces were deployed in the Caribbean, not to stop Castro's communist agents from spreading out across Latin America, but to prevent anti-Castro raids against the Cuban coast. Under pressure from Washington, Great Britain stopped Cuban resistance groups from using bases in the Bahamas for raids against Castro.[37]

The President's action in creating a sanctuary for the communists in Cuba — the unbelievable use of American military forces to protect a communist dictator from attacks by freedom loving Cubans prompted many concerned Americans to ask, "Which side is our government on?"

For committing the Cuban captives of communism to permanent slavery, for betraying his campaign promises to the American people, President Kennedy received no real guarantee that the Soviet missiles were removed. He received and accepted Khrushchev's promise. U. S. inspections were limited to surveillance by low-flying aircraft which observed "missile-like shapes" on the decks of several departing Soviet ships.

Within 30 days after Cuba was declared "free of Soviet missiles," Carlos Todd, editor of the Cuban Information Service, released maps and a detailed statement showing dozens of locations in Cuba where Soviet missiles were installed underground in caves, hidden from aerial reconnaissance flights.[38] Todd's evidence was ridiculed, just as his original reports about Soviet missiles and troops in Cuba had been denied by the Kennedy Administration.

Similar documented reports by other Cuban underground groups were publicized by Senator Kenneth Keating (R-NY) and other Congressmen. They were ridiculed by the Administration until finally the Senate Preparedness Subcommittee estimated, and the Administration confirmed, that a minimum of 17,500 Soviet troops were based in Cuba,[39] 10,000 more than Kennedy admitted were in Cuba before his pre-election "victory" over Khrushchev.

The surrender was not limited to the Western Hemisphere. When Khrushchev "agreed" to remove his missiles from Cuba, rumors circulated that President Kennedy had made a "deal" to remove U. S. missiles from Turkey and Italy. The Administration vehemently denied the reports. In January 1963, after the "crisis" was over, the Defense Department declared U. S. missile bases in Turkey and Italy "outmoded." The bases were closed.[40]

The influential chairman of the Senate Armed Forces Committee, Senator Richard Russell (D-Ga) recapped the disgraceful chain of events in a television interview on December 5, 1962. He said:

> Three months ago we were pledged to see that Castroism in this hemisphere was destroyed. We have now been euchred into the position of babysitting for Castro and guaranteeing the integrity of the communist regime in Cuba.
>
> We don't know for a positive fact that the missiles and bombers have been removed. I assume they have but all we have seen is a box they said contained a bomber and a long metal container that they said contained a missile. We have not had on-the-spot inspection.
>
> The Communists start out on a course of action they know is wrong, and then when you call their hand they say, "All right, we'll stop this if you'll give us something over here," and they know they have no right to it whatever. And that is what they did to us in Cuba.[41]

BERLIN

In June 1961, President Kennedy, meeting with Nikita Khrushchev in Vienna, became the fourth American President to go to the "summit." He returned for a TV report to the nation, and said:

> No new aims were stated in private that had not been stated in public on either side . . . Neither of us were there to dictate a settlement . . . There was no discourtesy, no loss of tempers, no threats or ultimatums by either side.[42]

A week later, Khrushchev revealed that he had given Kennedy a three-pronged ultimatum at Vienna. He demanded that Kennedy get Western forces out of Berlin by fall, recognize East Germany, and conclude a peace treaty with it.

After six weeks of silence, President Kennedy appeared on nationwide TV on July 25, 1961. He confirmed that his original TV report to the people had been untrue. He admitted that Khrushchev had issued the Berlin ultimatums at Vienna. He made a firm promise that American rights in Berlin were not negotiable.[43] The President asked for expanded defense spending, increased size for the regular Army, and the power to mobilize reserve forces. He summed up the meaning of the crisis saying:

> If we do not meet our commitment to Berlin, where will we later stand? If we are not true to our word there, all that we have achieved in collective security, which relies on these words, will mean nothing. And if there is one path to war, it is the path of weakness and disunity.[44]

Seventeen days later, the communists built the Berlin Wall, dramatically sealing off East Berlin in a flagrant violation of western rights. Despite Mr. Kennedy's pledge, and a stirring speech by Lyndon Johnson in West Berlin, the United States did nothing.

Shrewd observers had anticipated that the U. S. would not stand firm. Within days after President Kennedy made his pledge to stand firm in Berlin, Senator William Fulbright (D-Ark), chairman of the influential Senate Foreign Relations Committee and sometime administration spokesman, suggested that perhaps some "accommodation" could be arranged. Fulbright believed the source of the problem was the mass exodus of refugees from East Germany to the West which was "embarrassing to Khrushchev."[45]

While the President was asking for "sacrifice on the part of many citizens" to meet the threat of communism in Berlin, his administration was approving a 600% increase in export licenses for shipment of goods to communist countries. During the two weeks when the Berlin crisis was "hottest" the administration approved shipment of such "non-strategic" items as $2.5-million in railway equipment to communist Bulgaria, $1.5-million in synthetic rubber to the Soviet Union, and $700,000 worth of iron and steel scrap to communist Yugoslavia.[46]

At the same time mobilization of 100,000 National Guardsmen and reservists was being considered to "meet the communist threat," the American ambassador to Poland was officiating at the dedication of the world's most modern, most highly automated steel finishing plant. It was built for the communist Polish government in Warren, Ohio and American taxpayers "lent" the communists $2.5-million to pay for it.[47]

Many concerned Americans asked, "Can these be the actions of a government which considers communism an enemy, which means to stand firm in Berlin, or anywhere?"

THE CONGO

The story of the Congo, like that of Cuba, Laos, and other crises of the Kennedy Administration, has its roots in the Eisenhower era.

The Congo received its UN-ordered independence from Belgium on June 30, 1960. The first prime minister was the communist terrorist, Patrice Lumumba. Although supported by the United States and the United Nations, Lumumba's regime let the Congolese Army degenerate into marauding bands of terrorists.[48]

Murder, mayhem, rape, and pillaging spread through the rich jungle land. At Lumumba's invitation, hundreds of Soviet "technicians" swarmed into the country. Racist "black only" policies were instituted. Cannabilism resumed. Fiscal policies which were to lead to runaway inflation were adopted.[49]

After 11 days of such strife and turmoil, President Moise Tshombe proclaimed Katanga province of the Congo an independent country. He said, "We are seceding from chaos."[50]

During the following 30 months, Tshombe and the people of Katanga were subjected to diplomatic pressures, economic coercion, and UN-conducted, US-supported military actions to force Katanga to rejoin the Central government which even after Lumumba's death was communist-dominated.

Cyrille Adoula, the UN-US supported premier of the Central Congolese government, is labelled a "neutralist" but as a participant in Tito's Belgrade Conference in 1961, he voted for the vicious anti-American resolutions and announced he would follow the policies of the communist puppet, Patrice Lumumba.[51]

Adoula's cabinet was riddled with communists and pro-communists. Soviet-backed Antoine Gizenga was vice premier. Gizenga is a Prague-trained communist and successor to Patrice Lumumba. The Interior Minister, Christphe Gbenye, also trained in communist Czechoslovakia, controlled the police. Gizenga supporter, Reny Mwamba, was Minister of Justice.[52]

Reporters covering the Congo named three other cabinet ministers as pro-communists. The newspaper *Uhuru*, in Stanleyville, the capital of the communist province in Congo, boasted that Lumumbists won a majority of 23 of the 44 seats in the August 1961 elections.[53]

Tshombe rejected the US-UN ultimatum to join the Adoula government in September 1961, knowing that coalition government with communists leads to eventual communist control. This was his "last chance." The United Nations, with logistical support of the U. S. Air Force, attacked Katanga on September 13, 1961 to start an on-again, off-again war which was to last 18 months.

The UN action violated the Security Council's own directives on the Congo and Article 2, Section 7 of the United Nations Charter, which provides:

> Nothing contained in the present Charter shall authorize the United Nations to intervene in matters which are essentially within the domestic jurisdiction of any state.

Even so, the U. S. State Department defended the invasion as necessary to prevent communists from taking over the Congo. *However, Egide Bocheley-Davidson, a vicious procommunist follower of Patrice Lumumba, was named as the Central Congolese government's administrator for Katanga.*[54] Michael Tombelaine, assistant UN director for Katanga, is a French communist.[55]

Senator Thomas Dodd (D-Conn) protested on the Senate floor and declared that it . . .

> . . . is not the business of the UN to go about overthrowing anti-communist governments . . . It is difficult to believe that this action was taken in simple innocence.[56]

Congressman Donald C. Bruce (R-Ind) gave this evaluation:

> I charge that the U. S. State Department . . . is acquiescing in the communist takeover of the Congo. I fully realize the seriousness of that statement . . . I make no charges of treason. I cannot prove any. I simply say that over a period of years the tragic growth of communism and its victories in one area after another of the world forms a consistent pattern. What is wrong with our State Department?[57]

During the 18 month on-again, off-again war against Katanga, the United Nations committed unbelievable atrocities. At one point, uncivilized and untrained bands of Congolese soldiers, including communist supporters of Antoine Gizenga were transported to Katanga by the UN in US planes and unleashed. The two-week orgy of mass murder, rape, pillage, and cannibalism they carried out under the UN flag with the United States paying the bill is unequalled in modern times.[58]

. . . released untrue stories to the press which accused Struelens of offering a $1-million bribe to a Latin American country in exchange for diplomatic recognition for Katanga.[66]

. . . made public speeches smearing Congressmen who opposed the State Department's Katanga policy.[67]

. . . pictured all opposition to the UN brutality and atrocities in Katanga as the work of "ultra-conservatives" and those with financial interests in the Congo.[68]

The Senate committee questioned why the State Department denied the anti-communist Tshombe a visa to visit America while granting royal welcomes to numerous communist dictators and pro-communist puppets. At the time when Tshombe was denied entry to the U. S., the State Department granted visas to Holden Roberto, leader of the Angolan terrorist movement, and Mario de Andrade, leader of the communist faction among the Angolan terrorists.[69]

The Senate committee learned that de Andrade, as a communist, was ineligible for a visa, until the State Department and Attorney General Robert Kennedy ruled that his visit was in the best interests of the U. S. and granted a waiver.[70]

In commenting on the double standard under which the State Department welcomes communists and persecutes anti-communists, the Senate committee in its report said:

> There is unjustifiable inconsistency in a policy which arbitrarily excludes friends of the U. S. who are not excludable under the law, while granting visas to known communists and mass murderers, who are sworn enemies of this country, and whose exclusion is called for by law.[71]

Holden Roberto and Mario de Andrade were not the only enemies of the United States who were welcomed to America during the time when Tshombe was being persecuted and finally crushed by the joint UN-US action. Others were:

Dr. Cheddi Jagan, communist premier of British Guiana, received a royal welcome in Washington and a promise of $200-million in American foreign aid in August 1961. The press and TV buildup of his Washington visit equalled that given Fidel Castro in 1957-58.[72]

After Ben Bella, the FLN terrorist, established himself as dictator of Algeria and concluded economic, political and military alliances with Moscow and Peking, he was invited to Washington. President Kennedy greeted him on the White House lawn, honored him with a 21-gun salute, and promised him American aid. Ben Bella flew to Cuba the following day and was pictured kissing Castro.[73]

Americans who contrast the crushing of Tshombe, the harassment of Cuban freedom fighters, the destruction of the anti-communist government of Laos with the coddling of communist dictators in all parts of the world should recall a brief paragraph from President Kennedy's inaugural address and wonder at its meaning. He said:

> Let every nation know . . . that we shall pay any price, bear any burden, meet any hardship, support any friend, oppose any foe to assure the survival and success of liberty.[74]

In his first speech to Congress, President Johnson repeated these words of his predecessor — and pledged to continue the Kennedy policies.[75] Will President Johnson follow President Kennedy's words — or his actions? Less than 40 days after Johnson took office, the St. Louis Globe-Democrat reported on December 30, 1963 that U. S. customs officials had siezed a boat carrying bombs that anti-communist refugee groups planned to use against Castro.

INTERNAL SECURITY

Newspaper headlines were mainly occupied by Cuba, Laos, Berlin, and the Congo during President Kennedy's first two years. The rapid deterioration of safeguards against infiltration and subversion of the U. S. by communists, domestic and foreign, went almost unnoticed.

The return to government of the old "IPR crowd" alerted some Americans to vigilance. Close observers and careful students of communism watched apprehensively during the first year of the Kennedy-Johnson Administration as:

President Kennedy appointed Dr. James Killian, Jr. to coordinate and monitor the most important government intelligence agencies including the CIA, FBI and 30 other military and civilian security agencies.

Killian's "qualifications" to supervise the agencies which are America's front line of defense against communist infiltration and subversion include: (1) In 1947 he favored abolishing the Massachusetts legislative committee which investigated communist activities and protested listing of organizations as subversive by the Massachusetts attorney general (2) In 1948, Killian opposed a Massachusetts law which would have banned identified communists from teaching positions (3) He defended J. Robert Oppenheimer in 1954 when the Atomic Energy Commission withdrew his security clearance for close association with communists (4) As President of Massachusetts Institute of Technology, Killian rehired Professor Dirk Struik who had been fired from the MIT faculty because he was a communist (5) As President Eisenhower's chief scientific adviser, Killian was a major influence in having U. S. nuclear tests halted in September 1958.[76]

Another top security post was given to Salvatore Bontempo, a New Jersey politician. He was named to head the State Department's critical Bureau of Security despite a complete lack of any security experience — and a record of being indicted for criminal actions in disposing of surplus government property after World War II.[77] Bontempo finally resigned when Congressman Francis Walter (D-Pa) threatened an investigation.

The State Department Bureau of Security budget was slashed, however, so that 25 security agents and investigators had to be fired. John W. Hanes, a former CIA official and one-time head of the Security Bureau, labelled the cutback in the vital force as "either incompetence or a deliberate attempt to render the State Department security section ineffective."[78]

In November 1963, the several years drive to destroy the last remnants of a security program in the State Department culminated with the firing of Otto F. Otepka, chief of the Division of Evaluations in the Office of Security.

Otepka was a veteran security employee and dedicated anti-communist. He was fired by the State Department after he furnished the Senate Internal Security Subcommittee evidence to show that high State Department officials had lied under oath about security matters when they testified before the committee.[79]

Dozens of actions breached normal security procedures. Among them:

> Security investigations were waived on President Kennedy's orders for appointees to over 200 highly sensitive State Department positions.[80]

> Fingerprinting of alien nationals entering the U. S. was abolished. The State Department explained that the procedure had been "an affront to communist newsmen and UN employees."[81]

> Dean Rusk ordered a Polish communist admitted to the U. S. under the "cultural exchange" program, even though the Immigration Commission presented evidence that the man had been trained in Moscow to gather industrial intelligence information in the U. S.[82]

A return to the news of two names from the past, Lauchlin Currie and J. Robert Oppenheimer, along with the story of Owen Lattimore, related earlier, typify the approach of Presidents Kennedy and Johnson to security matters.

Lauchlin Currie had been FDR's Administrative Assistant for Foreign Affairs during World War II. In 1949, Currie left the United States and relinquished his citizenship to avoid testifying about his participation in a Soviet spy ring while on the White House staff.[83]

In 1961, the *Chicago Tribune* revealed that Currie was in South America administering the Alliance for Progress dollars the U. S. was providing to help "fight communism" in Columbia. The *Chicago Tribune,* after detailing Currie's participation in the World War II Soviet spy ring, said:

> This is the man who is planning how the dollars provided by a country which has stripped him of citizenship are to be employed in Columbia. It will be surprising if President Kennedy doesn't find out he has made an alliance for Communist progress in that country.[84]

In 1954, the Atomic Energy Commission withdrew the security clearance of Dr. J. Robert Oppenheimer, the scientific director of the World War II A-bomb project. The AEC determined that Oppenheimer had contributed large sums of money to the Communist Party during World War II, that his brother, his wife, and his mistress were Communist Party members, that Oppenheimer had recommended an identified communist for a job on the top secret A-bomb project, and that he had lied to security investigators about communist attempts to obtain nuclear data.[85]

In June 1961, the Organization of American States, of which the U. S. is the largest and most influential member, arranged to send Oppenheimer on a lecture tour of five Latin American countries. The State Department offered no objection even though Oppenheimer had no security clearance.

In fact, following the tour, Oppenheimer was a guest of honor at a formal White House Dinner. After this preliminary buildup, in December 1963, President Lyndon Johnson gave Oppenheimer the 1963 Enrico Fermi award of $50,000 in tax-free government funds. The award was granted by the Atomic Energy Commission in April 1963 with President Kennedy's approval.[86]

The *St. Louis Globe-Democrat* quoted administration officials as saying privately that the award was a first step in rebuilding Oppenheimer's "public image" and as a "test" of public reaction in preparation for his eventual return to a sensitive government job.[87]

One of President Johnson's earliest appointments was that of Abe Fortas as one of his top personal assistants. Fortas, a New Deal figure in the 1930's won fame in the late 1940's as a lawyer for loyalty and security risks such as Owen Lattimore.

Another of President Johnson's acts which caused dismay among concerned anti-communists was his appointment of Chief Justice Earl Warren to head the commission investigating the assassination of President Kennedy by a communist killer. The appointment of such a commission, headed by Warren, was suggested in the November 26, 1963 issue of the official communist newspaper, *The Worker*. Three days later, President Johnson appointed the commission, so loaded with "liberals" as to build suspicion of a planned coverup of any leftist involvement in the killing.

The New York *Daily News,* the nation's largest circulation newspaper, was quoted in the January 3, 1964 *Time* as calling for . . .

> . . . An all-out attack on Chief Justice Earl Warren's commission to investigate the Kennedy murder, plus a drive to persuade Congress to give Warren & Co. the heave.

The *Daily News* editorial said:

> In view of the Earl Warren Supreme Court's long-standing tenderness toward Communists, any report this commission may give birth to will be open to suspicion of pro-Communist and anti-conservative bias."

OPINION SUBVERSION

The return of the Oppenheimers, the Lattimores, and others to the fringes of government service creates an atmosphere which encourages further disregard of security procedures.

In addition, and very importantly, it tends to demoralize active anti-communists while conditioning the great majority of less informed Americans to believe that earlier actions in security cases were unjust "witchhunts;" that the internal threat of communism has been exaggerated.

For example, the *St. Louis Post-Dispatch* criticized Senator Thomas Dodd (D-Conn) for questioning Owen Lattimore's visit to Outer Mongolia. The newspaper implied that Dodd was continuing an unjust persecution of the one-time State Department adviser. The editorial said, "Professor Lattimore was *stigmatized* by the *McCarthyites* a decade and more ago." It adds about Lattimore, "It was *alleged* he influenced the State Department to regard the Chinese Communists as agrarian reformers."[88]

The editorial ignored the Senate Internal Security Subcommittee's verdict on Lattimore, which branded him "a conscious, articulate agent of the Soviet conspiracy."

Such twisting of facts and truth, the rewriting of history, has been termed "Opinion Subversion" by J. Edgar Hoover. It is one of communism's deadliest weapons in the battle against free men. Other actions of the Kennedy-Johnson Administration have similarly contributed to the subtle conditioning of the American mind to believe that "maybe communism isn't all bad." For example:

A longtime ban on the importation of the products of slave labor was lifted by the Administration. American stores were thereby opened to Russian crab meat, Polish hams, Yugoslavian and Hungarian baskets, Czechoslovakian glassware and Christmas tree ornaments. In the first year, communist products worth over $100-million were imported into America.[89]

The trade was a two-way proposition. Through sales of woven baskets, clothes pins, and other non-essentials in America, the communists earned the money to buy strategic goods here.

As an example, in 1961 officials in the Commerce Department overruled Defense Department protests and issued export permits to allow the Soviet Union to buy machine tools in America for grinding the precision ball-bearings for missile guidance systems.[90]

Alert Congressmen stopped the sale on five separate occasions but the units were finally shipped even after the Senate Internal Security Subcommittee proved the machines were available no where else in the world.[91]

When patriotic Americans tried to learn which companies were trading with the communist enemy, Commerce Secretary Luther Hodges, classified such lists "confidential" to protect the firms from "harassment."[92]

On March 17, 1961, with the approval of Secretary of State Dean Rusk, Treasury Secretary Dillon, Postmaster General Edward Day, and Attorney General Robert Kennedy, the President lifted a ban on importation and distribution of communist propaganda into the United States. The ban against *free* distribution of communist propaganda through the U. S. mails had been imposed by President Harry Truman 13 years earlier.[93]

In nine months, an estimated 8-million *packages* of communist propaganda materials from Russia, Poland, Czechoslovakia, and Red China were imported into the United States. Placed in the U. S. mail, *American taxpayers paid the postage* for delivering the Red propaganda to schools, churches, homes, and libraries all over the nation.[94]

When Congress moved to take action to bar importation of communist propaganda, the U. S. State Department encouraged U. S. printing firms to produce the official Soviet propaganda materials in this country. Haynes Lithograph Co., Rockville, Maryland, for example, with the full approval of the State Department publishes the official Soviet propaganda publication, *USSR*, which is sold on American newsstands.[95]

ANTI-ANTI-COMMUNISM

Alarmed by the disregard of internal security safeguards, Cuba, Laos, and the dozens of other "incidents" during the early months of the Kennedy-Johnson Administration, citizens in all parts of America started intensive anti-communist study programs.

Schools of anti-communism and cold-war forums, which sprung up in the last years of the Eisenhower Administration, were held in increasing numbers. It was at one of these schools, held after eight months of Kennedy leadership, that Senator Thomas Dodd (D-Conn) made the speech quoted in the first chapter of this book.

Unsolicited mail to Congress from the "grass roots" reached all-time proportions as awakening and angry citizens protested free distribution of communist propaganda through the mail, trade and aid to communist countries, and the other actions of appeasement.

The unrest spread, until, suddenly, the Administration accelerated what had been a quiet crackdown on anti-communist information programs. The government's actions were accompanied by a coordinated onslaught of highly inflammatory and grossly distorted attacks on the military, anti-communist leaders, and conservative groups in much of the nation's press.

CENSORSHIP

In Congress it was revealed that speeches of military leaders such as Admiral Arleigh Burke, chairman of the Joint Chiefs of Staff, were being censored to delete anti-communist remarks. Use of hard-hitting anti-communist films in military education programs was discouraged.[96]

A military officer was removed from his command for showing *Operation Abolition*, a filmed documentary of communist-inspired riots in San Francisco. The film had been produced by a Congressional committee.[97]

Cold war anti-communist seminars at which military officers were scheduled to learn about the communist menace were cancelled at Indianapolis, Fredericksburg, Glenview Naval

Air Station, San Antonio, Shreveport, and the Panama Canal Zone.[98]

The isolated incidents began to form a pattern which indicated a planned suppression of anti-communist information. Then, in late July 1961, it was disclosed that Senator William Fulbright (D-Ark) had prepared a highly secret memorandum earlier in the year which was the basis for the Administration's drive against anti-communism.[99]

In the memorandum, one of the most extraordinary documents ever distributed in Washington, Fulbright voiced such views as:

> Fundamentally, it is believed that the American people have little, if any need to be alerted to the menace of the cold war.[100]

Alerting the people is a dangerous step, according to Fulbright, for . . .

> . . . the principal problem of leadership will be, if it is not already, to restrain the desire of the people to hit the communists with everything we've got, particularly if there are more Cubas and Laos . . . Pride in victory, and frustration in restraint, during the Korean War, led to MacArthur's revolt and to McCarthyism.[101]

The Fulbright memorandum was a cynical appraisal of the ability and right of the American people to be informed on U. S. foreign policy.

Congress tried to investigate. The Senate Armed Services committee showed in testimony, which totaled over 3,000 printed pages, that speeches were being censored, that military training programs on communism were being "softened," and that military officers were persecuted for tough anti-communist views.[102]

The committee assembled over 200 printed pages of anti-communist remarks which had been deleted from just a few of the 1,500 speeches which were censored during the last part of the Eisenhower Administration and the first months of the Kennedy regime. Senator Strom Thurmond (D-SC) cited ten speeches prepared by Lt. Gen. Arthur Trudeau from which anti-communist phrases were deleted or softened by censors.[103] Deleted phrases included: "the steady advance of communism" . . . "insidious ideology of communism" . . . "the Soviets have not relented in the slightest in their determination to dominate the world and destroy our way of life."

Congress was unable to learn specifically who ordered the censorship because the Administration and its spokesmen took the "executive fifth amendment."

State Department and military censors were ordered not to answer questions about the censorship of specific speeches. Names of censors actually responsible for deleting anti-communist remarks from individual talks were withheld from Congress by Presidential order.[104]

Censorship continues and it is not limited to military officers. Even Agriculture Secretary Orville Freeman, an ultra-liberal, was muzzled by the State Department. A speech he planned compared the failures of the slave system of agriculture in the Soviet Union with the successes of the relatively free farms in America. These references were censored.[105]

Other government employees felt the sting of the anti-anti-communism drive.

Don Caron, a forest ranger employed by the Department of Agriculture, was forced to resign from his $8,000 a year forestry service job rather than stop writing a column on the menace of communism for a weekly newspaper.[106]

Caron's superiors in the forestry service stated that . . .

. . . the editorials reflect a zealous and almost fanatical patriotism and an active effort to awake the public to the dangers of communism . . . regardless of all else, the whole subject matter is surely controversial.[107]

Ordered to stop writing the column, which he based on Congressional sources and FBI reports,[108] Caron resigned from the forestry service.

Five months before, President Kennedy in his first State of the Union message to Congress had said:

Let every public servant know . . . that this Administration recognizes 'he value of dissent and daring, that we greet healthy controversy as the hallmark of healthy change.[109]

Under his Administration, words had no relation to action. Those who dared to dissent to condemn communism or defend America were censored, muzzled, or driven from government service.

MOSCOW-DIRECTED

Concerned by the government attacks and the almost total commitment of the press, radio, and TV to the drive against anti-communism, the Senate Internal Security Subcommittee scheduled hearings. Edward Hunter was invited to testify.

Hunter is one of the world's leading experts on psychological warfare, and the author of the authoritative book, *Brainwashing from Pavlov to Powers.*

Referencing his remarks to the communists' own publications, Hunter reported that the development of a healthy,

vigorous grass roots anti-communism movement in the United
States was of serious concern to the Kremlin. Hunter showed
that the vicious attacks launched against anti-communists in
the United States during 1961 were . . .

> . . . a Red anti-anti-communist drive, that was openly ini-
> tiated, under orders issued to the communist forces of the
> world, especially to those in the United States, through the
> Red manifesto of December 5, 1960.[110]

The Red manifesto Hunter exposed was issued December
5, 1960 in Moscow at the conclusion of the strategy conference of the 81 communist parties of the world, including the
Communist Party, USA. After acknowledging the growth of
the anti-communism movements, the Moscow manifesto
ordered:

> To effectively defend the interests of the working people,
> maintain peace and realize the Socialist ideals of the working
> class, it is indispensable to wage a resolute struggle against
> anti-communism — that poisoned weapon which the bourgeoisie
> uses to fence off the masses from socialism.[111]

Hunter introduced articles from domestic communist publications in which Gus Hall, general secretary of the Communist Party, USA, relayed the Moscow directive to Party
members for implementation.

Hall proposed a "unity of the left" — a coalition of communists, liberals, and progressives — to defeat the "fascist
network" responsible for the anti-communist movement in
America. In communist jargon, "fascist" is the label for all
active anti-communists. Hall called for unified attacks by
the left on the leadership of the "fascist network" including
Senator Barry Goldwater (R-Ari), the John Birch Society,
Congressional committees which investigate communism,
military officers, and those labor union officials who actively
oppose communism.

The Communist Party chief disclosed the role that the
Kennedy-Johnson Administration could play in killing the
anti-communist movement. Hall's article, published in the
official communist organ, *The Worker,* criticized some Kennedy actions, but advised the comrades . . .

> . . . it would be a serious mistake to consider the Kennedy
> Administration as embarked at present on the fascist road.
> If the tactical problem is solved correctly, it will be possible
> to slam the door on the ultra-right. defeat it, and force a
> shift in policy upon the Administration itself in the direction
> of peace and democracy.[112]

Hunter analyzed the article for the Senate committee.

pointing out that Hall employed "peace" and "democracy" in their dialectical materialist sense. "Peace" indicates a state which arrives when all sides accept communism. "Democracy" is the police state form of dictatorship existing in the Soviet Union.[113]

Within days after Hall triggered the attack on the "ultra-right" the campaign spread rapidly. The "unity of the left" against anti-communists which Hall proposed developed almost immediately. Hunter showed that within a week after Hall's orders went out, similar attacks appeared in major magazines, "liberal" newspapers such as the *Washington Post, New York Times,* and the *St. Louis Post-Dispatch,* and on the wire service of the Associated Press.[114]

In short, the tremendous smear campaign by government officials, the press, radio, and TV against anti-communists followed the exact line put out by Moscow.

As a result of his study, Hunter predicted that the communist effort to smear The John Birch Society would be followed by a campaign linking every other effective conservative anti-communist organization to it. He pinpointed a book, *The Fascist Revival,* published by the Communist Party, USA, which purports to tell "the inside story of the John Birch Society." Hunter said:

> The virulent tone of the booklet, indicates that the Communist Party would like to create a new Pavlovian trigger word for this period in its psychological warfare, and believes "Birchite" might be put into the language this way, replacing "McCarthyite" . . . the communists now seek to create a new scare word.[115]

Tactics of the press, leftist organizations, and the communists in the 24 months after Hunter made his prediction attest to his skill at foreseeing communist strategy.

The Administration's attack against those opposed to communism reached a peak on November 18, 1961. Despite Hunter's warning that the anti-anti-communism drive was inspired in Moscow, President Kennedy himself joined the assault. In a speech in Los Angeles, California, Kennedy said of anti-communists:

> Now that we are face to face again with a period of heightened peril . . . the discordant voices of extremism are heard once again in the land. Men who are unable to face up to the danger from without are convinced that the real danger comes from within . . . They look suspiciously at their neighbors and their leaders . . . they find treason in our finest churches, in our highest court.

But you and I and most Americans take a different view of our peril. We know that it comes from without, not within. It must be met with preparedness, not provocative speeches.[116]

Just 20 days after President Kennedy made his attack on conservative anti-communists, FBI Director J. Edgar Hoover set the record straight. In a speech on NBC-TV, he said:

The communist threat from without must not blind us to the communist threat from within. The latter is reaching into the very heart of America through its espionage agents and a cunning, defiant, and lawless Communist Party, which is fanatically dedicated to the Marxist cause of world enslavement and destruction of the foundations of our Republic.[117]

Ironically, just two years and four days after President Kennedy denied the existence of an internal communist threat in his speech in Los Angeles, he was cut down on the streets of Dallas by a sniper's bullet. It was fired by Lee Harvey Oswald, a self-admitted Communist.

President Kennedy's speech was full of contradictions. He ridiculed as "fanatics" those who say "peace conferences fail because we were . . . deceived by the Russians." He voiced scorn for those who attribute the communist hold on Eastern Europe to "the sellout at Yalta" and the loss of China to "treason in high places." Yet, 13 years earlier on June 6, 1948, this same John Kennedy made a speech which the *Boston Globe* reported under the headline, "Kennedy Says Roosevelt Sold Poland to Reds."

A year later, in the speech quoted in the opening pages of this chapter, young John Kennedy said of the loss of China, "What our men have saved, our diplomats and our President have frittered away."

As President, Kennedy labelled those who voice the same ideas "fanatics" . . . "discordant voices of extremism" . . . and "sowers of seeds of doubt and hate . . . fear and subversion."

NATIONAL DEFENSE

In ridiculing Americans who believe that communism is a threat internally, President Kennedy said that the real danger "comes from without" and that "it must be met with preparedness . . . to make more certain than ever before that this nation has all the power it will need to deter any attack of any kind."

Few Americans would disagree with the need for maintaining military superiority, yet, less than 60 days before making his statement in Los Angeles, President Kennedy had proposed a plan for the general and complete disarmament of the United States.

The offer was made in Kennedy's speech to the opening session of the United Nations on September 25, 1961. It was formalized a few days later by publication of State Department Document 7277, entitled, *Freedom From War: The United States Program for General and Complete Disarmament in a Peaceful World.*

Under the official, published, three-stage disarmament plan, nuclear tests would be banned, production of nuclear weapons and their delivery systems (manned bombers, missiles, etc.) would be halted, existing stocks of weapons and atomic warheads would be transferred to the United Nations, development of anti-missile missiles and similar *defensive* weapons would be abandoned.[118]

Use of outer space for other than peaceful projects would be prohibited, conventional armed forces and weapons would be reduced by transferring control over U. S. and other troops to the United Nations so "no state (including the U. S.) would have the military power to challenge the progressively strengthened UN Peace Force."[119] Even shotguns and hunting rifles owned by private citizens could be affected.[120]

Senator John Tower (R-Tex) took issue with the entire disarmament concept. In a speech on the Senate floor on January 29, 1962, he said:

> At a time when Western civilization is confronted by an extreme militaristic threat looking forward to world conquest, I think it is naive and unrealistic to be preoccupied with the question of disarmament. We know that the communist conspiracy has no intention of co-existing with us. We know that they are bent on domination of the whole world.[121]

Senator Tower quoted an editorial from a Dallas, Texas newspaper which labelled the disarmament document one of the most incredible proposals ever to emerge from the "foggy corridors of the State Department." The editorial concluded:

> As skeptical as I have always been of the measure of good sense and loyalty within the State Department I never would have believed that these people we call our diplomats could so completely and unabashedly advocate the surrender of American rights and sovereignty until this bulletin appeared . . . if more of the American people knew about this scheme there would be a nationwide uproar that would make the reaction to the Alger Hiss scandal look like another era of good feeling by comparison.[122]

Most Americans haven't known what is happening — and

many of those who do laugh off the entire disarmament proposal. A typical reaction to the disarmament proposals has been, "Don't worry, they're just talking."

In the face of such disbelief, Senator Joseph Clark (D-Pa) attempted to "set the record straight." Clark "refuted" Senator Tower's statement that the communists were not interested in co-existence. He denied that the disarmament plan was "dreamed up in the foggy corridors of the State Department." Clark said that State Department Document 7277, with its proposal for complete disarmament of the United States, is . . .

> . . . the fixed, determined, and approved policy of the Government of the United States. It was laid down by the President of the U. S., John Fitzgerald Kennedy, in a speech he made before the United Nations on September 25 of last year.[123]

Six weeks after Senator Clark's statement, the Administration offered the Soviet Union a formal treaty incorporating the disarmament proposals in Document 7277.[124] Clark further stated that the proposal for total and complete disarmament is not only the policy of the Kennedy-Johnson Administration but . . .

> . . . is also the kind of program which Congress envisioned when, last summer, it passed the statute creating the Arms Control and Disarmament Agency.[125]

Congress passed Public Law 87-297 creating the agency one day after Kennedy made his disarmament proposals to the United Nations. It is charged with managing disarmament negotiations, conducting technical research in the disarmament field, and instituting a public relations campaign to "condition" the American people to accept disarmament.[126]

During its first year of operation, the Agency reported that it was unable to fill all requests for information on disarmament, but . . .

> . . . Agency officials did participate in over 100 meetings, panel discussions and study groups in 1962. In addition, such informational materials as articles for commercial journals, scripts for educational television programs, network and local TV and radio programs were prepared and briefings and interviews were arranged with agency officials for correspondents of public information media.[127]

The degree of danger inherent in the operation of the Disarmament Agency, apart from its propaganda function, is a subject of controversy even among conservatives. Buried in the routine "enabling" provisions of the Act, Section 47 (b) grants authority to the President to transfer to the Disarmament Administration *any activities or facilities of any Government Agency*. Many believe that under this provision, and subject only to the cumbersome Congressional veto, American weapons could be placed under the control of the Director of the Disarmament Agency.

That such fears are not completely unfounded was shown on March 9, 1963 when Senator Barry Goldwater (R-Ari) disclosed that the Disarmament Agency was considering a massive American-Soviet "bonfire" in which 30 American Air Force B-47 bombers and 30 Soviet Badger bombers would be destroyed. The Agency denied Goldwater's charge. However, two days later, Secretary of State Dean Rusk admitted that such a project was being "considered."[128] Such destruction of weapons is provided for in Section A, 2c of Stage I of the Draft Treaty on disarmament submitted to the Soviet Union at the Disarmament Conference in Geneva on April 18, 1962.[129]

The "bomber burning" incident is one of many indications that the disarmament proposals of State Department Document 7277 are being implemented unilaterally by the United States government. The actions are taken surreptitiously with each step given a logical justification. Only by carefully evaluating the erosion of the overall U. S. military position over a several year period does the pattern become obvious. In the 1961-63 period, the Kennedy-Johnson Administration took these actions:

> . . . refused to spend money appropriated by Congress for a speed up in the development of the high-flying, supersonic RS-70 nuclear bomber.[130]

Defense Secretary McNamara justified his defiance of Congressional mandates by explaining that the RS-70 was unnecessary *because missiles and conventional jet bombers equipped with the Skybolt air-to-ground missile would do the job cheaper.*

This rather logical explanation was poked full of holes when the Administration stopped all production of long range manned bombers and cancelled production of the Skybolt missile, over the objections of competent military authorities.[131] In addition it was announced that . . .

> . . . manned bombers (B- 47's and B-52's) stationed at air bases in Morocco, France, England and Spain would return to the U. S. and these bases would be closed [132]

At about the same time in the spring of 1963, 45 American

missile launching bases in Turkey and Italy were declared "obsolete" and closed.[133]

Each of these decisions — cancellation of the Skybolt missile project, the halt in production of manned bombers, the closing of bomber and missile bases in Europe — were justified by the Kennedy-Johnson Administration on the basis that soon to be available Minuteman missiles and the nuclear missile-firing Polaris submarine provided adequate deterrents against communist attacks. There were three major discrepancies in these comforting words:

> Planned deployment of Minuteman missiles was reduced from 2,000 to 950; negotiations for Polaris submarine bases in Spain and Italy bogged down; loss of the one known Polaris base in Northern Scotland is likely when the Labor Government takes power in England.[134]

And so it goes. The RS-70 was abandoned for the manned bomber and the Skybolt missile — the bomber and the Skybolt are cancelled to be replaced by Minuteman missiles and the Polaris submarine, which are in turn cutback.

Conventional armed forces and purely defensive weapons systems have not been immune. Defense Secretary McNamara admitted to Congress that his plan to "streamline" the National Guard and Organized Reserves, in effect, eliminated eight National Guard divisions and 750 units of the organized reserve.[135]

The Nike-Zeus anti-missile missile was designed to seek out and destroy enemy missiles high in outer space before they could reach American cities. The Nike-Zeus had its first successful tests in November 1961.[136] Since then, it has been shelved.[137]

Defense Secretary McNamara explained to Congressional critics that a more sophisticated defense system against missiles, the Nike-X, was on the drawing boards. However, the Nike-X, if it works, won't be operational until 1969. Meanwhile, American cities are defenseless against possible Soviet missile attacks.

While the U. S. Defense "high command" was debating whether to proceed with development of the Nike-Zeus or the Nike-X, the communists developed their own anti-missile missile (or stole the design of the tested Nike-Zeus). On April 17, 1963, the Defense Department admitted that the Soviet anti-missile missiles deployed around Leningrad have the capability to intercept and destroy American Polaris missiles.[138]

Once the Soviet Union protects its cities against retaliatory attacks by American missiles, it can, at any time, issue the ultimatum, "Surrender or Die." That is the trap into which the Kennedy-Johnson Administration is leading America. Khrushchev expects that America will surrender. Robert Frost, the American poet, interviewed Khrushchev in 1962 and reported:

> Khrushchev said American liberals were too soft to fight.[139]

Senator Barry Goldwater (R-Ari) summed up what has been happening. On March 14, 1963, he said:

> Not one new weapons system has been proposed under the present Administration. The RS-70 has been abandoned. Skybolt has been dropped, manned bombers are being phased out, Nike-Zeus is being delayed, the Dyna-Soar is being re-examined for possible junking. This is not only stagnation, *this is Disarmament.*

While it was all happening President Kennedy was denouncing anti-communist "extremists" who look suspiciously at their leaders. He was telling the American people that the real communist threat "comes from without" and "must be met with preparedness . . . to make more certain than ever before that this nation has all the power it will need to deter an attack of any kind."

President Johnson appears committed to continuing the dismantlement of the American military establishment. Among his first acts as President were approvals of the complete abandonment of the B-70 and the Dyna-Soar. Within ten days after he took office, Johnson's administration announced the closing of 30 military bases in the United States and overseas — and the strategic navy shipbuilding and maintenance yards in Philadelphia and Boston. By the end of 1963, Johnson ordered withdrawal of the last strategic bombers based in Japan — and a return to the U. S. of other strategic Air Force units in the Far East.[140]

NUCLEAR TEST BAN

While American striking forces were being dismantled, American superiority in nuclear know-how was also being eroded away at the nuclear test ban talks in Geneva. While the United States talked for five years, the communists tested.

In the talks, under both Kennedy and Eisenhower, there were massive concessions to the communists, a continual erosion of the American position. For example:

> In a series of concessions, the U. S. agreed to accept fewer and fewer "monitoring stations" to detect possible nuclear

test cheating. Over a five year period, demands for control stations were reduced from 180 to 8.[141]

After reducing the number of monitoring stations far below the minimum "safe" level, further concessions were made:

> The U. S. agreed that checks in the Soviet Union could be made by "tamper-proof" black boxes — scientific instruments *which the communists would be trusted to install and maintain themselves.*[142]

Under the original proposals, whenever control systems detected radio-active fallout, or suspicious earth tremors, an international team of experts would make an on-site inspection of the area to determine whether an illegal nuclear explosion had occurred.

The U. S. agreed that the inspections could be made by teams of "experts" from Ghana, Outer Mongolia, or other communist satellites, without American or western representatives participating. The most serious concession involved the administration of whatever inspection and control organization might ultimately be established:

> A communist request for veto power over the budget and personnel of the international control and inspection organization was granted by the U. S., making any final agreement worthless because the Soviet Union could stop *any* spending for inspection.[143]

The implications of these and other concessions became so ominous that on February 21, 1963, Senator Thomas Dodd (D-Conn) made a lengthy speech in the Senate outlining the dangers. He said:

> We have made these concessions piecemeal, so that our position at any given moment has never been too different from our position 3 months previously. It is only by going back to the beginning and laying our concessions end to end that the terrifying scope of our retreat becomes apparent.[144]

The negotiations and concessions continued even after the communists showed their bad faith by breaking the three year "gentleman's agreement" not to test while the talks were proceeding. On September 1, 1961 in the midst of negotiations, the communists embarked on the most massive series of tests in history, climaxing on October 20, 1961 with the explosion of a 58-megaton bomb. Experts said the preparations for the tests had been underway for at least one year — while Soviet diplomats sat at the conference table "negotiating" a test ban. On November 8, 1961, President Kennedy told the American people:

The Soviet Union prepared to test (nuclear weapons) while we were at the table negotiating with them. If they fooled us once, it is their fault, if they fool us twice, it is our fault.[145]

On March 2, 1962, Kennedy told a nationwide television audience:

> We know enough about broken negotiations, secret preparations, and the (Soviet) advantages gained from a long test series never to offer again an *uninspected* moratorium.[146]

Despite the President's words, the talks and concessions continued. Even so, the communists, strangely, wouldn't accept a treaty in which they, in effect, would determine whether or not they were cheating. They held out for a no-inspection system at all. On March 8, 1963, Senator Barry Goldwater (R-Ari) in a Senate speech asked whether . . .

> . . . the Administration is engaged in an attempt to arrange a test ban without any inspections . . . when you look at the concessions we have already made in this area, you can see we are certainly headed in that direction.[147]

Eight months before, Senator Strom Thurmond (D-SC) predicted the ultimate outcome. He said:

> . . . we should have learned long ago in trying to negotiate with the communists — that the Soviets never accept our initial offers of appeasement. They know we will be back again, with hat in hand, making further concessions toward their position.[148]

Senator Thurmond was right. In July 1963, the United States agreed to a *no-inspection* nuclear test ban treaty which prohibited tests in outer space, under water, and in the atmosphere.[149]

The treaty was hailed as a "great break in the cold war." President Kennedy called it "the first step toward limiting the nuclear arms race."[150]

Actually, the treaty was nearly identical with one proposed by the communists 18 months earlier. On November 27, 1961, the Soviet Union offered the U. S. a treaty providing that . . .

> . . . all testing in the atmosphere, in outer space, and under water should be banned indefinitely. No international detection system is required because enough countries have systems adequate to detect all nuclear explosions.[151]

U. S. experts rejected that pact, contending that not all atmospheric tests could be detected, that detection of underwater tests was "extremely difficult," and that nuclear blasts in outer space could be effectively shielded by using test rockets with lead "wings" to absorb radiation.[152]

American Secretary of State Dean Rusk assailed the Soviet plan for an uninspected test ban as a . . .

> . . . transparent propaganda gesture put forward in a vain hope to mislead and deceive world public opinion.[153]

Eighteen months later, all the earlier technical objections were brushed aside, and Dean Rusk asked the U. S. Senate to ratify a nearly identical no-inspection test ban treaty, saying:

> If the promise of this treaty can be realized, if we can now take even this one frail step along a new course, the frail and fearful mankind may find another step and another until confidence replaces terror and hope takes over from despair.[154]

The drastic change in Rusk's position — and that of the Kennedy Administration — was in accord with the strategy proposed by Paul H. Nitze, who was Kennedy's Assistant Secretary of Defense for International Affairs and President Johnson's first Secretary of the Navy. In an essay published just before his appointment in 1961, Nitze indicated that many believe that continuing negotiations with the communists are vital to survival. Having accepted this viewpoint, Nitze said, the only logical corollary is that . . .

> . . . if we cannot get them to agree to our viewpoint, we must accept theirs if we are to survive.[155]

That's what Averell Harriman did in making a no-inspection test ban agreement in Moscow in July 1963. The test ban is only the first step. A few days before that agreement was made, William C. Foster, director of the Arms Control and Disarmament Agency, said:

> Everyone feels that if we can't negotiate a test ban — when we are so close — that we can't negotiate any other part of the disarmament program.[156]

The Administration looked upon Khrushchev's agreement and his apparent willingness to discuss other parts of the disarmament program as a "hopeful sign." President Kennedy said:

> There is hope that it may lead to further measures to arrest and control the dangerous competition for increasingly destructive weapons.[157]

Careful students of communism were not so hopeful. They recalled the prediction made by Dimtri L. Manuilski at the Lenin School of Political Warfare in Moscow in 1930. A student, Zack Kornfeld, later broke with the Communist Party and told the story. He reported that Manuilski, who later served as Russia's UN delegate, told the class:

> War to the hilt between communism and capitalism is inevitable. Today, of course, we are not strong enough to attack.

Our time will come in 20 to 30 years. To win, we shall need the element of surprise. The bourgeoisie will have to be put to sleep. So we shall begin by launching the most spectacular peace movement on record. There will be electrifying overtures and unheard of concessions. The capitalist countries, stupid and decadent, will rejoice to cooperate in their own destruction. They will leap at another chance to be friends. As soon as their guard is down, we will smash them with our clenched fist.[158]

THE "NO-WIN" POLICY

As appeasement followed appeasement, Senators in both political parties, some military leaders, and a few syndicated columnists raised charges that the Kennedy-Johnson Administration's foreign policy was based on a "no-win" concept.

A few more aggressive critics of the Administration charged that the President and/or his State Department were actually engaged, knowingly or unknowingly, in a planned program of surrender to communism.

Most newspapers ignored the charges, or ridiculed those who spoke out.

Finally on May 3, 1962, a high administration official, Walt Whitman Rostow, in a speech in Minneapolis, said:

It is sometimes asked if our policy is a no-win policy. Our answer is this — we do not expect this planet to be forever split between a communist bloc and a free world. We expect this planet to organize itself in time on principles of voluntary cooperation among independent nation states dedicated to human freedom. It will not be a victory of United States over Russia.[159]

At the Special Warfare School at Ft. Bragg, N. C., Rostow expressed the same "no-win" idea, and added:

It will not be a victory of capitalism over socialism.[160]

Under Secretary of State George Ball, in testimony before the Senate Armed Services Committee, explained why the Administration believes freedom will prevail. He said:

I think one cannot rule out, looking down the long course of history, that changes may take place in the individual nation states which make up the Communist bloc which will transform them from being dangerous, because they are exponents of a militant, aggressive, international communism, to the adoption of postures which will make them easier to live with in the world. [161]

Is such an outcome possible? Will communist leaders "mellow?" Years ago, Lenin foresaw this outcome for the world struggle:

> As long as capitalism and socialism exist we cannot live in peace: in the end one or the other will triumph — a funeral dirge will be sung over either the Soviet Republic or over world capitalism.[162]

Is it possible that present day communists have forsaken Marxism-Leninism and are "mellowing?" Here's what Khrushchev says:

> Anyone who thinks we have foresaken Marxism-Leninism deceives himself. That won't happen till the shrimps learn to whistle.[163]

Even so, the Kennedy-Johnson Administration based nearly every foreign policy decision — in Laos, Cuba, Africa, Geneva, Berlin — on the assumption that communists have "mellowed," despite all the evidence to the contrary. If American leaders persist in refusing to pursue a victory goal while the communists base their actions on the premise that either capitalism or socialism must triumph, then surely America will lose.

Senator Barry Goldwater (R-Ari) in his forthright book, *Why Not Victory?*, says of the "no-win" policy:

> I doubt if this nation ever before has found itself in a battle for her very existence where any public official or group of officials automatically foreclosed the possibility of victory . . . the opposite of victory is defeat — not coexistence or compromise. For the first time in our history that glorious word victory seems to be slipping out of our national vocabulary.[164]

Willard Edwards, the distinguished Washington correspondent of the *Chicago Tribune,* pieced the story together. He revealed in a two-part article that a top level staff working under State Department Policy Planner, Walt Whitman Rostow, had formulated a 285-page policy draft as a guide for cold war decisions.[165]

The Rostow master plan is based on the assumption that the Soviet Union is "mellowing" and that the way is open for meaningful agreements between the communist and noncommunist world — *if we can convince the communists that we mean them no harm!*[166]

Basically, Rostow's manifesto envisions that communist leaders have abandoned their goals of world conquest. It is essentially an updated version of the misguided strategy and advice Roosevelt accepted from Alger Hiss, Averell Harriman, and Harry Hopkins at Yalta, Teheran, and Cairo.

Those "mistakes" placed 800-million Poles, Hungarians, Chinese and Czechs in communist slavery. The world situation has reached a point where the next "mistake" won't enslave more Czechs, Cubans, or Viet Namese, but Americans.

The Rostow manifesto, as exposed by Willard Edwards, admits that the evidence, in the form of words and deeds by communist leaders, directly contradicts the assumption that communists are "mellowing." It proposes, therefore, a massive program of "indoctrination" to "educate" Congress and the people to the new "approach" using planted news stories, appearances before Congressional committees, speeches and articles by Administration officials.[167]

The propaganda department established within the framework of the Arms Control and Disarmament Agency is a prime example of the policy in practice. Rostow's own speeches and those of State Department officials George Ball and Harlan Cleveland are part of the "educational effort." Others can be cited. Dr. Ralph K. White, for example, is head of the Soviet Division of the United States Information Agency. Speaking to the American Psychological Association in September 1961, Dr. White said:

> . . . the avowed goals and values of the Russians are pretty much the same as ours . . . the U. S. must understand that the Russians genuinely look upon the United States as an aggressor . . . the Soviets fear the U. S. because it is allying itself with the Germans who attacked Russia during World War II.[168]

Senator Thomas Dodd (D-Conn) demanded that White be fired for equating the goals and values of murderous communist leaders with our own. Nothing was done.

NEWS MANAGEMENT

The propaganda effort to indoctrinate the American people to accept the Rostow dream that the communists are "mellowing" is part of an unprecedented effort to "manage the news," which started early in the Kennedy-Johnson Administration.

Contradictions between President Kennedy's words and Administration actions on Laos, Cuba, Berlin, the need for military strength, and the right of government employees to speak their minds have been recounted. The completely false and untrue stories government officials released to smear friends of the United States such as Moise Tshombe and his press representative in America, Michel Struelens, were exposed by a Senate committee.

Much of the news media accepted the Administration efforts to "manage the news" but finally became "restless" over the provably false statements released officially during the Cuban crisis. Criticism of the press grew until finally on December 6, 1962, the Assistant Secretary of Defense for Public Information, Arthur Sylvester, blatantly proclaimed that government had "an inherent right to lie." In a speech to New York newsmen, he said:

> . . . it would seem basic, all through history, that it's an inherent government right, if necessary, to lie to save itself.[169]

Administration spokesmen hedged on whether President Kennedy sanctioned the concept of "government by lie" which Sylvester proclaimed, but Sylvester retained his high position.

Sylvester's pronouncement confirmed what many Americans already knew. Statements by any government official mean nothing. The American people can have no faith, no trust in anything told them by their government leaders.

An official policy of "government by lie" is in itself serious. The implications it holds are frightening when coupled with other indications that the Administration had rejected all traditional concepts of morality as the basis for its rule.

Kennedy's assistant, Arthur Schlesinger, Jr., in an article in the *Partisan Review* in 1947, gave an insight into the morals of liberalism. He said that liberalism . . .

> . . . dispensed with the absurd Christian myths of sin and damnation and believed that what shortcomings man might have were to be redeemed, not by Jesus on the cross, but by the benevolent unfolding of history. Tolerance, free inquiry, and technology, operating in the framework of human perfectibility, would in the end create a heaven on earth, a goal accounted much more sensible and wholesome than a heaven in heaven.[170]

Liberal standards of morality, as enumerated by Schlesinger in 1947, were reiterated by another high government official in 1962. Assistant Secretary of State for International Organization Affairs, Harlan Cleveland, on a TV interview said:

> . . . we find that in trying to figure out what to do next, that general codes of ethics, prescriptions that is to say, that have been written down by someone else, by our church or our parents, or the books we read, or scripture, that these general prescriptions really aren't awfully useful in deciding what to do next.[171]

William Penn warned early Americans of the pitfalls in such a policy. He said:

> The nation which refuses to be governed by God will surely be governed by tyrants.

How Has It Happened?

> *Yes, we did produce a near perfect Republic.*
> *But will they keep it, or will they, in the enjoy-*
> *ment of plenty, lose the memory of freedom.*
> *Material abundance without character is the*
> *surest way to destruction.*
>
> — *Thomas Jefferson*

WHAT HAS HAPPENED to that intangible something called the American spirit? When Barbary pirates on the north coast of Africa tried to blackmail our nation when it was less than ten years old, Americans rallied to a cry of "Millions for defense, but not one cent for tribute."

Today, we grovel before a bearded dictator and offer tractors, drugs, food, and money in tribute. Our leaders tell us they will lie to us to stay in power — and we do nothing.

What has happened to the bold young nation which fought a war in 1812 against the world's mightiest power to protect a handful of its citizens from harassment on the high seas?

Today, 400 American boys rot in Red Chinese prisons, deserted after a war which ended in 1953. Thousands of other Americans are in the hell of Russian slave labor camps. Is it a sign that America is too apathetic or decadent to care when those who protest such injustice to fellow Americans are labelled "crackpots" and "extremists?"

What has happened to the noble American breed which was personified in the legend of Nathan Hale? He was a 21 year old school teacher who volunteered to go behind British lines and collect information for George Washington in the Revolutionary War. When caught, he faced death with a rope around his neck and these words on his lips:

I only regret that I have but one life to give for my country.

Today, we hear news speeding around the world from a communist courtroom in Moscow, where another young American accused of espionage says:

I didn't know what I was doing. I know now I was risking
world peace. My superiors were responsible.

Released several years later from his Russian prison, U-2
pilot Francis Gary Powers returned to America. Central
Intelligence Agency officials announced that he had "carried
out his mission." A "grateful" American people paid him
$45,000 in back salary for his *heroism* and Powers said:

One thing I always remembered was that I was an American.

Who is this new creature who calls himself an American?
Gary Powers is not an isolated case. Why is he tragically
typical of his, and my, generation? Are these the young men
who should be leading the fight to protect ourselves, our
children's future, and our heritage from godless communism?

Here is a professional, and very unflattering, evaluation of
a typical American. Written by the Chief of Intelligence of
the Chinese Peoples Volunteer Army during the Korean
War to his superior in Peiping, it fell into American hands:

The American soldier has weak loyalty to his family, his
community, his country, his religion, and to his fellow soldier.
His concepts of right and wrong are hazy and ill-formed. Op-
portunism is easy for him. By himself he feels frightened and
insecure. He underestimates his own worth, his own strength,
and his ability to survive.

There is little understanding of American political history
and philosophy, the federal, state, and community organizations, state and civil rights, freedom safeguards, checks and
balances and how these things allegedly operate within his
own system.

He fails to appreciate the meaning of and the necessity for
military or any other form of organization.[1]

It would be easy and reassuring to pass this capsule indictment oft as communist propaganda. However, without use
of physical torture, drugs, intensive psychological treatment,
coercion, or any of the other tactics usually associated with
brainwashing, the Chinese communists made collaborators of
one-third of all American POW's who fell into their hands
during the Korean war.[2]

This shocking record so astonished and concerned military
authorities that a full-scale inquiry was conducted. One
thousand of the 4,000 prisoners returned from Korea were
studied. Investigators found that some Americans had broadcast anti-American propaganda, informed on other prisoners,
wrote articles, letters and stories praising life under communism, confessed to "germ warfare" and other atrocities and
generally cooperated with their captors in every way.[3] With
others, the "collaboration" was not so complete.

For the first time in American history, of the 7,000 POW's in captivity in Korea, not one escaped, even though security measures were lax.[4]

In the early months of captivity, four out of every ten Americans died. This was the largest death rate for any group of Americans in any kind of captivity since the American revolution. A frightening number died, not from maltreatment, battle wounds, or starvation, but from a new disease Army psychiatrists termed, "Give-Up-Itis." A 20-year old American would refuse to eat, tell the others to leave him alone, pull his blankets over his head, and be dead in 48 hours.[5]

Without personal responsibility for their own lives, they had no thought of helping their fellow prisoners when they were sick or in trouble.

Deaths occurred when fellow Americans, objecting to the stench of a "buddy" weakened by dysentery, picked him up bodily and threw him out to freeze to death in the snow and 30-below zero weather. Questioned after release, other prisoners who witnessed the event but did not participate were asked why they didn't stop the murder. "It wasn't our affair," was a typical answer.[6]

These products of a supposed Christian nation had lost all concepts of decency, all sense of concern for their fellow man.

The record was so untypical of American prisoners in previous wars that the Army searched for answers.

In contrast to the disquieting performance of the Americans, all of the 229 Turks captured in Korea and subjected to the same treatment and conditions as American POW's, survived to *march* back through the gates at Panmunjon. Not only did they survive — but not a man among them collaborated in any way with the communists![7]

Major William Mayer, U. S. Army Phychiatrist, who participated in the lengthy and detailed study of American collaborators in Korea has described the techniques used to produce the sorry record.

Simple rewards were offered to the prisoners by their communist captors for seemingly "unimportant" types of collaboration. Soon, many were "going along." "Why not," they'd say, "everyone else is doing it."[8]

"Indoctrination and re-education" was accomplished in simple "discussion periods." American-produced books and texts were used which emphasized all that was bad in America. The 12-page course "outline" given each man was prepared in America, at a communist-operated school, the

Jefferson School of Social Science in New York city.[9] If the "student" didn't have a solid foundation in American history, government, and economics, much of the material made sense and sounded reasonable.

There were no drugs, physical torture, or highly developed hypnotic techniques — just subtle pressures for *conformity*.[10]

This was the "brainwashing" to which one-third of the American POW's in Korea succumbed. Major Mayer said:

> Frankly, it did everything the Communists wanted it to do. It didn't turn anybody into a communist because it wasn't designed to turn anybody into a communist. A small percentage of the people in the world are communists. The great majority are acquiescors. The great majority are simply cowed and somehow pushed along by this system *which doesn't look like something you can fight;* it's not very dangerous looking; *it just controls you.* You don't have to be a coward to give in to it. The majority of Americans (in Korean prison camps) in a sense did give in to it.[11]

Mayer continued his summation of the activities of American POW's:

> The majority of Americans, more than half in these camps never did anything they could really be criticized for. But just doing nothing has never been the way that America in 168 years got the work done which produced this fabulous society. When we get to the point where we just do nothing and enjoy it, maybe we've become an old country and not a new one and maybe we are well on the way down the western slope. This is a valid question for us to debate: whether our own success can destroy us?[12]

The Army study found that Americans who fought in Korea were a fair cross-section of young American males and slightly better educated than the troops who fought in World War II.[13]

However, they were a strikingly different group of human beings than those who fought in that earlier war less than 10 years before. They fit the evaluation of them written by a Chinese communist intelligence chief to an alarming degree.

This change in the American male, and his sister, had occurred in a very short time in the history of a nation. The collaborator in Korea had a brother five, eight, or ten years older who distinguished himself on the battlefields of World War II, and in prison, if captured. Actions of the communists substantiate this conclusion. Ignoring men over 30 as "hopeless reactionaries," they concentrated their indoctrination program at men in the 18 to 30 age group.[14]

In civilian life, the counterparts of the Korean collaborators have been responsible for the doubling of the crime rate since World War II. Since 1957, the crime rate is increasing five times faster than the population. Juvenile delinquents now commit 43% of all crimes.[15] With their sisters, they have been responsible for tripling the rate of illegitimate births in the 20 years between 1940 and 1960.[16] They have provided a market for an unprecedented volume of filthy and indecent literature — and permit much of it to be displayed openly in newsstands, family drug stores, and distributed through the U. S. mails. Divorces have skyrocketed, alcohol consumption climbs, and there is increasing narcotics use and addiction.

These failures are products of American schools, churches, and homes.

It is true that most Americans, like a majority of the American POW's in Korea, haven't done anything for which they can be criticized. They haven't done anything.

As one country after another has slipped, or been pushed behind the Iron Curtain, they have done nothing.

Their money is used to send foreign aid to the communist enemy. They do nothing.

In their reactions, Americans are like a majority of the POW's in Korea. They do nothing to be criticized for. At least 98% of all Americans are opposed to communism. Yet, they watch elected and appointed officials give continual aid and comfort to the enemy — and they do nothing.

As Major Mayer pointed out, the communist "brainwashing" in Korea wasn't designed to make communists out of Americans. If it succeeded in making them "go along," it did its job. Similarly, communists aren't interested in making all Americans, or any sizeable segment of them, communists. If Americans just "go along" and do nothing, communism will win without firing a shot.

What has transformed Americans who were once rugged individualists into a conforming, moldable, do-nothing mass?

FBI Chief, J. Edgar Hoover, who has so often decried the moral decay in our society, has also expressed concern about the failure of American prisoners in Korea. In 1959, in a speech to the National Strategy Seminar, Mr. Hoover said:

> The behavior of these prisoners of war was less an individual failure than it was an indictment of our entire society which had not prepared them adequately for their head-on collision with communist indoctrination . . . We must not ignore this forceful example of the impact of communist psychological pressures. Our continued survival may depend

upon the action we take now to insure that all citizens, not only military personnel, are fortified against the continuous communist ideological assault.

Mr. Hoover quoted a Presidential Commission's report on the Korean POW's which stressed the failure of our homes, schools, churches, and patriotic organizations to educate Americans in the principles which underly our way of life.

The report of the Presidential Commission said pointedly:

> The uninformed POW's were up against it. They couldn't answer arguments in favor of communism with arguments in favor of Americanism because they knew so little about America.

What the Chinese communist intelligence chief in Korea had said about Americans is largely true. How has it happened?

A close look at the basic institutions of America, institutions which are almost universally respected by our citizens, would be in order. What are the goals and guiding principles of America's educators, churchmen, government leaders and officials? How have they failed in the job of inspiring young Americans to become useful citizens committed to preserving and extending freedom?

Chapter VI

Education

> *America is reaping the consequences of the destruction of traditional education by the Dewey-Kilpatrick experimentalist philosophy . . . Dewey's ideas have led to elimination of many academic subjects on the ground that they would not be useful in life . . . The student thus receives neither intellectual training nor the factual knowledge which will help him understand the world he lives in, or to make well-reasoned decisions in his private life or as a responsible citizen.*
>
> — *Admiral Hyman Rickover*[1]

WHO WAS THIS MAN, Dewey, who is so roundly criticized by the renowned Hyman Rickover, the "father" of the nuclear submarine?

John Dewey was an educational philosopher. His experimental philosophies of education were first tried in a model school at the University of Chicago before 1900. They were dismal failures. Children learned nothing. Undismayed, Dewey left Chicago in 1904 and went to Teachers College, Columbia University where he became the dominant figure and the most influential man in American education.

His influence can be measured by the realization that under Dewey's guidance fully 20% of *all* American school superintendents and 40% of *all* teacher college heads received advanced degrees at Columbia. They adopted Dewey's experimental theories, which came to be known as "progressive education," in the schools of the nation. Under the pretext of improving teaching *methods*, they changed *what* was taught to American children.

What did Dewey believe? In his writing and teaching, Dewey rejected fixed moral laws and eternal truths and principles. He adopted pragmatic, relativistic concepts as his guiding philosophy. Denying God, he held to the Marxist concept that man is without a soul or free will. Man is a biological organism completely molded by his environment. Dewey believed that because man's environment is constantly changing, man also changes constantly. Therefore, Dewey concluded, teaching children any of the absolutes of morals, government, or ethics was a waste of time.

On this amoral philosophy, he developed his teaching formulae, commonly labelled, *Progressive Education*.

Dewey published, *My Pedagogic Creed*, in 1897. In it he saw the destruction of a child's individualistic traits as the primary goal of education. Once this was accomplished the youngster would conform or adjust to whatever society in which he found himself. Ability to "get along with the group" became the prime measuring stick of a child's educational "progress."[2]

Taken to a logical conclusion, Dewey's theory would have the child who finds himself in the company of thieves become a thief also. The tendency to justify immoral or unethical conduct by rationalizing that "everybody does it" is rooted in Dewey's teaching. Dewey summarized his theories, saying:

> Education, therefore, is a process for living and not a preparation for future living.[3]

Dewey laid the foundation for the future "destruction of traditional education" decried by Admiral Rickover when he said:

> We violate the child's nature and render difficult the best ethical results by introducing the child too abruptly to a number of special studies, of reading, writing, geography, etc. out of relation to his social life . . . the true center of correlation of the school subjects is not science, nor literature, nor history, nor geography, but the child's own social activities.[4]

Strict acceptance of Dewey's theories would eliminate teaching world geography unless the child can take a trip around the world. History would be eliminated from the curriculum, because it is past and will not be relived by the student.

In practice, Dewey's theories, as modified by his disciples, have eliminated the teaching of strict rules of grammar. The student learns grammar by "living" (talking) with the "group," or by reading literature. Old fashioned drill in spelling, the ABC's, penmanship, multiplication tables, and other basics has been deemphasized in favor of "learn by doing." Depending on the degree to which progressive education methods are carried, "learn by doing" can mean "learn not at all." Many parents have become dismayed to realize that children who have not memorized the ABC's through old-fashioned drill have difficulty in using a dictionary or telephone book without haphazardly paging through. They don't know that "M" comes after "L" and before "N," etc.

The *group* idea is the nucleus of the progressive system. No child is permitted to forge ahead of another. This would hurt the *group*. Promotions become automatic. Nobody is left behind because of poor work. This would disrupt the *group*. Grading and graded report cards are frowned upon. Grading promotes competition. Competition breeds rivalry and encourages students to excel and rise above the *group*. When competition is not permitted, children get the idea that personal excellence and trying to get ahead is not worthwhile.

Rosalie Gordon, author of the widely circulated, *What's Happened to Our Schools?*[5] said of progressive education:

> The progressive system has reached all the way down to the lowest grades to prepare the children of America for their role as the collectivists of the future . . . The group — not the individual child — is the quintessence of progressivism. The child must always be made to feel part of the group. He must indulge in group thinking, in group activity.[6]

She explains Dewey's obsession with the group and group activity by saying:

> You can't make socialists out of individualists.[7]

Dewey was a socialist.[8] At the climax of his career in 1950, he became honorary national chairman of the American counterpart of the British Fabian Society,[9] the League for Industrial Democracy.

A NEW SOCIAL ORDER

While at Columbia University, Dewey gathered about himself a group of young educationalists who called themselves, *Frontier Thinkers*. In the forefront of this group were Dr. George Counts, professor of education, and Dr. Harold Rugg. Known as the "hard" progressivists, they were to have a measurable and lasting effect on the nation's schools.

While Dewey's theories had been concerned chiefly with teaching methods, Counts and Rugg added the concept of using the schools as an instrument for "building a new social order."

Counts was the director of research for a 17-volume study of American education produced by the American Historical

Association.[10] Financed by the Carnegie Corporation, the Counts-directed study was to serve as the authoritative guide for revamping the philosophy and concept of American education. The final volume, issued in 1934, contained the recommendations of the five year project, of which the following is typical:

> Cumulative evidence supports the conclusion that in the United States as in other countries, the age of individualism and laissez-faire (freedom-Auth.) in economy and government is closing and a new age of *collectivism* is emerging.[11]

Of the Counts-directed study, the British socialist, Harold Laski, writing in *The New Republic*, said:

> At bottom, and stripped of its carefully neutral phrases, the report is an educational program for a socialist America.[12]

Laski is an authoritative commentator. He later became head of the British Fabian Society. Counts' hatred of free American economic and political traditions and his socialist goals were stated openly in a paper he presented to the Dewey-founded Progressive Education Association in Baltimore, Maryland in February 1932. Counts said:

> Historic capitalism, with its deification of the principle of selfishness, its reliance upon the forces of competition, its placing of property above human rights, and its exaltation of the profit motive, will either have to be displaced altogether, or so radically changed in form and spirit that its identity will be completely lost.[13]

Dr. Counts made clear that the changes he envisioned would result in:

> . . . a coordinated, planned and socialized economy.[14]

Accomplishing such a drastic remaking of America would involve many changes, Counts admitted. He said:

> Changes in our economic system will, of course, require changes in our ideals.[15]

Counts saw no wrong in abandoning even the traditional concepts of morality to achieve his goals. He pointed out in his book, *The Soviet Challenge to America*, that even in Russia . . .

> . . . new principles of right and wrong are being forged.[16]

Counts obsession with achieving a socialized, planned economy and the methods he was apparently willing to accept to realize it were plain in the foreword he wrote for his translation from Russian into English of *New Russia's Primer* by M. Ilin, a communist textbook for junior high school students. Counts said:

A single glance at the contents of the book convinced me that here was a document of rare quality. Practically every page carried the work of genius.

It presents the major provision of the Five Year Plan (Russian) with extraordinary clarity and charm — but perhaps most important it reveals the temper of the revolutionary movement (communist) and the large human goals toward which it is consciously building.[17]

Counts' praise for the communist program could hardly have been more glowing. Very few of even the most dedicated apologists for the Soviet Union would publicly find the goals of the Soviet communist state to be "human." Counts continues:

Mr. Ilin has shown by example how textbooks might be written. In this competition, however, Mr. Ilin has certain clear advantages. The revolutionary struggle has placed in his hands some very powerful aids. It has generated a great system of planning organization through which society is endeavoring to shape its own future . . . This translation is designed to acquaint adults, teachers, and educators, with a phase of the Russian experiment which in the long run may prove to be far more important than those sensational aspects of the revolutionary struggle which are emphasized in both the daily press and even the more serious publications. I trust it will serve this purpose and at the same time contribute to a better understanding of the American people of the greatest social experiment of all time.[18]

The "sensational aspects of the revolutionary struggle" which Counts found unimportant include the murder of millions of Russians who resisted state planning and control of every aspect of their lives. Although not a communist, Counts' tolerance of Soviet murder was, like that of most Fabian socialists, a product of his admiration for state planning. This "end" justified for Counts and many other advocates of planning the murderous "means" used in Russia to bring it about. Twenty years later, Counts became disillusioned with Russian communism, although he has retained his socialist views.

To achieve the "new social order," Counts, in 1932, called for teachers of the nation to provide the impetus. In his monograph, *Dare the School Build a New Social Order?* Counts wrote:

That the teachers should deliberately reach for power and then make the most of their conquest is my firm conviction. To the extent that they are permitted to fashion the curriculum and procedures of the school they will definitely and positively influence the social attitudes, ideals and behavior of the coming generation.[19]

In "reaching for power" the *Frontier Thinkers* moved in two directions. They rewrote the textbooks. They gained the prestige of the largest professional teachers organization by capturing the top jobs and control of the National Education Association. At the 72nd annual meeting of the NEA in Washington, D. C. in July 1934, Dr. Willard Givens, then a California school superintendent, in a report entitled, *Education for a New America*, said:

> We are convinced that we stand today at the verge of a great culture . . . But to achieve these things many drastic changes must be made. A dying laissez-faire must be completely destroyed, and all of us, including the owners, must be subjected to a large degree of social control.[20]

A year after delivering this call for destruction of free enterprise and individual freedom (laissez-faire), Givens was named executive secretary of the NEA, a position he held for 17 years until his retirement in 1952.

TEXTBOOK REVISION

Meanwhile, another of the *Frontier Thinkers,* Dr. Harold Rugg, continued the job of indoctrinating teachers and preparing teaching materials designed to "influence the social attitudes, ideals, and behavior of coming generations." In his book, *The Great Technology,* written for teachers in 1933, Rugg said:

> A new public mind is to be created. How? Only by creating tens of millions of new individual minds and welding them into a new social mind. Old stereotypes must be broken up and new "climates of opinion" formed in the neighborhoods of America.[21]

What climate of opinion would Rugg create? On page 171 of his book, he said:

> We know, now, that a large and growing group of middle men and manipulators of sales, money, investment, and credit have interjected themselves into our economic system . . . Most of them, however, are exploiters. The postulate follows that the economic system can be operated efficiently and humanely only by elimination, re-education, and assignment to productive work of the parisitical members of this group of middlemen.

Clearly, Rugg was proposing the destruction of the small businessman and complete government control of every citizen's life and employment. Later in his book, he defined how the schools were to be used to transform American political and economic institutions and create the new "public mind" which would accept complete government control of the individual:

> . . . through the schools of the world we shall disseminate a new conception of government — one that will embrace all of the collective activities of men; one that will postulate the need for scientific control and operation of economic activities in the interests of all people.[22]

Note that Rugg did not say "a new type of government" but a "new conception of government." Rugg proposed that this could be accomplished in three ways:

> *First and foremost,* the development of a new philosophy of life and education which will be fully appropriate to the new social order; *Second,* the building of an adequate plan for the production of a new race of educational workers; *Third,* the making of new activities and materials for the curriculum.[23]

It was in the area of new materials, textbooks, and teaching aids, that Rugg achieved greatest influence. The *Conclusions and Recommendations* of the American Historical Association's 17-volume report on education, of which Counts was research director, provided the opening. It proposed to consolidate the traditional subjects of history, geography, sociology, economics, political science, etc. into one composite course, called "social studies."

The idea was widely adopted. Completely new textbooks were needed. Rugg wrote them. All traditional presentations of subject matter was scrapped, and a variety of economic, political, historical, sociological, and geographical data was lumped into one textbook. With such a conglomeration of material in one book, the deletion or slanted presentation of key events, basic truths, facts and theories was not so evident.

Five million school children "learned" American political and economic history and structure in the 1930's from 14 social studies textbooks Rugg authored.[24] He also produced the corresponding teachers guides, course outlines, and student workbooks.

So blatant was the downgrading of American heroes and the U. S. Constitution, so pronounced was the anti-religious bias; so open was the propaganda for socialistic control of men's lives in Rugg's textbooks that the public rebelled.[25] Rugg, himself, told what happened in an open letter to President Roosevelt in 1942. He proposed to FDR that it would be a "thrilling experience" to sell the American people

on the need for "social planning" through a massive program
of government sponsored adult education. Rugg said:

> I know for I tried to do it during the great depression in
> my *Man and His Changing Society* — a series of books which
> was studied by some 5,000,000 young Americans until the
> patrioteers and the native Fascist press well-nigh destroyed
> it between 1939 and 1941.[26]

Rugg's textbooks went too far, too fast for complete public
acceptance. They were replaced by those of other authors
somewhat more skillful in the subtle promotion of socialism.

In 1940, the National Education Association began promoting a set of "social studies" texts known as the *Building
America* series.[27] They were replacements for the discredited
Rugg series. They had been widely adopted when a few
years later the Senate Investigating Committee on Education
of the California legislature condemned the NEA-sponsored
series for subtly playing up Marxism and destroying American
traditions.[28] The Senate committee report . . .

> . . . found among other things that 113 Communist-front
> organizations had to do with some of the material in the
> books and that 50 Communist front authors were connected
> with it. Among the authors are Beatrice and Sidney Webb,
> identified with the Fabian Socialist movement in Great
> Britain.[29]

Seven years after these disclosures, the texts were still in
use in the school systems of several states.[30]

Today, the typical text is cleverly done. Direct attacks on
basic truths are avoided when possible. However, the destructive influence of Counts, Rugg, and the other socialistic
Frontier Thinkers is clearly discernable.

CLASS HATRED

The presentation of American history as a *class struggle*
by widely-used textbooks is a striking example of the continuing direct influence of Dr. George Counts on today's schools.
Once America was relatively free of class hatred.[31]

The progressivists realized that it would be impossible to
pit one class against another for political gain, if such classes
did not exist, or were without basic antagonism. Dr. George
Counts proposed that the schools should disrupt this stabilizing influence in America. In the magazine, *The Social Frontier*, he wrote:

> In view of the absence of a class mentality among workers,
> it would be reasonable to assume that it is the problem of
> education to induce such a mentality rather than to take an

existing mentality and base a course of action upon it.[32]

This cruel and cynical admonition to the educators of America to purposefully promote class strife and bitterness was an open acceptance of Lenin's strategy of "incite one against another." Twenty years later, most textbook authors were carefully following Counts' advice. Class hatred is induced in students by presenting American history as a prolonged class struggle. Read these examples:

Craven and Johnson in their textbook, *The United States: Experiment in Democracy*,[33] tell the student:

> The *upper class,* numerically weak, consisted of those who owned so much wealth that they did not have to engage in manual labor. They generally wore *finer clothes* to set themselves off from the *masses.* (pg. 60)

The class struggle theme continues through the book. In describing the American Revolution, the authors say:

> The rest of the *upper class* people joined in the American cause, but with the full intention of checking later the aspirations of the *average citizen* for a more democratic way of life. (pg. 103)

Todd and Curti, in writing their *America's History*,[34] laid the foundations for presenting American history as a class struggle in this way:

> They (the founding fathers) were determined to keep control of the government in the hands of the *well-to-do,* whom they considered more stable, more judicious, and more temperate than the *poorer,* and *less educated people.* (pg. 173)

This is the Marxist view of American history, first propagated early in this century by Charles Beard in *An Economic Interpretation of the Constitution.* It is followed blindly today by most textbook writers, even though Beard later repented and repudiated his interpretation as faulty.

Faulkner, Kepner and Merrill in *History of the American Way*,[35] use the same theme to describe the Constitutional Convention:

> . . . the delegates were *conservative* or slow to change. And that is easy to understand. They were the *property holding class* . . . Two important groups were not well represented . . . First, the *common man* was not represented by any delegate who was a mechanic or a small farmer or the like. Secondly, most of the Revolutionary "radicals" were absent. (pg. 71)

The delegates were "conservative" in that they drew upon the accumulated wisdom and experience of the past in framing the Constitution of the new nation. To describe them as "slow to change" is absurd. They were largely the group which

instigated, financed, and fought the American Revolution.
Another deceit perpetrated by the authors is in failing to tell
the student that at the time the Constitution was written over
90% of *all* Americans were *property holders.*

This handling of the U. S. Constitution by textbook writers
demonstrates a commonly-used propaganda technique. Instead of directly attacking the provisions of the Constitution,
they are ignored, and the motives of the men who wrote it
are impugned.

F. A. Magruder in his *American Government*[36] uses a
different technique. Instead of smearing the men who wrote
the Constitution, he openly admits that important Constitutional safeguards are being by-passed today. The student is
given the impression that such infringement on constitutional
guarantees against an all-powerful government is "sophisticated and progressive." Magruder says:

> The principle of checks and balances in government is not
> held in such esteem today as it was a century ago. The people
> no longer fear the officers whom they elect every few years.
> (pg. 73)

The people of Germany elected Hitler in 1933. Because
they ignored the checks and balances of the German constitution, they never had an opportunity to vote him out. This,
the student doesn't learn from Magruder.

The class struggle theme runs like a thread through most
textbook presentations of U. S. History. Dumond, Dale
and Wesley in *History of the United States,*[37] describe the
period of great industrial growth in the late 19th Century
this way:

> The real issue was whether the government would once
> again serve the needs of the *toiling masses* rather than the
> *interests of special groups.* (pg. 525)

ANTI-FREE ENTERPRISE

With the foundation for the class struggle firmly laid, business, free enterprise, and profits are painted as the source of
all evil, just as Counts, Rugg, and other *Frontier Thinkers*
recommended. Craven and Johnson, in their text, say:

> Corporate industry represented a greater investment of capi-
> tal and consequently a greater concentration of power in
> politics than the slaveholders had ever dreamed of possessing.
> (pg. 422)

If this subtle equating of business with slaveholding was not
an adequate condemnation, the authors recite in an approving
manner this quotation by Lincoln Steffens:

Big business was, and still is, the current name of the devil, the root of all evil, political and economic. (pg. 516)

Steffens is quoted and praised in many texts. Students are not told that Steffens was a vocal supporter of the American Communist Party who said, "Communism can solve our problems."

Gavian and Hamm in *The American Story*[38] defame business and stir class hatred by quoting Mary Lease, an English socialist, who said:

Wall Street owns the country. It is no longer a government of the people, by the people, and for the people, but a government of Wall Street, by Wall Street, and for Wall Street. The parties lie to us . . . the people are at bay; let the bloodhounds of money who have dogged us thus far beware! (pg. 401)

Gavian and Hamm do not counter-balance this quotation by pointing out that nearly every American family has a stake in Wall Street. Over 25% of American families own stock in industry directly. Almost all others share in some way through private insurance policies, company pension plans, or union welfare programs whose assets are invested in Wall Street.

The class struggle theme is the vehicle used to openly advocate cradle-to-grave welfare care for all. Magruder equates opposition to the welfare state with selfishness of the few. In a section blatantly entitled, *Welfare of the People from the Cradle to the Grave*, Magruder says:

The United States has increasingly *curbed the selfish* and provided for the *welfare of the many*. The Government has established the Children's Bureau to look after the welfare of *every* child born in America. (pg. 15)

Magruder's text, *American Government*, is a study in propaganda techniques in itself. The class struggle idea is reinforced in this passage which uses a false premise to discourage thrift, saving, and family responsibility and justify welfare payments for all:

Because of sickness, accidents, and occasional unemployment it is *difficult or impossible* for a laborer who has reared a family to save from his meager wages (This is untrue-Author). And it is more just to place all the burden of supporting those who have been unfortunate, *or even shiftless*, upon everybody instead of upon some dutiful son or daughter who is not responsible for the condition. (pg. 339)

With the school children of America being educated in this philosophy, is it any wonder that total government expenditures for welfare have risen from under $5-billion annually during the depths of the depression to $35-billion in 1961, the most prosperous year the nation has ever experienced?

IN THE LOWER GRADES

Indoctrination in the availability and "rightness" of the "free" handout is not limited to high school students. The brainwashing starts today in the first grade. Recall the story, if you are old enough, in the first grade readers about the hardworking little squirrel who gathered and stored nuts for the winter. The story had a moral: Work hard and save wisely for uncertain days ahead.

For today's six-year old, that story has been rewritten. The new version is entitled, *Ask for It*.[39] In it, a little squirrel named Bobby, ate nuts from a tree during the summer. Other squirrels suggested that Bobby put some nuts away for winter. As Bobby Squirrel didn't like to work, he ignored the advice.

Winter came and one morning Bobby awakened to find the world covered with snow — and all the nuts were gone from the tree. He got awfully hungry but remembered that a boy who lived in a *white house* had taken some of the nuts from *his* tree during the summer. Bobby went to the *white house* and gave a squirrel call. A door opened and a "fine brown nut" rolled out. Bobby Squirrel learned his lesson. The story concludes:

> "Well!" thought Bobby. "I know how to get my dinner. All I have to do is ask for it."[40]

This story is in the first grade reader, *Our New Friends*, published by the Scott, Foresman and Company in 1956. The authors are Gray, Monroe, Artley, and Arbuthnot. It is approved for use in most states.

Magruder's high school text, *American Government*, as mentioned earlier, uses nearly every classical propaganda trick to confuse students into accepting socialism. Consider this non-sequitur under the heading, *Medical Service Under Our System of Free Enterprise*:

> In a democracy we believe in evolutionary methods rather than the revolutionary methods of a dictatorship; and under our system of free enterprise, competition improves the standard of service and tends to reduce the cost. *Therefore, instead of jumping right into socialized medicine,* why not have the Government support projects such as the following. (pg. 670)

If free enterprise medicine works so well, and Magruder acknowledges that it does, why consider socialized medicine at all, either immediately, or by the backdoor approach Magruder recommends. He advocates approaching socialized medicine *gradually* through such steps as federal aid for training doctors, federal funds for hospital construction, and government payment of hospital costs for lengthy illnesses.

INTERNATIONALISM

Since World War II, propaganda for World Government under the United Nations has been added to textbook agitation for the collectivist society envisioned by Counts and Rugg.

The drive, spearheaded in America by the National Education Association, is part of a world-wide movement by UNESCO (United Nations Educational, Scientific, and Cultural Organization). It received the official blessing of President Truman's Commission on Higher Education. The Commission's report, issued in 1947, had these recommendations:

> The role which education will play officially must be conditioned essentially by policies established in the State Department in this country, and by ministeries of foreign affairs in other countries. Higher education must play a very important part in carrying out in this country the program developed by UNESCO . . . The United States Office of Education must be prepared to work with the State Department and with UNESCO.[41]

What was the UNESCO program which the Presidential Commission recommended that American schools should implement? Embodied in the nine-volume UNESCO study, *Towards World Understanding*, it is the blueprint for conditioning American children for the day when their first loyalty will be to a socialistic one-world government under the United Nations.

The work of Counts and Rugg laid the foundation for the first two steps — the destruction of the U. S. Constitution and free economy — so that America could be easily merged into a socialistic world federation.

UNESCO's Director General, under whom the plan was prepared, was Julian Huxley, an atheistic philosopher and member of the Colonial Bureau of the British Fabian Society.

The goal of UNESCO was stated plainly in the study's first volume. It recommended that children should be educated in . . .

> . . . those qualities of citizenship which provide the foundation upon which international government must be based if it is to succeed.[42]

Under Huxley, UNESCO envisioned that destruction of children's love of country and patriotism was the first step towards education for world citizenship. The report said on the opening page of Volume V, *In the Classroom with Children Under Thirteen Years of Age:*

> Before the child enters school his mind has already been profoundly marked, and often injuriously, by earlier influences . . . first gained, however dimly, in the home.

The attack on home and parents continues. On page 9, the teacher is told:

> The kindergarten or infant school has a significant part to play in the child's education. Not only can it correct many of the errors of home training but it can also prepare the child for membership, at about age seven, in a group of his own age and habits — the first of many such social identifications that he must achieve on his way to membership in the world society.

After such guarded references to the "injurious influence" of the family on the young child, the UNESCO study makes it plain that the errors of home training include parental encouragement of patriotism. On page 58, the guidebook for teachers says:

> As we have pointed out, it is frequently the family that infects the child with extreme nationalism. The school should therefore use the means described earlier to combat family attitudes.

Among the "means described earlier" are the suppression of American history and geography which might enhance pro-American sentiments of the children. UNESCO gives specific suggestions in Volume V, page 11, on how this can be done:

> In our view, history and geography should be taught at this stage as universal history and geography. Of the two, only geography lends itself well to study during the years prescribed by the present survey (3-13 years). The study of history, on the other hand, raises problems of value which are better postponed until the pupil is freed from the nationalist prejudices which at present surround the teaching of history.

Translated, this means that if the grade school student is taught American history objectively he is very likely to realize that the American system of government, economics, and social values outstrip those found anywhere else in the world. Three pages later, UNESCO admits that detailed study even of foreign countries will lead the student to the conclusion that America is a better place to live. This problem is solved by recommending that teachers obscure the truth from their pupils in this way:

> Certain delicate problems, however, will arise in these studies and explorations. Not everything in foreign ways of living can be presented to children in an attractive light. At this stage, though, the systematic examination of other countries and manners can be postponed, and the teacher need seek only to insure that his children appreciate, through abundant and judicious examples, that foreign countries, too, possess things of beauty, and that many of them resemble the beauty and interest of his own country. A child taught thus about the different countries of the world will gradually lose those habits of prejudice and contempt which are an impediment to world-mindedness.

Thus, UNESCO recommends the deliberate "under education" of children. The student who does not know or understand the accomplishments of America and the shortcomings of the rest of the world is more likely to accept a "world government." The student who knows nothing of the horrors of the communist system in Russia and the failures of socialism everywhere it has been tried might well agree to a communist-influenced socialistic one-world government.

Such deliberate "under education" is a theme which runs through the entire UNESCO program. Karl W. Bigelow, another professor of education at Columbia, and a UNESCO board member, directed a seminar on Volume II of the *Towards World Understanding* series. The UNESCO seminar report, *The Education and Training of Teachers,* recommended:

> Therefore, we regard it as a matter of first importance for social and international living that educators should be more concerned with the child, and the healthy development of his body and mind, than with the content of the various subjects which go to make a school curriculum . . . Because of failure to adopt a wise approach to child growth and development, the primary school still tends to function as if it were an institution *for the abolition of illiteracy.*

Should the school's primary function be the teaching of reading, writing, and arithmetic (the abolition of illiteracy) or the "conditioning" of the child for "social and international living?" Bigelow's thesis, expressed in this UNESCO publication, is a simple restatement of John Dewey's original progressivist theories. The ultimate result can only be the "under education" of the child. The graduates produced by such "education" do not have the *basic* knowledge on which to make sound judgments. If they do not understand the source of America's strength, they cannot see the fallacies of a world collectivist order.

In short, UNESCO recommends that schools be converted into indoctrination centers for the production of emotionally-conditioned children who react like Pavlov's dogs rather than reason and think logically. The best selling book, Rudolf Flech's, *Why Johnny Can't Read*,[43] exposes the results of such under-education in one curriculum area.

Teacher training institutions, textbook writers, and professional education organizations picked up the theme of "education for world citizenship." Dr. Willard Givens, executive secretary of the National Education Association, joined the board of directors of the U. S. Commission for UNESCO.

Professional education journals and faculty members at Teachers College, Columbia University started agitating for mandatory revision of textbooks to conform to UNESCO standards, *even before the standards were publicly announced*. Writing in the *NEA Journal* in April 1946, Issac Leon Kandel of Teachers College, Columbia University, said:

> Nations that become members of UNESCO accordingly assume an obligation to revise textbooks used in their schools . . . unilateral efforts to revise the materials of instruction are futile. The poison of aggressive nationalism injected into children's minds is as dangerous for world stability as the manufacture of armaments. In one, as in the other, supervision by some kind of international agency is urgent.[44]

Textbook revision to obliterate national history and geography, downgrade patriotism and love of America, and build a tolerance for the communist enemy in Russia has been accomplished in line with UNESCO recommendations. A review of widely-used textbooks establishes this fact.

Patriotic impulses are generally belittled and equated with extremism, in line with UNESCO proposals for overcoming "injurious parental influences." In *The United States: Experiment in Democracy,* the authors, Craven and Johnson, say:

> In the 1920's many Americans were *excessively nationalistic and intolerantly patriotic* . . . The official (Ku Klux) Klan literature reflected the average middle class in its assertions of "100 per cent Americanism." (pg. 662)

Note the linking of the "middle class" and patriotism with the Ku Klux Klan. This is typical. Another text, *History of the American Way,* by Faulkner, Kepner and Merrill, says:

> . . . there was an increase in the number of *so-called "100 per cent Americans"* whose behavior was quite un-American

and undemocratic. The Ku Klux Klan for example. . . . (pg. 650)

Gavian and Hamm in their high school text, *The American Story*, put it this way:

> National feeling was very strong, and it was often shown in undesirable ways. The strong nationalism of the years following the war (WWI) was commonly expressed in such slogans as "America First" and "One Hundred Per Cent Americanism."

Decent Americans deplore fanaticism. However, with discussions of patriotism in textbooks limited to such slurring passages it is no wonder that love of country, one of man's most noble attributes, is in such disrepute; that today the citizen who is moved to express a patriotic remark feels impelled to preface it by saying, "I don't want to sound like a flag waver, but . . ."

Belittling references to patriotism in textbooks are not the only methods used for downgrading love of country. Display of the American flag in the classroom is neglected in many areas. The pledge of allegiance to the flag was once a standard exercise for opening the school day. This practice has been discarded to such a degree that in 1961 members of the California State Legislature felt compelled to pass a law requiring that the pledge of allegiance or the singing of the Star Spangled Banner be used daily. The bill passed — *but by only one vote.* A similar bill was passed in Illinois in 1963 — but was vetoed by the governor.

The downgrading of American heroes contributes to national disillusionment. Todd and Curti in their *America's History,* have this to say about George Washington:

> Outwardly Washington seemed to most people somewhat cold and overdignified. After his death *American patriots developed a myth of his godlike qualities* . . . (pg. 184)

After 15 or more years of such anti-patriotic propaganda in the schools, J. Edgar Hoover felt impelled to speak out. At Valley Forge on February 22, 1962, he said:

> Too often in recent years, patriotic symbols have been shunted aside. Our national heroes have been maligned, our history distorted. Has it become a disgrace to pledge allegiance to our flag — or to sign a loyalty oath, or pay tribute to our national anthem? Is it shameful to encourage our children to memorize the stirring words of '76? Is it becoming opprobious to state "In God We Trust" when proclaiming our love of country?

What we desperately need today is patriotism founded on a real understanding of the American ideal — a dedicated belief in our principles of freedom and a determination to perpetuate America's heritage.[45]

Recall that UNESCO recommended that textbooks should be revised to play down those facts about foreign countries which are unattractive. Similarities rather than differences between countries were to be emphasized. In this way, UNESCO said, children "will gradually lose those habits of prejudice and contempt which are an impediment to world mindedness." Compare that UNESCO recommendation with the description of the communist government of Russia in F. A. Magruder's text, *American Government*. Magruder says that socialism in Russia is "an example of totalitarianism" but then proceeds to describe it this way:

> Under the Constitution of 1936 the Government is a federation. It is a Union of 16 Soviet Socialist Republics (USSR) . . . the powers are divided between the Union and the member republics *somewhat as those of our Union are divided between the United States and the States.* Suffrage (voting) is granted to men and women 18 years of age and over. The voters directly or indirectly elect the two houses comprising the Supreme Council. This body legislates and also chooses the Presidium, consisting of a chairman and 36 members which carries on the government. There are also Ministers *comparable to our Cabinet members.* (pg. 37-8)

At no point is the student told directly that the Soviet voter is given no choice, that the only candidates on the ballot are those selected from above by the Communist Party.

In describing the collective farms in Russia, Magruder says:

> The members of each collective have a sort of town meeting to determine policies and elect the manager. (pg. 38)

Magruder in line with UNESCO advice to "avoid the unattractive," does not mention that 10-million small Russian farmers were murdered before the remainder "accepted" the collective farm idea.

The summary of Magruder's discussion of the Russian communist government has the subtitle, *Swing from the Radical to the Conventional.* Under this heading, he says:

> The Revolution of 1917 was fourfold: governmental, economic, religious and moral. An absolute monarchy was replaced by Soviets (Councils) dominated by a dictator, but the Constitution of 1936 granted direct suffrage (voting). (pg. 40)

From this passage, the student would assume that Russia no longer has a dictatorship. With such textbook descriptions of the Soviet Union, it is reasonable to believe that students might lose the "prejudice and contempt" for communism which UNESCO cites as "an impediment to world mindedness."

In the treatment of American foreign policy, the origin and growth of world communism, and the influence communist agents have had in influencing U. S. foreign policy toward communist objectives, discernable textbook bias is the rule rather than the exception. Outright falsehoods are not uncommon.

Textbooks impart false information about the establishment of the communist state in Russia. Lenin and the Bolsheviks are given credit for overthrowing the tyrannical Czarist regime. The Czar was actually overthrown by Kerensky who established a constitutional republic, *which was subverted and siezed by the communists*. But Dumond, Dale and Wesley, in *History of the United States,* say:

> At the end of World War I the source of greatest danger was thought to be Russia, where after centuries of oppression the masses revolted and established a communist regime . . . (pg. 698)

Harlow in *Story of America*[16] described the rise of the totalitarian state this way:

> In 1917 revolutionists in Russia overthrew the government of the Czar and established a communist nation. (pg. 557)

The cruel, harsh, inhumane methods used in the Russian communist state are ignored or deliberately distorted, while Soviet progress is praised. Mowrer and Cummings in *The United States and World Relations*[17] are guilty in this way:

> Notable progress has been made in many sections of the country (Russia), particularly in those that are remote from Moscow, as shown by the really remarkable expansion in the Arctic. (pg. 157)

In accordance with the UNESCO instructions to disregard the "unattractive," students are not told that the "remarkable expansion in the Arctic" has been accomplished largely by the 20-million inmates of Soviet slave labor camps. The Mowrer and Cummings book points up the problem. On the surface it is anti-communist. But in the presentation of factual information it builds the attitude in the student that the Soviet system has its merits.

The pro-Soviet bias of textbooks becomes obvious when descriptions of Nazism are compared with passages on communism. Nazi methods, governmental structure, and plans for world conquest were similar to those of the communists.

Not a handful of Nazis remain in the world. We are threatened by a world-wide communist conspiracy of 33-million fanatically-dedicated revolutionaries who have enslaved one-billion people. Yet, while textbook writers use justifiably vicious words to describe Nazism, the communists get a "neutral" appraisal. Harlow is typical. He writes of "brown-shirted Nazi gangsters" and "black shirted Fascist plunderers" in describing the rise of totalitarianism in Germany and Italy. Of Communism, he writes:

> Meanwhile, Russia had *organized* the Union of Soviet Socialist Republics and was ruled by a handful of Communist Party members led by Joseph Stalin. (Pg. 606)

The bias becomes obvious in the treatments of the role of Russia and Germany in World War II. Of the early part of the war when Russia and Germany were still allies, Gavian and Hamm use these words to describe the joint destruction of Poland:

> . . . While the *Nazis* quickly *overran* the western half of Poland, the Russians *occupied* the eastern half. (pg. 595)

Todd and Curti use almost exactly the same words, adding a few modifiers to describe the Nazis:

> While the *Nazi storm troops quickly overran* the western part of the country (Poland), *Russian armies occupied* the eastern half. (pg. 757)

Note that German armies are described as Nazi storm troops while the Russian armies are not called *Communists* or the *Red Army*. Communism has rightly been described by J. Edgar Hoover as "Red Fascism." As such it deserves equally condemnatory textbook treatment with Nazism.

The Yalta Conference, one of the most sordid episodes in American diplomatic history, gets only passing mention in textbooks although agreements made there by Roosevelt, Stalin and Churchill resulted in the enslavement of 700-million people by the communists.[48] Here is how several textbook authors describe the agreements which resulted in communist domination of Poland, Yugoslavia, Hungary, Bulgaria, Rumania, China, and six other nations. Craven and Johnson say:

> In February 1945, Roosevelt met with Churchill and Stalin at Yalta to make plans for the final blows against Germany and Japan. (pg. 824)

Gavian and Hamm in *The American Story* say:

> At the Yalta Conference . . . Roosevelt, Churchill and Stalin outlined a plan for dividing both Germany and Austria. (pg. 670)

Faulkner, Kepner, and Merrill in their text go even further in distortion by omission. They say:

> At the Yalta Conference . . . . Russia, Great Britain, and the United States agreed that the liberated peoples should "create governments of their own choice." (pg. 688)

Dumond, Dale and Wesley come closest to telling the student that there might be something in the Yalta story worth studying. They say:

> Some agreements between Russia, Great Britain, and the United States as to the postwar treatment of Germany were made at Yalta, though details still remain in dispute. (pg. 788)

Alger Hiss, a communist and adviser to Roosevelt at Yalta, is ignored as an influence on the Conference and the agreements made there. This is typical of the textbook "blackout" on high level infiltration and subversion of the U. S. Government by communist agents.

Texts written in the 1950's ignore or belittle the influence of Hiss, Harry Dexter White, Owen Lattimore, and other high level agents. If their part in directing American policies toward communist objectives was thoroughly discussed, the student would likely gain an impression that communists were too treacherous to trust in any world government. If the continuous string of over 50 agreements broken by the communists since World War II were detailed, the student might rightly decide that negotiation of further agreements is unwise.

If the true story of U. S.-Soviet relations were told, students would never accept textbook propaganda for a United Nations world government and disarmament. Yet, these themes run through the textbooks from which students are supposed to learn about *American* government. Magruder, on the first page of his book says:

> We know that unity of our own states brought peace and strength to our country. We believe that similar cooperation will bring peace and goodwill to the nations of the world.

Magruder ignores the conditions which made unity possible in America, conditions which do not exist in today's world. They included a 500-year heritage of seeking freedom under English common law from 1215 when the Magna Charta was signed; common language, religious and racial heritage; agreement on an economic system; and true acceptance of a common goal of freedom.

Today, nearly one-third of the "new" nations of the world have no traditional concepts of law. Some have not completely rejected cannibalism. Only a handful of United

Nations members have concepts of private property and freedom similar to those which made America strong. Racial and religious differences further complicate the problem. Even if all these obstacles could be brushed away, the international communist conspiracy with its goal of world domination makes any form of unity, except eventual slavery for all, impossible.

Ignoring all these facts, Magruder repeats the same illogical reasoning on page 14 of his text:

We have peace in the United States because we have agreed to federal laws and have an army to enforce them. When we have definite international laws and an army to enforce them, we shall have international peace. When atomic bombs are made only by a world government and used only by a world army, who could resist?

Who could resist? Certainly not the United States if the "neutralist" Afro-Asian block united, as usual, with the communist countries and voted *democratically* to place all Americans in slavery. Would it be wrong? Perhaps. But it would be democratic.

Yet throughout the book, the student is conditioned to accept world government, without discussing whether it would be good or bad. Finally, in the last two chapters, Magruder spells out in detail the specific steps which should be taken to prepare for world government. They include:

Give the UN absolute power to regulate international trade and commerce. (pg. 715) Immigration control now handled by each country would be relinquished to the UN along with the power to arbitrarily remove people from one part of the world and settle them in a place a UN planner determines their skills, etc. are needed. (pg. 716)

Place control of the Panama Canal under the United Nations. (pg. 716) Establish an international police force strong enough that no nation can resist its orders. (pg. 716-7) Give the UN power of taxation. (pg. 717) Place broadcast stations, press, speech, etc. under UN control to insure development of "cooperative" public opinion (brainwashing). (pg. 718)

As fantastic as many of these proposals sound, they were taught to the children of America as long as 12 years ago. Today, they are being discussed seriously as steps to be taken by the U. S. Government.

All those who support such programs are not communists. Those who write such textbooks, put them into school systems, and vehemently defend them when they are exposed are not communists, or even pro-communists. They are misguided socialist idealists consumed with the idea of solving world problems through a one-world socialist government. They believe that, if all human differences (economic, religious, political, etc.) can be eliminated, all mankind's problems will disappear as well. In striving for this idealistic goal, they emotionally banish all fact and reason. Past communist treachery, which would be an obstacle to world socialistic brotherhood, is pathologically ignored.

Under the protective cover offered by the misguided one-worlders, the communists have been able to operate in the schools of America.

As early as 1940, the Rapp-Coudert Investigating Committee of the New York State Legislature disclosed that the 11,000 member Teachers Union in New York city was under complete communist control. Over 1,000 communists were teaching in New York city schools.[49]

In the committee's final report, it was stated:

> The communists and those under their influence in the Teachers Union comprised nearly one-fourth of all personnel in city colleges.[50]

After exposure by the Rapp-Coudert committee, communist influences in the schools lessened for a brief period. However, in 1952, the Senate Internal Security Subcommittee learned that no real cleanup had been accomplished. In a series of hearings on subversive influences in education the committee learned that 500 or more communists were still teaching in New York city. Administrative red tape, Supreme Court decisions, and opposition of teacher organizations have hampered efforts to utilize the information developed by the investigations.

Efforts to remove communist teachers from positions of influence have been strongly opposed by such influential organizations as the American Association of University Professors.[51]

Decisions of the U. S. Supreme Court have made nearly impossible the job of concerned school authorities in cleansing their own ranks. In the case of *Sweezy vs. New Hampshire*[52] the Warren Court reversed the New Hampshire Supreme Court and held that the Attorney General of New Hampshire exceeded his authority in questioning Professor Sweezy about suspected subversive activities. Questions which the Court said that Sweezy properly refused to answer included, "Did you advocate Marxism at that time?" and "Do you believe in communism?"

In the case of *Slochower vs. Board of Education of New York*[53] the Court reversed the decisions of three lower courts and held that it was unconstitutional to discharge a teacher because he took the Fifth Amendment when asked about communist activities. The court ordered Slochower, an identified communist, rehired in his position at Brooklyn College and granted him $40,000 in back pay.

Through the combined actions of the communists, and the disciples of Dewey, Counts, Rugg, and other *Frontier Thinkers,* many of our schools have become instruments for producing the "new social order." These criticisms do not apply equally to all 40,000 school systems in the United States.

Because of local control over the schools, alert parents, informed school board members, and patriotic school administrators and teachers in many areas have been able to unite to do an outstanding job in their schools.

For this reason, the "progressivist" thinkers are actively advocating a massive program of federal aid to education which would ultimately remove control of the schools from the local level and transfer it to Washington. The appointment of one "progressivist" thinker as head of the Office of Education would insure that the amoral, socialistic theories of Dewey, Counts, and Rugg could be permeated into those schoolhouses and textbooks which have thus far been immune.

Because control of the schools is at the local level, the job of insuring that they remain sound, or making them so if they are not, must be done locally. However, the parent, school administrator, or organized group which opposes, or even questions, the theories and methods of the progressivists is likely to bring down a storm of attacks, smears, and vilification.

The National Education Association's *National Commission for the Defense of Democracy Through Education,* can, and will, rush its trained propagandists to the scene. Charges of socialist bias in education is vehemently denied, or ridiculed. *The Pasadena Story,* an impressive publication issued by the NEA Defense Commission when parents in Pasadena, California rebelled at the indoctrination of their children, is typical. Of the Pasadena parents, the report says:

> They apparently claim that this country has already moved into, or is rapidly moving toward, some form of socialism, collectivism, or statism. They contend that subversive elements have sifted into public education and that many teachers are seeking to change the American way of life. They charge that John Dewey's progressive education is an instrument designed to break down American standards and weaken the fabric of American society . . . They oppose certain educators who they

assert are seeking to indoctrinate the youth of the country for a changed social and economic order.[54]

This report was issued in June 1951 by the National Education Association. The NEA executive secretary at the time was Willard Givens who himself had publicly stated:

> We are convinced that we stand today at the verge of a great culture . . . But to achieve these things, many drastic changes must be made. A dying laissez-faire must be completely destroyed, and all of us, including the owners must be subjected to a large degree of social control.[55]

Today, the NEA's Defense Commission, in Gestapo-like fashion, maintains a "blacklist" of individuals and organizations which publicly question or criticize the quality of education. The NEA Commission for "Defense of Democracy" in its 1961 annual report admitted:

> About 1,000 requests for information concerning individuals or groups thought to be causing trouble for the schools or the profession were received during the year. Several new fact sheets and information bulletins concerning critics of education were prepared. The Commission has, probably, the most complete files of their kind of critics of education.[56]

The *Tulsa Tribune,* after determining that a dossier on its editor was in the NEA files of "critics of education," asked editorially:

> What is the function of the National Education Association — to improve the education of America's children or to stifle criticism of present educational methods.[57]

Chapter VII

Subverting Our Religious Heritage

For, if the trumpet give an uncertain sound, who shall prepare himself for the battle?
— *I Corinthians, 14:8*

THE WEAPONS OF HATE AND FEAR by which the collectivists have moved a generation of Americans to sell their freedom and integrity for security would never have worked had American roots in basic Judaic-Christian traditions not first been severed. God could not be replaced by Government as the source of all blessings until moral concepts were first blurred.

The collectivists, no respecters of institutions, no matter how sacred, planted their roots in the churches of America before the end of the 19th Century.

Dr. Walter Rauschenbusch and Dr. Harry F. Ward were probably the most responsible for the "revolution in religion." They replaced the Bible-based belief that man was individually responsible to God for his own salvation with a concept of "social salvation." Rauschenbusch was a turn-of-the-century theologian and Ward was professor of Christian Ethics at New York's influential Union Theological Seminary for 25 years.

Analyzed, the "social salvation" which collectivist theologians teach is basically a restatement of the Marxian dogma of Economic Determinism — "change the economic environment and man will be transformed." A theology based on the message of Christ teaches that through true acceptance of Him and His teachings, man is changed, and can, in turn, change the world and correct its ills.

Rauschenbusch spelled out his break with traditional Christianity clearly when he wrote:

> . . . we differ from many Christian men and women who believe that if only men are personally converted wrong and

injustice will gradually disappear from the construction of society. It does not appear such to us.[1]

Dr. Rauschenbusch graduated from Rochester Theological Seminary in 1885. He was a confirmed socialist even before making a trip to Europe in 1907 to visit with Beatrice and Sidney Webb, founders, with atheist George Bernard Shaw, of the British Fabian Society. Rauschenbusch was a shrewd practitioner of the Fabian methodology who realized that if he identified socialism as such in his preaching and teaching, many people in the church would be repelled. Therefore, in his new "theology" Rauschenbusch promised a "Kingdom of God on Earth."[2] As early as 1893, Rauschenbusch wrote:

> The only power that can make socialism succeed, if it is established, is religion. It cannot work in an irreligious country.[3]

Major Edgar Bundy, in his comprehensive and well-documented book, *Collectivism in the Churches,* said of Rauschenbusch, "Socialism, thus, was his first concern. Religion was only a means toward achieving socialism."[4]

What effect has Rauschenbusch had on the Church in America? Here are the words of Dr. A. W. Beaven, a former president of the Federal Council of Churches of Christ in America, written in 1937:

> It is clear, it seems to me, that the greatest single influence on the life and thought of the American Church in the last 50 years was exerted by Walter Rauschenbusch.[5]

Rauschenbusch and his "social gospel" provided the philosophy for the collectivist movement which has drained much of American Protestantism of its effect on man and his life. Dr. Harry F. Ward contributed the organizational and conspiratorial genius to the movement.

Ward is an identified communist.[6] In 1908, he was the founder of the oldest, officially-cited communist-front group in America, the Methodist Federation for Social Action.[7] A year later, he played a part in organizing the Federal Council of Churches, forerunner of the present day, National Council of Churches. He has been an organizer or promoter of nearly every important communist-front activity in America since. In September 1961, while in his 80's, this durable old man was the keynote speaker at an officially-sponsored communist rally in New York which protested the action of the Supreme Court in branding the Communist Party USA as a communist-controlled organization.[8]

Identified under oath as a communist by Benjamin Gitlow,[9]

first head of the Communist Party USA; Manning Johnson, one-time leader of the Party's Negro Section;[10] and several others, Ward was branded as the "Red Dean" of the religious field before a committee of the U. S. Congress. Ward posed as a Methodist but for 25 years he infected hundreds of young ministers of all denominations with his blasphemous ideas as a professor of Christian Ethics at Union Theological Seminary. He also served at Boston School of Theology at Boston University.

Ward recruited pupils, associates and disciples to his crusade[11] to produce, in his words:

> . . . a changed attitude on the part of many church members concerning the purpose and function both of the Church and Christianity.[12]

Among his closest associates and most devoted pupils in the religious field were such conspirators as the Rev. Jack McMichael, Rev. Charles Webber, Rev. Alanson Smith, Dr. Willard Uphaus, and Rev. Lee Ball.[13] The controversial Methodist bishop, G. Bromley Oxnam, was Ward's pupil, secretary and one-time apologist.[14]

THEIR DISCIPLES

What effect have these Marxist conspirators, Fabian and communist had on the Church, its people, its theology, and its teaching?

In 1960, a controversy developed over an official U. S. Air Force Reserve Training Manual which warned Air Force personnel that communists, their dupes and sympathizers had infiltrated into churches. Church groups protested vehemently and Congress investigated. Richard Arens, staff director of the House Committee on Un-American Activities, testified during the hearings as to the evidence of communist activity in the religious field. He said:

> Thus far of the leadership of the National Council of Churches of Christ in America, we have found over 100 persons in leadership capacity with either Communist-front records or records of service to Communist causes. The aggregate affiliations of the leadership, instead of being in the hundreds as first indicated, is now, according to the latest count, into the thousands, and we have yet to complete our check, which would certainly suggest, on the basis of authoritative sources of this committee, that the statement that there is infiltration of fellow travelers in churches and educational institutions is a complete understatement.[15]

Such consistent collaboration with communists, knowingly

or unknowingly, by the leadership of the largest church-related organization in America is a chilling revelation to most Americans. The Chairman of the House Committee on Un-American Activities, Congressman Francis Walter (D-Pa) stated when opening the hearings on the controversial Air Reserve Training Manual:

> This is not to say that these persons are necessarily consciously supporting communist enterprises, but the net result is, for all practical purposes, the same.[16]

What is the net result? The National Council of Churches, its subordinate organizations, and the leaders of many of its affiliated denominations and their publications consistently parallel or follow the Communist Party line, as exposed by J. Edgar Hoover.[17] The collaboration is particularly evident on such issues as disarmament,[18] recognition of Red China and its admission to the United Nations,[19] opposition to the committees of Congress which investigate communist infiltration, subversion, and agitation,[20] anti-anti-communism,[21] and in the promotion of visits to America by communist "churchmen" from behind the Iron Curtain.[22]

How important are the churchmen, who, wittingly or unwittingly, support communist fronts and causes? How many are there?

An independent group of Methodist clergy and laymen, Circuit Riders, Inc.[23] have analyzed the influence achieved in the Church by the collectivists. From public records, newspaper ads sponsored by communist fronts, the letterhead lists of sponsors of cited subversive groups, signers of communist-circulated petitions, etc., Circuit Riders, Inc. has compiled and published names of over 7,000 ministers and theological school professors who have supported communist fronts and causes.

These 7,000, some of whom have supported 100 or more communist causes, and some of whom have been duped but once, comprise only a small segment of the more than 200,000 Protestant ministers in America. Are they important then?

An analysis of the "hierarchy" of the six denominations included in the Circuit Riders study, religious publications, and theological school faculties show that in typical Fabian and Communist fashion they hold positions of influence and control far out of proportion to their numbers.

For example, the Congressional hearings on the much-smeared Air Reserve Training Manual cited the names of a few leading fellow-travelers in the ministry. They included: Walter Russell Bowie who has affiliated with 33 communist fronts and causes, Henry J. Cadbury, with nine, George Dahl with 18, Leroy Waterman with 20, and Fleming James with a verified total of 25 affiliations with communist fronts and causes.[24]

These five men, and 25 others with records of support for communist causes, served on the committee of 95 Bible scholars, translators, and theologians who produced the Revised Standard Version of the Holy Bible.[25] While less than three per cent of Protestant ministers have affiliated in any way with communist fronts and causes, on this one important project nearly 30% of the participants have been so affiliated.

In their translation ten years ago, these Church "liberals" laid the foundation for current attacks on the validity of the Virgin Birth of Christ and the questioning of the Deity of Christ which are currently the rage in "modernist" theological circles. In the translation of the Old Testament, these scholars changed the prophetic passage in Isaiah 7:14 which reads:

> Behold, a virgin shall conceive, and bear a son and shall call his name Immanuel.

In the "new" version, copyrighted by the National Council of Churches, this beloved passage reads:

> Behold, a young woman shall conceive and bear a son and shall call his name Immanuel.[26]

Through control of religious organizations and magazines, Sunday School literature, prominent seminaries and journals of theological thought, they guide the thinking and paralyze the action of thousands of other dedicated men of God — by controlling the information they get.

CHURCH LITERATURE

Here is an example of the influence of these collectivist thinkers. The *Christian Century* is perhaps the most widely distributed and most influential publication for Protestant clergymen. The magazine's editorial policy is viciously anti-anti-communist,[27] opposes Congressional investigation of communist subversion,[28] disseminated the line that Chinese Communists were "agrarian reformers" and promotes the big government concept that a central authority should do all things for all men. The magazine was a stalwart supporter of Fidel Castro. In fact, three months *after* Castro himself announced to the world on December 2, 1961 that he had been dedicated to communism since his teens and that his revolution had been a communist one, the *Christian Century* on March 6, 1962 said:

Fidel Castro's powerful position as the president of the Cuban Agricultural Reform Institute has been turned over to Cuban Communist Carlos Rodriguez. . . . The question which now arises is whether Castro controls or is controlled by the new president of the C.A.R.I. . . . Have the communists now completely captured Cuba and are they retaining Castro as a showpiece? Is it possible that a man as vain and as courageous as Castro would turn over leadership without a struggle? Has there been such a struggle and has the Cuban Communist Party won it?[29]

That these thoughts should be voiced in an influential church paper three months after Castro *himself* announced that he was a Communist, and almost three years after his firing squads executed thousands of Cubans, is utterly fantastic. This complete refusal to face reality and facts is hardly a qualification for an influential church editor.

Not all propaganda which finds its way into church literature and publications is so obvious. The *Adult Student,* official Sunday school publication of the General Board of Education of the Methodist Church, in the September 1962 issue presented an "objective" study of Communism.[30] Through omission, distortion and clever use of adjectives, and outright attacks on those who are trying to *do* anything about the threat of communism many Methodists were mislead or had their concern about communism dulled.

Admittedly, communist theory was presented authentically. However, communist theory has played only a minor role in the growth of world communism. Communist tactics of infiltration, subversion, bribery, lies, bluff, brutality, treason, and murder are played down or ignored as the force which has spread communism around the world. A certain tolerance of communism and its leaders is implied or stated. Here is an example:

First of all, we deceive ourselves if we visualize communism in stark black-and-white terms, as absolute evil opposed to our absolute good.[31]

Marx is pictured as a "humanitarian" and "devoted husband and father."[32] This whitewashing of Marx by a widely distributed church publication ignores the starvation death of three of his infant children and the unhappy suicides of two others while in their teens. Further, Marx is equated with Jesus as a revolutionary. Under the heading, "Two Revolutionaries," the *Adult Student* says:

Jesus and Marx each lived in a time of social crisis . . . each believed that a new order lay within the reach of man

. . . Both recognized . . . the need for social and moral reform . . . Both revealed a messianic sense of destiny . . . both men drew on their heritage of Old Testament prophecy to denounce evils in the world . . . Thus Marx and Christ were revolutionary leaders.[33]

The article presents the outright communist argument that we are no better than the communists in this way:

How easily, in personal judgments or national policies, we too slip into the same moral relativism! We condemn a "communist foothold" ninety miles from Florida, yet support a military outpost five miles from Red China.[34]

The writer conveniently ignores that communist forces are in Cuba by virtue of a bloody military overthrow of an existing, elected government. Communist military forces in Cuba are threatening to aggressively spread slavery throughout Latin America. The Nationalist forces on Quemoy and Matsu are an outpost of the free world, a deterent necessary only because of Chinese Communist threats to swallow up Formosa and the rest of Southeast Asia.

CORRUPTING CHRISTIAN DOCTRINE

The most tragic effect of the Harry F. Wards, and like thinkers, in the theological schools has been the warping of the basic precepts of Christian doctrine until it is no longer an effective force in man's life. The result is seen in our society. It was observed in Korea where hazy concepts of right and wrong were found in men who had no firmly held, fundamental religious convictions.

Redbook magazine, in its August 1961 issue, published an article which sparked more than a little discussion among Bible-believing Christians, clergy and theologians. Based on interviews with 100 students at eight leading seminaries, the article found:

. . . that 56% of the young ministerial students do not believe in the virgin birth of Jesus Christ . . . that 11% said "No" when asked, "Do you believe in the divinity of Jesus?" . . . that many of the 89% who said "Yes" wanted to define divinity to suit themselves. Belief in the immortality of man ranked as a major belief of only 2% and only 1% were convinced there will be a Second Coming of Christ. While only 29% believe in a real heaven and hell, 46% believe that Jesus ascended physically into heaven as described in the Gospels of Mark and Luke. (This is a contradiction in itself as twice as many reported believing in the Ascension into heaven as believe in heaven).[35]

This disintegration of the basic tenets of Christianity is the outgrowth of "modernist" theologians who deny the divine inspiration of the Bible. With many Christians rejecting their intellectually bankrupt concepts, a new and even more insidious movement, the "neo-orthodox," has arisen. Admitting the divine inspiration of the Scriptures, the neo-orthodox theologian leaves each man free to "interpret" the Bible for himself.

Such interpretation has led to the hazy concepts of right and wrong Army investigators found among American POW's who collaborated in Korea. It has contributed to the general breakdown of moral standards in our society which has resulted in a 100% increase in the rate of illegitimate births in 20 years and sexual promiscuity among young people. The Church, with its watered down "interpreted" doctrines, has failed to stem this tide.

An official publication of the General Board of Education of the Methodist Church, *Workers With Youth,* in the September 1961 issue, suggested that adult leaders use films at young people's meetings and social events. The teacher's guide advised:

> . . . it would be unrealistic to demand that such dramas be immaculate before they can qualify for such viewing. For under guidance, we learn from the sordid and pathological.[36]

Today's young people are over-exposed to the "sordid and pathological" from every side without its being presented in church programs as well. The tone of the advice given Methodist youth leaders is further demonstrated by this excerpt from the same article:

> For many people, the church has become a symbol for repression, for restriction, for a desperate fear of wrong . . . Perhaps it is far better for youth to risk moral stumbling than to shrivel into barren and empty spirits, alone with their regrets.[37]

The church should be the one last bulwark against decaying morals and the permissive, experimentalist attitude toward sex reflected in movies, literature, news media, and TV. The use of false alternatives: risk moral stumbling *or* shrivel into a barren, empty spirit is a typical collectivist weapon for destroying traditional truth.

The decay of the church as a vital moral force would be serious even without the drift toward "neutrality" by church leaders in the battle between east and west. A moral vacuum is being created in which those dedicated to the destruction of our society can work unimpeded. Admiral Ben Morrell, decorated Navy veteran, founder of the World War II Seabees, and outspoken conservative philosopher, describes the dilemma in this way:

> We urge people to go back to church; but there they frequently find that the very forces which have impaired our traditional beliefs have also affected the source of those beliefs, the church itself. The contemporary religious scene is in a state of confusion. Many of our prominent and articulate churchmen and some of our most influential church bodies have favored socialization of our national life and have urged that more power be placed in the hands of government.[38]

Over the years, those who have attempted to question the "drift to the left" in the Church have been subjected to ridicule, persecution, and continual efforts to stifle such discussion. At the height of the smears against anti-communism in the press of the United States, *Look* magazine, in the April 24, 1962 issue, published an article, *The Rightist Crisis in Our Churches.* The author, the religious editor of the United Press, ridiculed charges of infiltration of church organizations and cited as his authority, William C. Sullivan, assistant director of the Federal Bureau of Investigation. The article quotes Sullivan as saying:

> It can be stated factually and without equivocation that any allegation is false which holds that there has been and is, on a national scale, any substantial Communist infiltration of the American clergy . . . There can be no doubt as to the loyalty of the overwhelming majority of the clergy of our nation.[39]

Sullivan is, of course, correct. No responsible critic has charged that any *substantial* part of the clergy is communist or pro-communist. Even the largest estimates of the knowing or unknowing participation of clergymen in communist fronts is under 5% and this is far from substantial. However, the remarks of the assistant director of the FBI are widely circulated to discredit those who are concerned that a small hardcore of clergymen who are serving something or someone other than God dominate church organizations, publications, etc. at the top. Sullivan's quoted words come from a 90 minute speech he delivered at the Highland Park Methodist Church in Dallas, Texas on October 19, 1961.

The balance of Sullivan's speech is ignored by those who ridicule the threat of communism in the churches. Sullivan listed nine reasons why clergymen succumb to communist appeals. They include:

Failing to recognize obvious communist propaganda in petitions, open letters, clemency appeals, pamphlets, etc. . . . mistaken notions that clergymen can work with communists for peace, civil rights, ending racial discrimination, etc. without harming religion and strengthening communism.

Confusing the values of communism with those of Christianity . . . confusing the social doctrines of Karl Marx with those of Jesus Christ . . . a tendency to reject or drastically dilute the supernatural content of religion in favor of a naturalistic form of humanism which can make it hard to logically take a strong stand against communism.

Show a proneness to join organizations without questioning their real sponsorship, direction, policies, etc. . . . making statements and drawing conclusions relative to foreign policy, economics, and domestic politics which exceed their field of competence.[40]

A good example of the final point was the 400 laymen and 200 clergymen who participated in the Fifth World Order Study Conference in Cleveland, Ohio, Nov. 18-21, 1958. They unanimously passed a resolution in favor of diplomatic recognition of Red China by the U. S. and the seating of the communist Chinese government in the United Nations. The Conference was dominated by officers, staff personnel and members of the General Board of the National Council of Churches.

J. Edgar Hoover, in a series of articles in the fundamental church publication, *Christianity Today,* outlined the communist strategy of deceit in their potent attack against the Churches. Mr. Hoover said:

"Look," the communists are saying, "we are tolerant of religion, we do not want to attack your faith. Rather, let's work together on issues in which we are both interested — peace, civil liberties, economic justice. We communists are believers in love, justice, and the brotherhood of man. Let's not fight but work together.

Here is the deadly "come along" of communism, directed today at the Christian pulpit. This enables the Party to move close to unsuspecting ministers and laymen who see only the exterior verbiage and not the concealed danger. How does the Party work here? In many ways: encouraging churchmen to endorse, support and even participate in communist-front groups, Communist-sponsored petitions; *to neutralize clerical opposition to communism.* (If a minister can be influenced to keep silent about the dangers of communism, the Party has gained.)[41]

How many churches today are effectively opposing communism? In his article Mr. Hoover asks the clergy who read the magazine:

> Have you encouraged members of your church to read about communism and to learn of its evil nature? Have you urged formation of discussion groups to acquaint men and women with the challenge.[42]

Unfortunately, much of the clergy in America has not heeded this sound advice. It appears they have been largely neutralized in the fight, one of the communist goals Mr. Hoover outlined. Patriotic clergymen have been misled into opposing anti-communist programs of all sorts by the anti-anti-communist propaganda in the religious press and a sincere desire to avoid "controversy" — and opposing communism can be controversial.

Chapter VIII

The Press, Radio and TV

> *Our republic and its press will rise and fall*
> *together.*   — *Joseph Pulitzer*

THE NEWS MEN OF AMERICA must share with the U. S. Department of State the responsibility for the fall of China, the butchering of Budapest, Castro's rise in Cuba, and the destruction of the anti-communist forces in Indonesia, Laos, Algeria and the Congo.

If alert, conscientious reporters had rejected official State Department press "handouts" and "briefings" and dug out the known and documented backgrounds of Castro, Ben Bella, and Mao Tse-tung, these communist dictators wouldn't be in power today in Cuba, Algeria, and China.

If the American press had consistently informed the American people about the repeated failures, mistakes, and stupidity of the State Department, the mess in Washington would have been cleaned up years ago. Communism would not be threatening America today from an armed stronghold just 90 miles from Florida.

Walter Trohan, distinguished chief of the *Chicago Tribune* bureau in Washington, charitably attributes press failures to the "system" in Washington. In an article entitled, *Decline of the Fourth Estate,*[1] first written in 1951 and republished ten years later, Trohan said:

> In Washington, where a thousand newspapermen ply their trade, there is mounting suspicion that members of the press have begun to grow weary of the exacting watchdog role and have been attaching themselves to the First Estate, the ruling class.
>
> The simple truth is that the press has given up on fact-hunting for the less arduous and frequently more profitable role of interpreting what has gone before and predicting what is to come, in conformity with the Administration's pattern.

Trohan described how the press is seduced with high living, first-name treatment by the "greats" of government, expense-paid press trips abroad, "tips," and "leaks" on important stories, and off-the-record "briefings" by high officials. Such invitations and access to news sources are not available to the conscientious newsman who asks embarrassing questions. Trohan continued:

> The temptations to abandon reporting in favor of revealing are many . . . it is far easier to run through the grist of official handouts than to grub for news . . . Once a reporter convinces himself that he can bring his readers great news from these handouts, he has little or no compunction in lengthening the stride of his dispatches to take in the propaganda.
>
> It is not difficult to convince a reporter that it isn't the news but the way he writes it that counts. Especially when he finds that those who hew the line most consistently are acclaimed as journalistic greats . . . and when he becomes aware that Pulitzer prizes go to reporters taking handouts from law firms defending loyalty suspects or from a foreign nation.

The sins of the press are not limited to printing what it is handed. Instead, the American press has ignored, and at times deliberately covered up, the disclosures of repeated stupidity, if not treason, in high places.

The press handling of the story of William Arthur Wieland, whose part in bringing Castro to power was detailed in Chapters I and III, is a clearcut example.[2]

At the presidential press conference on January 24, 1962, a woman reporter asked why William Wieland and another man had been appointed to key State Department positions. The *St. Louis Post-Dispatch* account of the incident was typical of press coverage of the incident. It was written by Anthony Lewis of the *New York Times* News Service. It said:

> President Kennedy vigorously defended two State Department employees yesterday against a newspaper woman's charges that they were security risks. He rebuked the reporter, Mrs. Sarah McLendon, when she made the accusation at his press conference. He personally vouched for clearance of the two men and said he hoped they would continue to serve without detriment to their character by your question.[3]

The story quoted the President as saying that he and Dean Rusk had personally examined Wieland's record and found him suited for his assignment. The report continued:

> Mrs. McLendon did not say what lay behind her charge that the two men were security risks.[4]

Such reporting might be excused if Lewis, the writer, was not aware of Wieland's record during 15 years in the State Department. That he had the information became obvious in the final paragraphs of the long article, which said:

> The Senate Internal Security subcommittee had made public accusations against Wieland. These were contained in testi-

mony before the committee by three former ambassadors in Latin America, William D. Pawley, Robert C. Hill, and Earl E. T. Smith.[5]

The story used generalizations from the testimony about Wieland in this way:

Pawley charged that Wieland, while director of the State Department Office of Caribbean-Mexican Affairs between 1958 and 1960, had assisted the overthrow of the Fulgencio Batista government of Cuba by Fidel Castro.

Pawley said Wieland had done so by buying the idea of not selling arms to either side in the revolutionary conflict. He also said that Wieland had a "close association with Herbert Matthews of the New York Times."

Hill attributed what he termed "wrong decisions" on Cuba to Wieland. He said Wieland was either "a damn fool or a communist, and I don't think he was a communist."

Smith mentioned Wieland's name in a long list of persons whom he criticized for helping in the overthrow of the Batista regime.[6]

If this was all the evidence against Wieland, Mrs. McLendon's charge that he was a security risk was irresponsible. In creating this impression, the writer of the *New York Times* article ignored all the damning evidence against Wieland in the Senate reports, which was detailed in Chapter III.[7]

In ignoring this evidence, it can only be concluded that the New York Times writer was deliberately covering up for President Kennedy, Wieland, and the failure of the State Department security system.

The Wieland case is not the only instance where the press has supressed serious charges against Kennedy appointees.

The questionable record of Arthur Goldberg, Kennedy's first Secretary of Labor and Justice Felix Frankfurter's replacement on the U. S. Supreme Court have been ignored. *The Wanderer*, a St. Paul, Minn. Catholic newspaper, in its September 27, 1962 issue published charges that Goldberg had served a number of communist causes and fronts and had, as secretary of labor, appointed a communist to a government position.[8] The article charged that Goldberg had been president of the Chicago Chapter of the National Lawyers Guild. The Guild has been officially cited by the House Committee on Un-American Activities as "the legal bulwark of the Communist Party."[9]

Goldberg, the article charged, served as a sponsor of the Conference on Constitutional Liberties in America, designated as a communist front by the Attorney General.[10]

As Secretary of Labor, Goldberg appointed Walter Gellhorn

of Columbia University as official arbitrator for the International Organization of Masters, Pilots, and Mates, a labor organization representing key men in the Merchant Marine. Gellhorn, the article said, was identified as a communist by Louis Budenz before the House of Representatives Select Committee to Investigate Tax-Exempt Foundations.[11]

Does the past record of Mr. Goldberg inspire confidence of the American people when he is appointed as a Supreme Court Justice? Hardly. Justice Goldberg has never denied these affiliations, and despite their wide circulation by conservative groups, the nation's press has ignored them.

A similar "blackout" has been imposed on more serious charges against Adam Yarmolinsky, special assistant to Defense Secretary Robert McNamara.

During a 1962 Senate investigation, it was charged that Yarmolinsky had admitted to World War II Army security investigators that he had attended meetings of the Young Communist League. He denied joining the organization, but said, "They (the Young Communist League) believed and I was inclined to believe that a so-called Communist government was a desirable end."[12]

As an employee of the extreme left-wing Fund for the Republic, Yarmolinsky authored a vicious attack on Congressional committees which investigate communism and also security agencies such as the FBI which attempt to protect the nation from communist subversion.[13]

Yarmolinsky's parents have long records of support for left-wing causes which they continued even after their son was appointed to the number two spot in the Department of Defense. Yarmolinsky's father, Avrahm, who was born in Russia,[14] and his mother, a writer who uses the name Babette Deutsch,[15] have been charged with being members of the John Reed club in 1930.[16] More recently they signed a public appeal to President Kennedy in 1961 for Christmas clemency for Carl Braden and Frank Wilkinson.[17]

During 1962, Babette Deutsch was listed by the *New York Times* on a committee seeking freedom for the communist terrorist, David Siquieros, in Mexico,[18] and advocated abolition of the House Committee on Un-American Activities and its investigations of communists.[19]

Herbert Romerstein, a former undercover agent in the Communist Party, in his book, *Communism and Your Child*, recited some of these facts and said:

If a young GI in our armed forces had parents with records such as this, he would be the subject of an investigation to determine his loyalty.[20]

Press coverage of these aspects of the background of a top Defense Department official has been limited to ridicule of those who attempt to call attention to them.

Liberal or left-wing bias of the press is not a new development. The story of how the *Saturday Evening Post, Collier's,* and other influential publications dwelled on the shortcomings of Chiang Kai-shek's government while glorifying the communists is told in detail in Chapter III. The *Saturday Evening Post* published over 60 articles which promoted the communist line during this period.[21]

The "hatchet job" the *New York Times* did on Senator Joseph McCarthy discussed in Chapter III[22] was typical of the press coverage given the Wisconsin Senator's fight to expose communist infiltration in government.

These are not isolated cases.

The *Indianapolis News* called attention to the double standard in an editorial on April 11, 1962. The News said:

When the Columbia Broadcasting System staged its famous TV program called "Thunder On The Right" it devoted considerable attention to a house bombing in California.

The network, it will be recalled, ran a longish interview with a minister who had been critical of "right wing extremists," and who had had a bomb thrown at his house. The episode was treated as an example of what right wing agitation could lead to.

Not, of course, that anyone had identified the house bomber. But it was concluded, this was the kind of thing which happens in the emotional atmosphere created by the right-wing extremists. Even though it was unclear who executed the bombing, America's right wing revival was deemed ultimately responsible and judged accordingly.

The *Indianapolis News* editorial then called attention to the death by hanging of Newton Armstrong, Jr. Armstrong, 19, was the editor of a conservative student newspaper at San Diego State College in California. His father was a prominent member of the anti-communist John Birch Society. Armstrong's hands, when he was found hanging in a bedroom in his home, *were bound behind his back.* His death was finally labelled a "suicide" by the authorities.

After recounting the details, the *Indianapolis News* said that if the nation's press would apply the same standards to the hanging as they had to the bombing of the minister's home, then Armstrong's hanging was clearly the responsibility of "liberal" extremists. The News challenged CBS-TV with these words:

> We think it would make a compelling documentary by CBS; but we won't hold our breath waiting for it.

The nation's press exhibited the same double standard shown by CBS. The home bombing made headlines across the nation. The minister and prominent screen stars were interviewed on network news broadcasts. Without proof, right wing "radicals" and anti-communists were blamed. By contrast, the death of the Armstrong boy was ignored. Those who suggested foul play were ridiculed.

The news magazines have shown the same prejudice against anti-communists.

In its September 1, 1961 issue, *Life* magazine depicted Dr. Fred Schwarz, head of the Christian Anti-Communism Crusade, as a money hungry cynic. After a storm of public criticism, Life's publisher, C. D. Jackson, personally appeared on the platform of Schwarz' anti-communism school in Hollywood Bowl on October 16, 1961 and apologized. Jackson said:

> I believe we were wrong and I am profoundly sorry. It's a great privilege to be here tonight and align *Life* with Senator Dodd, Representative Judd, Dr. Schwarz and the rest of these implacable fighters against communism.[23]

Although Jackson apologized before the 10,000 people in the audience, *Life* did not print a retraction to be read by the 6-million subscribers who had seen the original smear. In fact, just six weeks after Jackson made his public apology to Schwarz, *Life* in its December 1, 1961 editorial, *Crackpots: How They Help Communism,* took another swipe at Schwarz and his efforts, saying that Dr. Schwarz and his Christian Anti-Communism Crusade attract "people who are too superheated to teach or learn anything."

C. D. Jackson, Special Assistant to former President Eisenhower, led the militant anti-McCarthy forces in the President's official family and eventually succeeded in masterminding the destruction of the Wisconsin Senator.[24]

Jackson's boss, Henry Luce, the owner of *Time, Life* and other publications is another Republican with an affinity for "liberal" causes. Luce served for a time as a trustee of the Institute of Pacific Relations[25] while Owen Lattimore and his associates were using the IPR to influence State Department far eastern policies.

Luce also conceived and financed the *Commission on Freedom of the Press.*[26] The commission spent $200,000 of Luce's money and in 1948 produced a five-volume report which was a blanket condemnation of the nation's press for its bias *in favor of big business, wealth and the status quo.*[27] Luce had selected the ultra-liberal Chancellor of the University of Chicago, Robert Hutchins, to head the commission. Ten of the 12 members had a total of 68 affiliations with communist front organizations.[28]

Life's sister publication, *Time,* has shown a similar tendency to be in the vanguard of those attacking anti-communists, while maintaining its reputation as an anti-communist, Republican-leaning publication.

In its October 22, 1951 issue, for example, *Time* "exposed" Senator Joseph McCarthy and used as "evidence" of McCarthy's wrong-doing his persecution of Gustavo Duran. *Time* stated, "Duran, never a Red, was definitely and clearly anti-communist," implying that McCarthy's charges were sheer fabrication. *Time* published this falsehood even though it had been furnished copies of the Military Intelligence Reports which showed that Duran, a State Department employee, had been a member of the Communist secret police in Spain in 1936-38 and had served the conspiracy in various European capitals during the 1930's.[29]

The editors of *Time* selected the March 10, 1961 issue to launch an attack on the anti-communist John Birch Society. The charges of Robert Welch, the society's founder, that Dwight Eisenhower was a tool or dupe of the communists had first been published in Chicago and Milwaukee newspapers eight months before during the 1960 Republican National Convention. Scattered left-wing organs repeated the "expose."

However, it was not until the charges against Welch and the John Birch Society were published in the February 25, 1961 issue of *People's World,* the official west coast communist newspaper, that *Time* and hundreds of other newspapers and magazines picked the story up.

Strangely, *Time,* even though its reporters had been supplied a full assortment of John Birch literature[30] made the *same* error as the communist *People's World* in identifying John Birch, for whom the society was named, as a *Navy* rather than an *Army* captain. Time also identified only three of the 26 members of the Council of the John Birch Society — *three of the same four mentioned in the People's World article*. Significantly, *Time* included the name of Adolphe Menjou in its list of Council members, as did the *People's World,* even though the *Time* reporter was furnished an up to date list and had been advised that Menjou had res gned several months before.[31]

The press, after headlining the attacks of nearly every left-wing spokesman against the John Birch Society, ignored the objective or friendly evaluations of the organization which were made in the following two years. For example, Ezra Taft Benson, secretary of agriculture in President Eisenhower's cabinet, made an evaluation of the John Birch Society which directly contradicts the nearly unanimous condemnations and "exposes" of the press. In a formal statement in *Church News*, the official publication of the Mormon Church, of which he is an elder, Benson said:

> I have stated, as my personal opinion only, that the John Birch Society is the most effective non-church organization in our fight against creeping socialism and godless communism.[32]

Benson's statement was ignored, or was buried in back pages of newspapers, as was the report of the only official investigation and evaluation of the John Birch Society. In 1963, the Senate Fact-finding Subcommittee on Un-American Activities of the California Legislature completed a two-year investigation of the John Birch Society and its activities. The report made some criticisms of statements made by the founder of the society, Robert Welch, but concluded:

> There is no question, as National Review points out, that he has stirred the slumbering spirit of patriotism in thousands of Americans, roused them from lethargy, and changed their apathy into deep desire to first learn the facts about communism and then implement that knowledge with effective and responsible action.[33]

Of the society's membership, the California Senate report stated:

> We have found the average member to have been concerned about the advances of the world communist movement and the advances of communist subversion in this country. The John Birch Society has provided the only organization with a militant program of study and action through which the frustrations of these people can be released . . . The average member is firmly convinced that the real threat is not essentially abroad, but that since our foreign policies are evolved here, and as they are influenced here, and since our retreat from one European crisis after another has been engineered in Washington, then the problem must be faced in this country.[34]

In conclusion, the Senate report said of the John Birch Society:

> We have not found the society to be either secret or a fascist organization . . . there have been instances of imprudent

activity and indefensible statements but such isolated occur-
rences are not typical of the organization as a whole . . .
We believe that the reason the John Birch Society has attracted so many members is that it simply appeared to them
to be the most effective, indeed the only organization through
which they could join in a national movement to learn the
truth about the communist menace and then take some positive
concerted action to prevent its spread.[35]

In contrast to headlines and front-page placement accorded
every unsubstantiated charge against the John Birch Society
since the communists triggered the anti-Birch campaign in
1961, very little attention was given to this official "clearance"
by a committee of the California Senate.

Volumes could and should be written on the press coverage
of President Kennedy's assassination by a communist killer.
Even after Oswald was captured and his Marxist affiliations
disclosed, TV and radio commentators have conducted a
continual crusade of distortion and smear to direct the blame
against right wing or conservative groups.

The bias in the press is not always intentional. It is not
necessarily deliberate. It is, to a degree, the natural result
of the basic education newsmen have received in American
schools coupled with a change in the fundamental concepts
of journalism. The net effect, however, is the same.

Traditionally, the job of the newsman was to report the
five "W's" — the who, what, when, where, and why. While
following these age-old precepts of the newspaper field, the
reporter covering a political speech, for example, told what
the speaker said. Opinions and explanations were left to the
editorial page.

About 20 years ago schools of journalism started teaching
prospective newsmen the technique of "interpretive reporting"
which had been popularized by the news magazine, *Time,*
and other Henry Luce publications.

The interpretive reporter, rather than faithfully recording
in an orderly way a speaker's words, instead explains the
"meaning" and "overall importance" of what is said. Such
interpretation is justified with the contention that the average
reader might not understand the report otherwise, that the
broadened latitude given the reporter permits him to bring in
explanatory background material and use a writing style which
is more lively and interesting.

The danger in such "interpretive reporting" is that the reporter may himself not fully understand the *meaning* of
what the speaker says. When an ultra-liberal reporter covers

the speech of a conservative speaker, or vice versa, the writer is in basic disagreement with the message presented. He would feel that the speaker was misleading his audience. The reporter would therefore feel it his duty, not to relate the speaker's words objectively, but to present the case in such a way so that the reader gets the "truth." The danger, of course, is that the reporter may not himself know the "truth" and the facts are never fully presented so that the reader may judge for himself.

The use and abuse of interpretive reporting was so widespread during the 1960 Presidential campaign that widespread criticism developed within the press itself in the months following the election. Four independent studies were made by news agencies or press related organizations of the campaign coverage.

Interpretive reporting by the Associated Press and United Press received detailed attention in an exhaustive study by Richard Pourade, editor emeritus of the San Diego Union. Completed almost a year after the election, Pourade's report reproduced portions of 140 daily AP and UPI dispatches which showed bias in the coverage of both candidates in the last five weeks of the campaign. In his summary, Pourade said:

> One of the most surprising features of the Associated Press coverage was the extent to which the so-called interpretive columns questioned the motives of the candidates, disparaged their remarks, and brought the doubt of the Associated Press on their integrity and character.
>
> Even if the benefit of the doubt were given to all wire service reporters covering the campaign, that they did their journalistic best to submerge their personal feelings, the fact remains that the editorial laxity granted them in their daily coverage resulted in emotional treatment too often keyed to the reporters' personal conviction.
>
> Wire service reporters set themselves up as a final judge of crowds, reactions, sincerity of statement, pertinency of the statements politically and ideologically, and passed judgements on the merits of the various proposals. To often, what the candidate had to say was buried beneath how the reporter personally evaluated it in the context of the whole campaign, and what he thought was the crowd's reaction to it.[36]

Earl Johnson, editor of United Press International, in a letter defending UPI's coverage, included a statement which said that the attitudes and reactions of reporters covering the candidates was disgraceful.[37]

The "disgraceful" behavior of the press was described by

Willard Edwards, Washington correspondent of the *Chicago Tribune,* in a comprehensive study he made of election coverage. Of the press corps assigned to Vice President Nixon's campaign, Edwards said:

Ninety per cent of this press corps, which ranged between 50 and 100 at various periods in the campaign, were all-out supporters of Kennedy. They were not only opposed to Nixon, they were outspoken in their hatred and contempt of him . . . it was loud and open. When Nixon was making a speech, there was a constant murmur or ridicule from many in the press rows just beneath the platform.[38]

THE MEN OF THE PRESS

Walter Lippmann is often acclaimed as the "Dean of American Newspapermen." His syndicated column appears in over 300 newspapers. His name on a book makes it a best-seller. Yet, since 1940, his "scholarly" appraisals of world affairs, his soothing, nothing-to-worry about evaluations of communist intentions have rarely been right.

Lippmann is a longtime leftist. As a student at Harvard, he joined the British Fabian Society in 1909.[39] He became president of the Harvard chapter of the Intercollegiate Socialist Society the same year and was a close associate of Felix Frankfurter.[40]

Today, Lippmann rather consistently opposes any action to free the captive peoples behind the Iron Curtain. When the Hungarian rebellion erupted in 1956, Lippmann was quick to caution against aid for the Freedom Fighters. In his October 26, 1956 column, he wrote:

It is not in our own interests that the movement in Eastern Europe should go so far that no accommodation with Russia is possible . . . In the interest of peace and freedom . . . we must hope for a time — not forever, but for a time — the uprising in the satellite orbit will be stabilized at Titoism.

In 1961, Lippmann, a longtime apologist for Castro, was shocked by the attempted invasion of Cuba at the Bay of Pigs and actually expressed relief when the try failed. In his May 2, 1961 column, Lippmann said:

Bad as have been the consequences of failure, they are probably less bad than would have been the indecisive partial success which was the best that could conceivably have been received.

Thirty-eight years after Walter Lippmann helped start the Intercollegiate Socialist Society chapter at Harvard, other influential editors, columnists, and Washington correspondents helped to found another leftwing political group, the Americans for Democratic Action in 1947.

The ADA's political platform advocates Red China's admission to the United Nations, transfer of all national armaments to a UN peace force, elimination of barriers on trade with communist countries, and a hands off policy towards Cuba.[41]

The domestic goals of the ADA include total state control of the economic life of the nation through application of the theories of the British Fabian economist, John Maynard Keynes. An end to loyalty checks for federal employees, elimination of loyalty oaths for students on government scholarships and a halt to Congressional investigations of communist activities are other goals of the ADA.[42]

Among the founders of this left-wing group was Marquis Childs, Washington correspondent of the *St. Louis Post-Dispatch*.[43] Childs writings are widely syndicated and he appears regularly as a panelist on the TV news interview show, "Meet the Press."

Other ADA founders included the Alsop brothers, Joseph and Stewart, whose columns are used by many newspapers.[44] They are also regular contributors to the *Saturday Evening Post*. Ken Crawford, now a featured columnist in *Newsweek* magazine, was an ADA founder, as was James Wechsler, editor of the *New York Post*.[45] Elmer Davis, influential newsman, author and head of the communist-riddled Office of War Information, and other lesser known newsmen were also founders of the ADA.[46]

All newsmen are not liberals or socialists. However, as in so many other fields, the key jobs, acclaim as journalistic geniuses, opportunity to write syndicated columns, and guest spots as panelists on TV news shows go to the liberals.

THE BROADCASTERS

Edward R. Murrow, one-time vice-president of CBS, and now head of the United States Information Agency, Howard K. Smith of CBS and ABC, and Chet Huntley of NBC have, by their associations, writings, and actions, marked themselves as biased liberals.

Edward R. Murrow's service to leftist causes dates back to 1935 when he served on the board of the Institute of International Education, an organization which encouraged young American school teachers to take their summer training at the University of Moscow — and subsidized their trips there.[47]

As the nation's top producer of TV news "documentaries"

Murrow pioneered the technique of "forgery by film." An ardent defender of Alger Hiss, Owen Lattimore, John Stewart Service and others discharged from government service for security reasons, Murrow's assistance earned him the praise of Owen Lattimore, who in 1950 in his book, *Ordeal by Slander,* said:

> Before I could speak for myself, Murrow kept the record straight by repeatedly drawing attention to the fact that nothing had been proved against me.[48]

Lattimore pointed out that Murrow consistently gave him "air time" to present his views. A year later, the Senate Internal Security Subcommittee found Lattimore to be "a conscious articulate agent of the Soviet conspiracy." Murrow's defense of Lattimore could possibly be excused as bending over backwards to be fair. However, when the subject of Murrow's broadcasts was the late Senator Joseph McCarthy, there was no fairness. The character assassination Murrow did in editing film to make McCarthy look like a giggling psychopath brought protests from even McCarthy's most bitter enemies.

The *Saturday Review's* Gilbert Seldes despised McCarthy but he was shaken by the viciousness of Murrow's "objective" film report. He said:

> The people who roared with delight should ask themselves quickly how they would have felt if the same technique had been applied to someone they liked — for example, to (Adlai) Stevenson.[49]

John Cogley, another vehement critic of McCarthy, writing in the liberal Catholic journal, *Commonweal,* pointed out . . .

> . . . the Murrow show has set a potentially dangerous precedent which those who are now applauding may find good reason to regret in time to come.[50]

Murrow's filmed defense of another security risk, J. Robert Oppenheimer, drew criticism from even Dorothy Schiff, publisher of the ultra-ultra-liberal *New York Post.* Mrs. Schiff said that the Oppenheimer case did not seem to present a clear-cut issue on which liberals could make a fight. Yet, she said:

> . . . Murrow asked Oppenheimer only questions that tended to put him in the best possible light. The impression left with the uninformed viewer was that of a hero and a martyr.[51]

Murrow's questioning of Oppenheimer avoided the fact that Oppenheimer's wife, brother, and mistress were communists, that Oppenheimer had contributed sums of up to $1,000 annually to the Communist Party, and that he had admitted lying under oath to government security agents when questioned during World War II when he headed the atom bomb project.[52]

Murrow carried his bias into government service. When the communists broke the nuclear test ban in September 1961, Murrow's *Voice of America* broadcasts which supposedly send a message of freedom behind the Iron Curtain handled the announcement this way:

Khrushchev, with aching heart, consented to test again.[53]

Howard K. Smith is another widely-heralded TV news commentator and producer of "documentaries."

Smith made headlines on November 11, 1962 when he brought Alger Hiss, convicted perjurer and one-time communist espionage agent, out of obscurity. Hiss was invited to participate in the Smith-narrated, *Political Obituary of Richard M. Nixon.* Hiss discussed the character and personality of former Vice President Nixon, who as a young congressman in 1948, played a large part in exposing Hiss as a communist agent.

Anyone familiar with Smith's views and writings would not have been surprised at his invitation to Alger Hiss. For instance, in his book, *The State of Europe,* published in 1949 when the cold war was four years old, Smith had this praise for the communist satellites of Eastern Europe:

Four years of "People's Democracy" — to sum up my conclusions — have probably yielded Eastern Europe a solid net gain. If the Communist regimes have been indistinguishable from their predecessors in political repression, they have been at least in the social and economic realms, an outstanding success.[54]

Smith exposed himself as a socialist in the same volume when he said:

The maintenance of the system of private enterprise is not only becoming technically less possible; it is rapidly losing its last moral justifications.[55]

Smith explained his inability to oppose communism in this way:

Whenever the merits and demerits of the Welfare State and its planned economy, the main point is that it is coming by one means or another. The only question is how long it will take and in what form it will come.

It is the inherent inevitability of this great mutation that has made it impossible for me to take a clear anti-Soviet attitude. A good deal of the Soviet economic and social analysis is shrewder and more to the point than much of the thinking about what is going on in the west. For all their distorted vision, the Soviets have seen the clear fact that the survival of Capitalism is impossible in Europe. They have certainly brought to the common man of Europe a richer life.[56]

In an earlier volume, *The Last Train from Berlin,* written in 1942, Smith said:

Russia looked better the longer I stayed and the more I saw.[57]

Smith has held honored and responsible posts with both CBS and ABC-TV networks. His views have been projected into American homes as objective news analysis. He has won the highest awards of the Journalism and Broadcast professions, the DuPont Award, the Overseas Press Club award for best radio reporting from abroad, the Sigma Delta Chi award for radio journalism, and a TV emmy.[58]

Chet Huntley, ace commentator and news analyst for NBC-TV, narrated an NBC "White Paper" on the controversy over welfare reforms instituted in the small city of Newburgh, N. Y. Entitled, "The Battle of Newburgh," it was broadcast on January 28, 1962.

The day following the program, Joseph M. Mitchell, city manager of Newburgh, issued an 18-point indictment of the program. He made these charges:

Approximately 60,000 feet of film was taken of which 2,000 appeared on the show. Statements of the prominent city leaders who *supported* the welfare reforms were edited out.

Biased witnesses, two former office holders and the husband of a welfare department employee, criticized the reform program. They were presented as typical Newburgh citizens without disclosing their personal involvements which caused them to oppose the welfare reform.

NBC filmed the principal defense of the welfare reform program in a bar which gave the impression that the only support for the reform program came from those who sit around bars drinking.

False figures were used in presenting the Newburgh budget, the entire city was pictured as a slum, and city officials were ridiculed by editing which presented their remarks out of context.

The program was built for emotional appeal rather than a calm examination of the facts. For example, the city manager was pictured saying, "No truly needy person has suffered." This was followed by a filmed sequence of a crying man.[59]

Five months later, the crying man voluntarily confessed to city officials how the "documentary" had been staged. In a tape-recorded interview with the city council, Thomas H. Weygant, said he had been paid $50 by NBC for his part in the "news" film. He had been carefully rehearsed on what to say and how to say it. NBC employees, Weygant said, had deliberately undressed his children before they appeared on the show to make it appear that he could not afford to clothe them.[60]

NBC denied the charges. The $50, they said, was a collection taken up by the cameramen to help the unfortunate, abused victim of the Newburgh welfare reform program.

Mitchell's most telling indictment of the NBC White Paper was the omission of any explanation of the 13 regulations which provoked the controversy.

Widely condemned by liberals as "cruel" and "inhumane" and praised by conservatives as long overdue, the Newburgh reforms included requirements that all able-bodied men on relief had to report for work in city maintenance departments; that those on relief who refused to accept offered employment would be denied further relief; that relief payments to any family could not exceed the take-home pay of the lowest paid city employee with the same number of children; and that relief be denied to mothers of illegitimate children who bear additional illegitimate children.[61] These provisions were not spelled out on the NBC "White Paper" so NBC viewers could not judge the reforms for themselves.

Chet Huntley, of course, was simply the commentator on the show. The words he spoke, the film he showed were the compilation of the producers, editors and writers of NBC news. The NBC "White Paper" series is a product of this teamwork. *The Battle of Newburgh* was the ninth NBC White Paper — and it was a typical production.

All newsmen are not biased. There are good publishers and conscientious reporters. Some of them are liberals — some are conservatives. However, they can't report the truth if they never get it. That's the spot many dedicated and responsible newsmen are in — without knowing it.

Rex Davis, veteran news director of the CBS-affiliate in St. Louis, KMOX, put the problem into words. He was interviewed by the *St. Louis Globe-Democrat* when he completed 16 years on the air in St. Louis and said:

> How do you know what's the truth? You try like the devil but you are dependent on the news services (for national and international news) and if they goof, what do you do?[62]

Another newsman put it this way: "If you can't trust your news sources, what can you trust?"

This states the problem. Thousands of working newsmen across the country, being conscientious themselves, attribute these same characteristics to the men who reach top positions on the AP and UPI news services. They depend on AP and UPI for the news they report to their own readers and listeners. They base their own judgments of world happenings on these "facts."

How reliable are these sources?

Wire service coverage of the 1960 presidential campaign and the criticism of it within the press has already been discussed.[63]

There are other examples. When Whittaker Chambers died in 1961, the AP obituary used so many "hate words" in describing Chambers that a number of newspapers protested. The *Sentinel Star* of Orlando, Florida published an editorial dissent and then lodged a formal protest with AP's general manager, Frank Starzel. The editorial said:

> The staid, powerful Associated Press handled the news of Whittaker Chambers in a peculiar way. Chambers, you may remember was a $30,000 a year senior editor of *Time* who, in 1948, put the finger on Alger Hiss, the State Department spy, and lost his job, his reputation, and his health. The only reason we can think of is patriotism. He made a clean breast of everything; he wanted to atone for his mistake by warning the U. S. of its danger.
>
> The AP's handling tends to indict him for being loyal to the U. S. The AP calls him a "turncoat communist." Turncoat is a despised appellation and the inference is that anyone who turns from communism should be despised. The AP says Chambers "tattled." Telling the truth is honorable, but, from childhood, we are taught that tattling is unworthy. The AP says Chambers "recited" to a "Congressional spyhunting committee." Here the inference is that he merely repeated a cooked-up story and that spy-hunting is not a serious matter.
>
> Whereas the AP calls Hiss "brilliant," it kisses off Chambers as being "pudgy, short and fat" and says "he lived with a woman outside of marriage." This was before he married a woman to whom he was devoted for 30 years until his death.[64]

The *Sentinel Star* editorial concluded with this observation:

> We are living in peculiar times, gentlemen of the Associated Press, when patriots are maligned.

We are indeed living in peculiar times. The maligning of patriots by the Associated Press and other segments of the communications industry is not limited to men like Whittaker Chambers. Even George Washington, the father of our country, is being downgraded.

On February 22, 1961, the Associated Press supplied its member newspapers with a feature story marking the birthday of our first president. It pictured George Washington as a gambling slavekeeper who was a sucker for con-man schemes.[65]

In September 1962, former General Edwin Walker went to Mississippi to observe the military forces which occupied Oxford to force the enrollment of James Meredith, a Negro, to the University of Mississippi. While in Oxford, Walker was arrested by military authorities and charged with inciting a riot, sedition against the United States, and other crimes.

The charges arose, in part, from Associated Press reports that Walker had incited students to riot against lawful authority and had led them in a charge against U. S. marshals. The AP account was written by a 21-year old AP reporter, Van Savell, who stated that Walker . . .

> . . . took command of a group of students, climbed a Confederate statue, and told the crowd that Governor Ross Barnett had betrayed Mississippi.[66]

The story quoted Walker as saying, while perched on the statue:

> But don't let up now. You may lose this battle but you will have been heard. This is a dangerous situation. You must be prepared for possible death. If you are not, go home now.

This AP news story was the one that most newspapers and radio stations used. It was repeated and rephrased countless times. A completely different story was told by United Press International. In a dispatch received on the St. Louis UPI teletype at 11:23 PM CDT, September 30, 1962, the same incident was described in this way:

> During a lull in the rioting, General Edwin Walker mounted a Confederate statue on the campus and begged the students to cease their violence. He said: "This is not the proper route to Cuba." His pleas were greeted with one massive jeer.[67]

Almost four months later, after Walker's illegal confinement in a mental institution, a series of court appearances and hearings, the federal grand jury at Oxford, Mississippi refused to indict him and all charges were dropped on January 21, 1963. Walker is suing Associated Press for $2-million, charging that he was libelled.

Walker's attorney, Clyde Watts of Tulsa, Oklahoma, has obtained a sworn statement from a deputy sheriff in Oxford, who was eating in the same restaurant as General Walker when news was received that students were rioting on the campus. Both Walker and the sheriff left the restaurant almost immediately. The sheriff's statement says that when he got into his car and turned the radio on he heard a news report that rioting students were being led by Walker — whom he had just seen leaving the restaurant.[68]

Another influence on working newsmen are the half dozen or so "prestige" newspapers which newsmen themselves rank as the "best" in the nation.

Of the ten newspapers which normally top the polls of journalism professors, newsmen and editors, only one, the *Chicago Tribune,* presents a consistently conservative viewpoint on *both* national and international affairs. Three other papers are moderately conservative on economic matters but tend to blind internationalism in coverage of foreign news. The other six, *The New York Times, Washington Post, St. Louis Post-Dispatch, Atlanta Constitution, Louisville Courier Journal,* and *Milwaukee Journal* are ultra-liberal in their viewpoint.

The *New York Times,* consistently rated as the number one newspaper in America, is frequently regarded as the source of all truth by intellectuals, college professors, working newsmen, many advertisers, and even some conservatives. The untruths in the *New York Times* coverage of Senator Joseph McCarthy, its buildup of Castro, its omission of key facts against William Arthur Wieland, and the pro-communist bias of its book review section during the tragic China period have already been noted.[69]

The *St. Louis Post-Dispatch* is normally ranked as the top newspaper in the midwest and the third or fourth nationally, behind the *New York Times* and the *Washington Post.* It was read daily by President Kennedy. Adlai Stevenson and other top officials have appeared in ads publicly endorsing the paper.

An independent audit[70] of the 210 issues of the *St. Louis Post-Dispatch* published in the January 16-October 17, 1961 period showed that the paper published 28 editorials on disarmament and nuclear testing, 21 on Berlin, 15 on Red China, 10 on Cuba, 7 on Laos, and 7 on the Congo. There were 23 other editorials on the internal communist threat.

An analysis of the position taken by the *St. Louis Post-Dispatch* in these editorials[71] showed that the paper . . .

. . . urged maximum concessions to achieve agreements based largely on mutual trust with the communists on disarmament and nuclear testing. The U. S. and Russia were blamed equally for the disarmament negotiations stalemate.

. . . advocated "accommodation" of communist demands on Berlin and trading away American rights for agreements which the communists might, or might not, keep.

. . . favored the admission of Red China to the United Nations.

. . . opposed any intervention in Cuba and condemned even feeble U. S. efforts to unseat Castro.

. . . spoke against U. S. aid to the anti-communists in Laos and recommended that the anti-communist government be forced to put communists into key positions in a coalition cabinet.

. . . approved UN efforts to crush the anti-communist forces of Moise Tshombe in Katanga and advocated a coalition government for the Congo with communists in key spots.

On the domestic scene, the *Post-Dispatch* during the same period published 23 editorials dealing with the activities of communists in the United States, attempts by Congress to investigate subversion, and educational efforts by public and private figures to alert people to the menace of communism. The *Post-Dispatch* position . . .[72]

. . . suggested the need to abolish the House Committee on Un-American Activities and halt congressional investigations of communism.

. . . contradicted J. Edgar Hoover's statement that riots against the House Committee on Un-American Activities in San Francisco were communist inspired.

. . . ridiculed a proclamation of Missouri's governor, John Dalton, declaring an anti-communism week in Missouri, claiming that communists were not a threat internally.

. . . condemned government rulings that the Communist Party, USA should register as an agent of a foreign power.

. . . linked all anti-communist movements with Fascism and the Ku Klux Klan.

. . . praised Senator Fulbright's memorandum which said that "the American people have little if any need to be alerted to the menace of the cold war" because the principal problem of government leaders is to "restrain the desire of the people to hit the communists with everything we've got" in Laos and Cuba.

The *Post-Dispatch* viewpoint differs little from those of other top "thought molding" newspapers, the *New York Times, Washington Post, Milwaukee Journal, Louisville Courier Journal*, etc.

Whether the slanting, distortion, and control of news is done by Fabian socialists, misguided idealists, or actual communists is not important. The result is the same.

Free, representative government is predicated on the assumption that the people, having the *facts*, will make the right decisions when they go to the polls. If the press abdicates its responsibility, the system will fail. Breaking through the "paper curtain" which screens most Americans from the truth is a primary challenge.

Chapter IX

Mental Health

> *The pretense is made that to do away with right
> and wrong would produce uncivilized people,
> immorality, lawlessness, and social chaos. The
> fact is that most psychiatrists and psychologists
> and other respected people have escaped from
> moral chains and are able to think freely.*[1]
> — *Dr. G. Brock Chisholm, first head,
> World Federation of Mental Health*

FOR THE RARE CITIZEN who escapes indoctrination in
the "new social order" in progressive schools; for the Bible-
believing Christian who rejects "theologians" who teach that
socialism is the new "Kingdom of God on Earth"; for all the
sturdy souls who hold to age-old concepts of right and wrong,
and are vocal about it, the collectivists have one final, ultimate
weapon. Declare them insane!

Fantastic? Not at all. Just as in the fields of education,
religion, press, radio and TV, the collectivists have succeeded
in infiltrating and twisting the honorable psychiatric and psychological professions to their own ends.

The "new leaders" in the psychiatric field propose to re-
educate the world's population using psychological procedures
to create a new breed of amoral men who will accept a one-
world socialistic government. They hold the weapon of commitment to a mental institution over the heads of those
"reactionaries" who rebel at accepting the "new social order."

It sounds unbelievable? Listen to the words of Dr. G.
Brock Chisholm, first head of the World Federation of Mental
Health, and later head of the World Health Organization of
the United Nations. His address, sponsored by the William
Alanson White Psychiatric Foundation was delivered in October 1945 in Washington, D. C. to a large group of psychiatrists and high government officials. Chisholm said:

> What basic psychological distortion can be found in every
> civilization of which we know anything? The only psychologi-
> cal force capable of producing these perversions is morality —

the concept of right and wrong. The re-interpretation and eventual eradication of the concept of right and wrong are the belated objectives of nearly all psychotherapy.

If the race is to be freed from its crippling burden of good and evil it must be psychiatrists who take the original responsibility.[2]

Chisholm has been obsessed for years with the idea that instilling concepts of right and wrong, love of country, and morality in children by their parents is the paramount evil. In another speech, he said:

The people who have been taught to believe whatever they were told by their parents or their teachers are the people who are the menace to the world.[3]

What besides concepts of morality and right and wrong does Dr. Chisholm consider to be a neurosis? He explains it in this speech:

Even self-defense may involve a neurotic reaction when it means defending one's own excessive wealth from others who are in need.[4]

Chisholm proposes that psychotherapy be used to eradicate such neuroses as a man wishing to defend his own private property in this way:

There must be an opportunity to live reasonably comfortable for all the people in the world on economic levels which do not vary too widely either geographically or by groups within a population. *This is a simple matter of redistribution of material wealth.*[5]

This is the basic Marxist concept that those who have, should have it taken away. How different are Chisholm's ideas from those of America's pioneers. Had they decided on some scheme of redistribution of the wealth, all would have stayed poor and hungry, because there was no wealth. Instead of redistributing what meager wealth was available, they conceived a system of government which safeguarded private property. Initiative was stimulated and people were encouraged to *produce*, and by producing, to *create* new wealth for themselves. In the process, all men benefited from more jobs, new products and services. In freedom, men have made more spiritual, moral, intellectual progress, and produced more material wealth for themselves and others than under any other system conceived by man.

The answer to the problem of poverty is not redistribution of wealth, or "cutting the pie" into smaller pieces. This is socialism. The true answer is stimulating people to create and produce more — making more and bigger "pies."

Chisholm and his "mental health" associates plan to achieve world-wide distribution of wealth. This means a world government in which all citizens can vote "democratically" to take away the wealth of every American and divide it up in little equal shares. All will then be poor.

Chisholm's ideas are not those of a single "crackpot." After expressing these views widely and frequently, he became head of the World Federation of Mental Health and the World Health Organization. Other psychiatrists and psychologists have similar views, officially expressed.

At the International Congress of Mental Health in London in 1948, prominent American "mental healthers" including Dr. George S. Stevenson, medical director of the National Association for Mental Health, Dr. Daniel T. Blain, and Dr. Harry Stack Sullivan served on the Preparatory Commission. Their goals were revealed in this declaration, published and distributed in the United States by the National Association for Mental Health:

> Principles of mental health cannot be successfully furthered in any society *unless there is progressive acceptance* of the concept of *world citizenship.* World citizenship can be widely extended among all peoples through applications of the principles of mental health . . . At a major turning point in world history there is an *obligation* on social scientists and psychiatrists to attempt this new formulation.[6]

Chisholm, in outlining his program for "enduring peace and social progress" said that psychiatry should meet this "obligation" by reaching people who matter with "clear thinking, talking, and writing." Who are the people who matter? Chisholm said:

> Teachers, the young mothers and fathers, the parent-teachers associations, youth groups, service clubs, schools and colleges, the churches and Sunday school . . . everyone who can be reached and given help toward intellectual freedom and honesty for themselves and for children whose future depends on them.[7]

Naturally, in speaking to such groups, the "mental health" advocate will seldom openly suggest abolishing right and wrong, private property, or loyalty to country. More likely, they talk of "adjusting to a changing world" and learning to "compromise." They may unfold the story of how one of nine Americans need psychiatric help. They cite the grievous need for increased funds for training "mental health" workers. How many times have you been exposed to the "mental health" pitch?

Chisholm's associates have achieved positions of great in-

fluence. He suggested working through PTA's. Professor
Harry Overstreet, and his wife, Bonaro, have served as consultants to the National Congress of Parents and Teachers
(PTA) and its magazine for many years. Here are excerpts
from one of Overstreet's many books, *The Great Enterprise*,
published in 1952:

> Through clinical experience, we have come to recognize one
> invariable characteristic of that sick condition of the mind we
> call neurosis: namely, Rigidity.[8]
> . . . the rigidity is found in several areas. In each one of
> these we can predict that the individual will respond with
> trigger-quickness and in exactly the same way. Sometimes,
> it appears, such persons have constellations of prejudice areas.
> A man, for example, may be angrily against race equality,
> public housing, the TVA, financial and technical aid to back-
> ward countries, organized labor, and the preaching of social
> rather than salvational religion.
> Try as we may, we can scarcely open up a subject that does
> not tap their permeative, automatic "againstness." Such people
> may appear "normal" in the sense that they are able to hold
> a job and otherwise maintain their status as members of so-
> ciety, but they are, we now recognize, *well along the road
> toward mental illness.*[9]

Using such criteria, the mental health experts estimate that
one out of nine, or five out of ten, and some say, every
American needs "mental health" care. Are you among them?
Do you hold rigidly to "outmoded" concepts of right and
wrong? Do you reject socialism? Do you oppose foreign aid
waste? Do you object to letting African cannibals vote on
how we should live under a world government? If so, you
are by "definition" well along the road toward mental illness
and in need of "treatment."

How do the experts hope to achieve control over you and
the other 25-million or more Americans they say need "care"?
Chisholm provided the answer:

> We may begin to speculate on the advisability that psychia-
> trists, once the necessary one, two, or three million are avail-
> able should be trained as salesmen and be taught all the
> techniques of breaking down sales resistance.[10]

How successful have they been? Think for a moment of
all the stars of TV, radio, the movies, writers, etc. (the people
who matter) who look upon their sessions with a psychiatrist
or analyst as a "status symbol."

How many of these public figures are in the forefront of
"peace" movements? How many are vocal advocates of uni-
lateral disarmament and nuclear test bans? Are they among

the "comedians" who were staunch and consistent supporters of Castro as a humane "reformer"? Are they the comedians who regularly poke "fun" at patriotism and conservative political leaders, ridicule God, and downgrade traditional concepts of morality?

For those too stubborn to succumb to the psychiatrist's super-salesmanship, Chisholm proposed one final remedy when he asked:

> Should attempts be made by the profession to institute *compulsory treatment* for the neuroses as for other infectious diseases?[11]

Since Chisholm offered this idea 18 years ago, legal systems have been established in a majority of states for involuntary and *compulsory* hospitalization and treatment of neurosis. The state laws have been based on a prototype bill published originally by the Federal Security Agency of the Public Health Service, now a part of the Department of Health, Education and Welfare.

Entitled, a *Draft Act Governing Hospitalization of the Mentally Ill*, it is, in fact, a skeleton bill designed for adoption uniformly by federal, state, and territorial governments to radically alter commitment procedures. The preface to the *Draft Act*, which has come to be known as the "model mental health law" was written by Dr. George Stevenson, participant in the London Conference.[12]

Few legislators who passed the "model mental health laws" realized that Chisholm, Stevenson and their associates define "mental illnesses" as a "sense of loyalty to a particular nation, a sense of loyalty to a moral code, strict adherance to concepts of right and wrong, opposition to foreign aid or communism."

Yet, today, if *you* hold these beliefs, two *examiners* who may or may not have psychiatric training or be doctors, can certify *you are mentally ill*.[13] If you won't consent to voluntary treatment, a police officer can arrest you. You can be subjected to three to five days of treatment of the psychiatrist's choosing *before you even get a hearing to protect your rights* in most states. Treatment can include electric shock treatments, chemotherapy, hypnosis, or conceivably, a frontal lobotomy. The procedures under which the *patient's* rights are "protected" are open to serious question. When the hearing is held to determine whether permanent commitment and further treatment is necessary, the patient need not be notified of the proceedings and may not be present if the psychiatrists "believe" such attendance would be injurious to the patient.[14] The court conducting the hearing need not be bound by the normal rules of evidence.[15] Basically, all that is necessary to "revoke" all the constitutional rights of any citizen is to accuse him of being "mentally ill."

"Loopholes" in the same laws permit the commitment of innocent, sane people by a greedy relative, a bored husband, or an "interested" friend. They were exposed by the *Reader's Digest* recently in an article, *The Tragedy of Sane People Who Get "Put Away."*[16] It said:

> Under faulty "reform" laws, thousands of normal men and women are being railroaded into mental hospitals every year.[17]

POLITICAL WEAPON

The threat of discrediting a conservative political leader by branding him as mentally ill, or committing an anti-communist to a mental institution has been used sparingly, but frequently enough to establish a frightening pattern.

Attempts were made to discredit Whittaker Chambers testimony when he unmasked the high State Department official, Alger Hiss, as a communist agent. A psychiatrist *who had never examined Chambers* took the witness stand and under oath branded him as a psychopath.[18] Such charges do not have to be made formally to be effective. The late Eleanor Roosevelt in her column *My Day* for August 4, 1948 branded the testimony of Elizabeth Bentley in exposing high government officials as communists as "the fantastic story of this evidently neurotic lady."

In 1957, an obscure Californian was committed to a mental institution because of public utterances against the United Nations. The examining psychiatrist testified at the sanity hearing that the man *did not come to conclusions of the community.*[19] Do you always agree with the majority?

To protect Hungarian Freedom Fighters who testified before the UN Committee on Hungary from possible Communist reprisals, Povl Bang-Jensen, a Danish diplomat and assistant secretary of the committee, refused to divulge their names. In addition, he charged, and documented, that errors were being written into the draft of the Committee's report which would make the document a laughing stock rather than a sharp indictment of communist terror in Hungary.[20]

To discredit and silence him, UN medical authorities circulated a report intimating that Bang-Jensen was "mentally ill." He was dismissed by Secretary General Dag Hammarskjold. Meanwhile, he had assembled evidence, from two Russians wishing to defect, that the communists had achieved working control of the highest policy-making levels in the UN Secretariat.[21]

Two years later, after his sanity had been established by a reputable psychiatrist,[22] and a long fight to get official recognition of his story, Bang-Jensen was found, shot to death near his New York home. Police quickly labeled the death a suicide.

The United States Senate Internal Security Sub-committee after an 18-month study of the case said:

> It is the opinion of this report, however, that the finding of suicide was based on incomplete evidence. There are too many solid arguments against suicide, too many unanswered questions, too many serious reasons for suspecting Soviet motivation and the possibility of Soviet implication.[23]

Note the pattern. First, an attempt to discredit the Dane with unfounded charges of "mental illness" and later a probable phony suicide, at which the Communists are past masters.

On April 25, 1962, Mary Kimbrough Jones, a secretary in the Department of Agriculture was sitting on a powder keg. Her boss had just been transferred and denied access to the office where the files contained information implicating top government officials in the $200-million Billie Sol Estes farm storage scandals. Already, one government official who had possibly stumbled onto such evidence had committed "suicide" by shooting himself *five times* with a cumbersome bolt action rifle!

Shortly before noon on April 25, police arrived in Mary Jones' office. They seized Miss Jones and transferred her to a mental hospital. Two days later, two government psychiatrists certified that she was mentally ill.[24] News reports were circulated that her own doctor had agreed with the findings. He denied these statements as false.

After a public clamor, and 12 days in isolation in a psychiatric ward, Mary Jones was certified as sane and released by the District of Columbia Mental Health Commission. Even so, ten days after her release as sane, the two psychiatrists, *without any further observation of the woman,* once again announced to the press that she was mentally ill. This was a blatant attempt to impugn her possible testimony in the Estes case.[25]

THE WALKER CASE

Major General Edwin A. Walker, a decorated war hero and outspoken anti-communist, was arrested while leaving Oxford, Mississippi on October 1, 1962 on orders of Attorney

General Robert Kennedy who was in Washington. Walker was charged with seditious conspiracy and insurrection, despite conflicting newspaper accounts of his actions. United Press said that Walker cautioned the crowds against violence. The Associated Press said he advocated rioting.[26]

A government psychiatrist in Washington, D. C. *who had never seen or examined Walker,* adjudged him "mentally ill" on the basis of newspaper stories.[27] Even before getting this long distance "diagnosis," the government spirited Walker out of Mississippi in a Border Patrol plane. He did not get to raise bail or obtain a lawyer. He was committed to the Federal Prison Medical Center at Springfield, Missouri for psychiatric examination, estimated to take 60 to 90 days.[28]

Even ultra-liberal groups were shocked at the crude violation of Walker's civil rights, and after eight days as a political prisoner, he was released. The case became too *hot* for the government to handle.

After release, Walker voluntarily submitted to a psychiatric examination and was pronounced "mentally sound" and "operating on a superior level of intelligence" by the head of one of the Southwest's largest psychiatric centers.[29] His final vindication came when a federal grand jury refused to indict him and the sedition and insurrection charges were dropped.

Walker's treatment, while outrageous, was legal under the provisions of the United States Code, Sections 4244, 4245, 4246, 4247, and 4248. Undoubtedly, they would be found unconstitutional if tested in the Courts. However, they are presently the law. Any citizen's rights could be denied just as Walker's were.

All psychiatrists do not accept the amoral, socialistic theories of Brock Chisholm and Harry Overstreet. Reputable psychiatrists learn whether psychological disturbances result from actual organic difficulties in the central nervous system for which rather specific therapy is available.[30] If not, attempts are made through counseling to reinforce the concepts of good and evil, right and wrong in the patient. With such help, the weight of current psychiatric evidence is that nature will itself be the best healing agent.[31]

The Chisholms faced by a patient overcome with guilt because of extra-marital relations, homosexual practices, or other anti-social tendencies will devote their efforts to convincing the patient that such actions are perfectly normal, that no guilt should be experienced.

This is an outgrowth of the materialistic, psycho-dynamic approach to understanding human behavior. This school holds that when an individual feels a drive (desires to do something) that the drive must be satisfied (regardless of moral principles) or resulting tensions will produce insanity.

Accepting this largely discredited theory, the psychiatrist's job is to destroy the stabilizing concepts of right and wrong and man's conscience which cause guilt when anti-social, immoral impulses are satisfied. Such treatment, like Dewey's theories of education, will ultimately produce a breed of amoral, Pavlovian men with minds conditioned to respond to physical stimuli (bread and circuses) of a "master psychologist" or master politician. Not relying on free will, morals, or conscience for guidance, such amoral, criminal minds are typical of the man Marx envisioned. Is it any wonder that Dr. G. Brock Chisholm's appointment as head of the World Health Organization was warmly sponsored by his friend, Alger Hiss?[32]

Within the psychiatric profession itself criticism has been mounting against the psycho-dynamic approach to human behavior. Dr. Dalbir Bindra, president of the Canadian Psychological Association, summed up the repudiations, saying:

> All that can be said now is simply that so far there exists no proof of the value of the psychodynamics approach. Thus, I believe that this approach has turned out to be a wrong lead and that any further research along these lines would be a waste of time.[33]

Even though thoroughly repudiated, ideas of the Chisholms and the Overstreets have achieved deep-rooted influence in schools, churches, PTA's as Chisholm advocated.

CHURCH ACCEPTANCE

For example, *Coronet* magazine, in a shocking article, *Religion and Sex: A Changing Church View,*[34] outlined the new, more permissive attitude of many liberal churchmen towards sex, pre-marital relations, adultery, etc. The article states:

> These thinkers have been influenced not only by recent Biblical scholarship, *but also by the findings of psychiatry —* especially the revelation of psychic damage that may be done by sexual repression.[35]

The article quotes a minister who was visited by a married man, troubled by guilt over an affair he was having with another woman. Adultery is a very serious Christian offense, the article points out. However, because the man's wife was a bedridden invalid, the minister with the "new" church view said:

There were no easy platitudes that applied here. The only function I could serve was to relive the man's feeling of guilt.[36]

The inroads made by the "mental healthers" in the field of education was spotlighted in *Life* magazine. An article, *The New Tests in Our Schools — The Three R's and a P (For Psyche)*, in the September 21, 1962 issue said:

In the first few weeks of the new school year several million pupils from the first grade through senior high school will open examination booklets that pose some surprisingly personal questions.[37]

Among the questions mentioned by *Life* were:

Are you too nervous? Most of the time I wish I was dead. I hear strange things when I am alone. I am afraid I am losing my mind.

Life pointed out that while State Education laws often prevent even a licensed physician from giving a child an aspirin tablet without parental permission, school testers can administer highly personal tests. Children's records can be marked "maladjusted" or "potential schizophrenic" without the parents ever being notified. Most parents, *Life* said, are amazed to learn that their child's "personality" is recorded in black and white in locked files outside the principal's office.

Psychological testing and counseling and guidance in the schools received a big boost as a result of the National Defense Education Act of 1958. This bill provided money for trained counselors and testing programs to assist students in selecting higher education opportunities.

That the program has fallen into the wrong hands was made clear by Congressman John Ashbrook (R-Ohio) on October 10, 1962 when he introduced HR 10508 which would ban psychological testing of students, without advance permission from parents. Ashbrook said:

I believe there is an urgent need for this legislation so that proper guidance and counseling will not be confused with brainpicking and interference.[38]

To support the need for legislation, Ashbrook cited examples of widely-used tests which include "difficult or impossible to answer questions—tests which pit loyalties of religion, home, and parents against each other." He cited these specific examples of loyalty-splitting questions from one "moral value" exam.[39]

Which is worse: (1) spitting on the Bible; (2) spitting on the American flag?

Which is more important: (1) taking the oath of allegiance to the United States; (2) joining a church?

Which is worse: (1) denying the existence of God; (2) laughing while the Star Spangled Banner is played?

Consider the conflict for normal youngsters forced to make these differentiations. Note the implied suggestions that it is "less bad" to spit on either the Flag or the Bible.

Often containing 300 or more questions, personality tests are depressingly negative in approach. A typical test is the Science Research Associates *Youth Inventory*. Form A of this test includes 30 to 40 questions which tend to destroy respect for and authority of parents and teachers. Students answer "yes" or "no" to these questions:

I can't discuss personal things with my parents. I feel there's a barrier between me and my parents. My father is a tyrant. I am ashamed of my parents' dress and manners. I hate school. I wish I could quit school now. My teachers play favorites. My teachers are too strict. Class periods are not well organized.

Sex questions with an abnormal slant are asked of sub-teen age children in the same test:

I wonder if I am normal in my sexual development. I think of sex a good deal of the time. I wonder if high school students should pet and make love. I want to know more about venereal disease.

Traditional religious beliefs and concepts of right and wrong are dulled or shaken in this way:

I'm bothered by thoughts of Heaven and Hell. I'm losing faith in religion. Is it wrong to deny the existence of God? Does it really pay to be honest? How does one set standards of "right" and "wrong?"

The Board of Educational Research, Ohio State University has developed a psychological test used widely in many states. Called *The Wishing Well*, it plants doubts about God and free enterprise in the *fourth grade students* to whom it is administered and stimulates fear of economic security, with questions like this:

I wish I could be sure that my father would always have a steady job. I wish I could know how you can believe that God is always right and at the same time believe that you should think for yourself. I wish I knew how you can make lots of money and still be a very good citizen.

Those concerned about the serious rise of juvenile delinquency and teen-age violence often ask, "Where do children get these ideas?"

Some ideas may came from a seven-part, 344 question test developed at the University of Kansas with a grant from the U. S. Public Health Service. It is administered to normal junior high school students. A section entitled, *Rules We All Break*, implies by the title that the listed actions are normal, expected behavior for teen-agers. Typical *Rules We All Break* according to this test are:

> Damage or disfigure furniture in schools. Steal goods from warehouses or storage houses. Puncture or cut automobile tires, bike tires. Tied up person with rope, string, or wire to a tree or similar object and then left them that way. Damage cemetery property. Become so angry that you threw things at or hit a teacher or principal or other school official. Taken part in fights where knives or switchblades were used. Injured or hurt someone not in your family, but arranged matters so that someone else got the blame.

There are 78 such *rules we all break* in the test. The normal, decent child might well get an inferiority complex through answering "no" to all of them.

Congressman Ashbrook in introducing his bill to require parental consent before administering such tests said:

> A parent could well ask what all of this has to do with the educational process. Suggestions often plant seeds of doubt. Children who are normal may begin to think they are not normal. To read all the questions (in a test) tends to give anyone an inferiority complex.[40]

Many competent school guidance counselors reject as "more harmful than helpful" such testing, which has its genesis in largely discredited psycho-dynamic, Freudian approaches to psychology. School psychologists in Denver, Colorado protested their use and dropped them.[41] Dr. Henry S. Dyer of the Educational Testing Service, Princeton, N. J. says:

> I take a dim view of current personality tests and I think the general public is being much too frequently taken in by the mumbo jumbo that goes with them.[42]

Yet, millions of school-age children are subjected to these brainpicking, psychiatric tests which implant doubts about God and religion, break down parental authority; downgrade American traditions and generally create a mood of sordidness, depression and cloudy thinking about right and wrong. These are exactly the goals set by Dr. G. Brock Chisholm as a goal for mental health programs.

So through the schools, churches, PTA's, changes in mental health legislation, and indiscriminate branding of patriotic Americans as mentally ill, these warped practitioners work to create the "amoral" man, the criminal mind which will accept a one-world socialistic government, as envisioned by Chisholm.

Chapter X

The Organized Labor Movement

*It is necessary to be able to withstand all of
this, to agree to any and every sacrifice, and
even — if need be — to resort to all sorts of
devices, maneuvers, and illegal methods, to
evasion, and subterfuge, in order to penetrate
into the trade unions, to remain in them, and to
carry on Communist work in them at all costs.[1]*
— *Nicolai Lenin*

ON JANUARY 20, 1934, Walter and Victor Reuther
wrote a letter from Russia where they were working and
studying the Soviet labor movement. Written to Melvin
Bishop, a close friend in Detroit who later became CIO
educational director, the letter said in part:

. . . the daily inspiration that is ours as we work side by
side with our Russian comrades in our factory, the thought
that we are actually helping to build a society that will forever
end the exploitation of man by man, the thought that what we
are building will be for the benefit and enjoyment of the working class, not only of Russia, but for the entire world is the
compensation we receive for our temporary absence from the
struggle in the United States.[2]

After further praise for Russian thinking and methods, and
vilification of American business leaders, the letter, which was
signed, "Vic and Wal," concluded:

Carry on the fight for a Soviet America.[3]

What Reuther believes today cannot be known. For years
after his return to America his close cooperation with and
sometimes leadership of the "communist" faction in the
United Auto Workers Union has been exposed in numerous
Congressional hearings.[4]

In the late 1930's, communists controlled 21 of the international unions affiliated with the CIO. Nearly one-half of the
members of the executive board of the CIO, its governing
body, were communists.[5] Lee Pressman, general counsel of
the CIO was a party member.[6] He has since broken with the

Party and remains in this high post. Despite exposure of the communist control of the CIO by congressional investigations in 1938-39, the communists remained in open control for at least seven more years.[7]

After World War II, when public feeling against communists and communism reached a peak, Walter Reuther publicly identified himself with the movement which expelled known communists from union posts. However, officers and members of union locals who tried to enlist Reuther's aid in breaking the communist hold in some UAW branches testified before Congressional committees that their requests to him were ignored.[8]

When Reuther's speeches are analyzed and the programs supported by his union are checked carefully, there can be no doubt that Reuther is, today, at least a dedicated promoter of class hatred and the socialist movement to control every aspect of American life. He is rarely found in the ranks of those who speak out vigorously against the communist menace.

In fact, just the opposite is true. At the United Auto Workers Convention in Atlantic City, N. J., May 10, 1962, Reuther and the executive committee of the Union passed a series of resolutions. They advocated measures which would so hamper attempts to control internal subversion that even the Communist Party, USA in its official publication, *The Worker*, expressed elation.[9]

The resolutions which Reuther rammed through the closely controlled executive committee (without permitting delegates representing UAW members across the country to vote on them) included:[10]

A request for clemency for the convicted communist, Julius Scales.

A call for abolition of the House Committee on Un-American Activities.

An expression of opposition to official government finding that the Mine, Mill & Smelter Workers Union is communist-dominated.

A demand that government action to deport aliens found to have been members of the Communist Party be halted.

A condemnation of Congressional efforts to stop the importation of Communist propaganda into the United States.

Two weeks after Reuther's UAW passed these resolutions, the United Packinghouse, Food and Allied Workers (AFL-CIO) convention passed essentially the same measures.

Contrast Reuther's record and actions with these remarks of George Meany, president of the AFL-CIO:

> The conflict between communism and freedom is the problem of our times. It overshadows all other problems. This conflict mirrors our age, its toils, its tensions, its troubles, and its tasks. On the outcome of this conflict depends the future of mankind.[11]

Basic differences between Meany and Reuther are reported to be the source of conflict between them, and the basis for recurrent reports that Reuther will, when strong enough, move to challenge Meany for the top spot in the AFL-CIO.

Reuther's concept of the function of organized labor differs sharply also with that of Samuel Gompers, founder of the American Federation of Labor, and champion of the rights of the working man as a self-reliant citizen. Contrast Reuther's anguished pleas for placing medical care for the aged under social security, a measure which has lead to socialized medicine in every country where it has been adopted, with this Gompers statement:

> Compulsory social insurance is in its essence undemocratic and it cannot prevent or remove poverty. The workers of America adhere to voluntary institutions in preference to compulsory systems, which are held to be not only impractical, but a menace to their rights, welfare, and their liberty. Compulsory sickness insurance for workers is based on the theory that they are unable to look after their own interests and the state must use its authority and wisdom and assume the relation of parent and guardian.[12]

Contrast Reuther's background as President of the Intercollegiate Socialist Society at Wayne University in Detroit[13] and his ardent championing of Keynesian and Fabian economics as a backdoor, "respectable" approach to socialism with another of Gomper's statements:

> I want to tell you socialists that I have studied your philosophy . . . I have heard your orators . . . I have kept close watch upon your doctrines for 30 years and know how you think and what you propose. I know too what you have up your sleeve. Economically, you are unsound; socially, you are wrong; industrially, you are an impossibility.[14]

Gompers, in his wisdom, had the true interests of American workers and their progress at heart.

He knew that socialists "had up their sleeve" only schemes for *control* of the workers of the world. This became sharply clear in an article by Arthur Schlesinger, Jr., assistant to President Kennedy, which set forth the plan for achieving socialism in America. Proposing a continuing series of "New Deals" as a backdoor approach to socialism,[15] Schlesinger, a "darling" of Reuther's CIO, said of labor:

> The trade union is as clearly indigenous to the capitalist system as the corporation itself, and it has no particular meaning apart from that system. In a socialist society its functions are radically transformed: it becomes, not a free labor movement, but a labor front. Even in England as Sir Walter Citrine remarked on joining the coal board, strikes can no longer be trade union instruments in a nationalized industry. Unions inevitably become organs for disciplining the workers, not for representing them.[16]

This state is rapidly approaching in America. The Administration's action in August 1963 which banned strikes in the railroad industry is a step in this direction. In a modern socialist state, labor terms are dictated by government officials — not negotiated at a bargaining table between labor and management.

POLITICAL ACTION

Before the 1930's, labor unions restricted their activities principally to the legitimate function of representing their members at the bargaining table and expressing union views when labor legislation was before Congress or state legislatures. Walter Reuther's mentor, the late Sidney Hillman, took the labor movement strongly into the political field. Hillman formed the broadly-based, labor-financed, National Citizens Political Action Committee (PAC).

Investigations by the Special House Committee on Un-American Activities in 1944 disclosed that 117 of the 141 members of the PAC national advisory board were leaders in other officially-cited communist fronts. The PAC was designated by the House Committee as a communist-front.[17]

After the PAC was discredited as a communist-front, the CIO formed the forerunner of today's, *Committee on Political Education (COPE)*. Through COPE, millions of dollars are collected from union members who believe in the free enterprise system. This money is used to finance and propagandize measures that will replace American traditions of economic and political freedom with socialist state control. The methods used have been described by President Kennedy's special assistant, Arthur Schlesinger, Jr.[18] Through COPE, Walter Reuther, who in the '30's advised his followers to "work for a Soviet America" is possibly the most powerful political figure in America.

He can mobilize a disciplined core of over 100,000 paid union organizers and business agents for political action.

They win their political battles, not by convincing 51% of the population that they are right, but through effective use of the time-tested methods developed years ago by the old-fashioned "ward heelers" and political bosses.

COPE's skilled organizers and their well-paid precinct workers determine on a block-by-block basis in advance of elections which voters will vote "right." They insure they are properly registered. On election day, all "friendly" voters are taken to the polls.[20]

In many elections, when half or less of those eligible actually vote, COPE can control the outcome by finding that 25% of the population which will vote, either blindly for a party label, or knowingly in favor of socialism — *and getting them to the polls.*

Applying these principles, in recent years COPE has elected sufficient Senators in normally conservative states to control the U. S. Senate. They have gained control of state legislatures and elected governors. Candidates pledged to the Reuther-COPE program have unseated conservative Congressmen in many parts of the nation.

While he can be politically non-partisan when it means defeat of an advocate of sound economics and limited self-government, Reuther is conceded to hold veto power over the Democratic nomination for President.

At the 1960 Democratic convention in Los Angeles, for example, TV news analysts made it clear that over one-third of the delegates were COPE-controlled. With over 25% of the delegates to any Democratic convention from the more conservative southern states, Reuther holds the balance of power in the controlling northern section of the Democratic Party.

Reuther's political stranglehold on the Democratic Party is not the only dangerous influence in the labor movement. Despite the well-publicized "cleanup" of the AFL and CIO in the 1940's when known communists were driven out, communists still control the unions in certain strategic areas of the economy.

The communist-control of the American Communications Association, whose members service many of Western Union's telegraph lines and the communications circuits from the Pentagon to key defense installations around the world was documented in an earlier chapter.[20]

Harry Bridges, the Australian-born communist leader of the

International Longshoremen's and Warehousemen's Union, has successfully fought government attempts to deport him and strip him of his power. With a word, Bridges can tie up all shipping of defense supplies, military equipment, etc. through the west coast ports. His communist associates in Hawaii have organized the dock workers, government employees, and sugar and pineapple plantation workers.[21] They hold a virtual political and economic stranglehold on the life of our 49th State.[22] Bridges' union was expelled from the CIO in 1950 as communist-dominated.[23]

Eleven other strategically-placed labor organizations were expelled at the same time, including the Mine, Mill and Smelter Workers, United Public Workers of America, United Farm Equipment and Metal Workers of America, and the United Office and Professional Workers of America.[24]

Russell Nixon, a top-ranking communist[25] has since 1941 been a top-rank official of the United Electrical, Radio and Machine Workers Union, except for periods when he has served in the government. Nixon's union, kicked out of the CIO in 1950, also represents workers in the key electronics, electrical and missile producing fields.[26]

Communists became entrenched in the labor field in the 1930's when Nathan Witt, a communist, became Secretary of the National Labor Relations Board, and Edwin S. Smith, another communist, gained a seat on the five-member board.[27] During this period rules were established which regulate labor-management relations even today. Witt hired and supervised hundreds of people to staff the regional offices of the growing NLRB. His influence is felt even today, years after he was publicly exposed.

American working men and union members are as loyal and dedicated to the United States as any group in the nation, and probably more so, on a percentage basis, than university graduates. Yet, their money, the prestige of their organizations, and their votes are frequently committed to the destruction of America. In a number of industries, sound thinking working men and dedicated union leaders have performed meritorious service in the difficult battle against communist infiltration. In other industries, the job still needs to be done.

The Tax-Exempt Foundations

*We all know that foundation aid can increase
measurably the pace of any social tendency,
but we don't seem to know when this artificial
acceleration ceases to be desirable.*
— *F. P. Keppel, President
The Carnegie Corporation*

FROM WHERE HAS THE MONEY COME to build and
finance the vast collectivist underground which reaches its
tentacles into education, the churches, labor and the press?

Amazingly, the fortunes of America's most successful ty-
coons, dedicated by them to the good of mankind, have been
re-directed to finance the socialization of the United States.

Two special Congressional committees exposed the extent
to which tax-exempt foundations are using their resources for
Un-American and subversive activity. Yet, apparently nothing
has been done to check this flow of millions of dollars annually into the hands of conspirators. In 1952, the investigation
was started by a Special Committee of the House of Representatives headed by Congressman E. E. Cox (D-Ga).[1] It continued in the 83rd Congress under the direction of Congressman Carrol Reece (R-Ten).[2]

Both efforts were hampered by lack of staff to do the
monumental research job necessary to unravel the complex
multi-billion dollar dealings of the foundations and their
interlocked agencies. Gross lack of cooperation from executive agencies of the government under President Eisenhower
and the foundations themselves slowed the studies.[3]

Even so, the investigations proved incontrovertibly that
money of American capitalists — Ford, Rockefeller, Carnegie,
Guggenheim, etc. — has largely financed those working for
the establishment of a "new world order."

The Reece Committee acknowledged the magnificent service
rendered by the foundations in medicine, public health, and
science. However, large sums have been wrongly committed

to "changing society." A handful of foundation executives reluctantly acknowledge the misdirection.

Raymond B. Fosdick, in *The Story of the Rockefeller Foundations*, quoted the Rev. Frederick T. Gates, long-time adviser to the Foundation and John D. Rockefeller, Sr., as follows:

> If I have any regret, it is that the charter of the Rockefeller Foundation did not confine its work strictly to national and international medicine, health, and its appointments. Insofar as the disbursements of the Rockefeller incorporated philanthropies have been rigidly confined to these two fields (medicine and public health) they have been almost universally commended at home and abroad. Where they have inadvertently transgressed these limits, they have been widely, and in some particulars not unfairly condemned.[1]

What have been the transgressions for which foundations "have been widely and not unfairly condemned?" The Reece Committee found that grants in the social sciences and international affairs were almost totally committed to "liberals" who advocate the socialization of America and world government. Direct grants have been made to communists and socialists. Foundation executives have exhibited a naivete about communism which has already contributed directly to one tragedy, the loss of China to the communists.[5]

Frederick P. Keppel, President of the Carnegie Corporation, admits that foundation funds can "change" America. In his book, *The Foundation, It's Place in American Life*, he wrote:

> We all know that foundation aid can increase measurably the pace of any social tendency, but we don't know when this artificial acceleration ceases to become desirable.[6]

How have foundation grants been used to "accelerate" social tendencies? Here are some of the ways uncovered by the Reece committee:

> Aggregate contributions of over $4-million were made by six American foundations to the London School of Economics. Beatrice and Sidney Webb founded the school as the international "headquarters" and intellectual center of the Fabian socialist movement.[7]

Foundation grants made possible the writing and publication of anti-American, anti-free enterprise books and texts:

> The Carnegie Corporation financed the writing and publication of *The Proper Study of Mankind*. Written by Stuart Chase, the book praised the communist agents, Harry Dexter White and Lauchlin Currie, and outlined an "ideal" society in which the individual is suppressed. Over 50,000 copies of

the book were distributed by the Carnegie Foundation to libraries and scholars. One of Chase's earlier books recommended that profit-making be punished by firing squads.[8]

When advised of these facts and of Chase's record of support for more than 20 Communist fronts and causes, Dr. Charles Dollard, president of Carnegie Corporation, defended the selection of Chase to author the book. In a statement filed with the Reece committee, Dollard said that Chase was "an extremely able writer."[9]

The Carnegie Corporation made continuing grants to the communist-fronting Professor Robert A. Brady,[10] to finance study and ultimately a book, *Business as a System of Power*. The book's theme, as stated in the foreword, was:

> . . . capitalistic economic power constitutes a direct, continuous and fundamental threat to the whole structure of democratic authority everywhere and always.[11]

The movement to socialize America via education discussed earlier was largely financed by foundation funds. The Reece Committee found:

> The Rockefeller and Carnegie funds provided the financing for the radical movement in education lead by Counts, Dewey, Kilpatrick and Rugg. Direct grants were made to the National Education Association, Progressive Education Association, American Historical Association, and to the center of the revolutionary movement, Teachers College, Columbia University.[12]

The 17-volume study on American education directed by Dr. George Counts, termed later by British Fabian leader Harold Laski as "an educational program for a socialist America," was financed by a $340,000 grant from Carnegie.[13]

Foundation grants have financed the gigantic program of revising textbooks to serve socialist ends. For example:

> The Rockefeller Foundation provided over $50,000 to finance the *Building America* textbooks series. The California Senate's Investigating Committee on Education condemned these texts for playing up Marxism and destroying traditional concepts of American government.[14]

The California Senate committee determined that 113 communist front organizations contributed material to the Rockefeller-financed *Building America* texts. Works of over 50 communist-front authors were included. Beatrice and Sidney Webb, founders with George Bernard Shaw of the British Fabian Society, were among the authors. One of the writers renounced his American citizenship to become ambassador to the United Nations from communist Poland. Broadly promoted for years by the National Education Association, the textbook series was still in use in a number of states in 1954.[15]

In its final report, the Reece Committee observed:

It would be interesting to aggregate the total funds poured by the foundations into the dissemination of leftist propaganda and compare it with the trickle which flowed into the exposition of the fallacies and frailties of collectivism.[16]

INTERNATIONAL RELATIONS

The role of the foundations in "Changing America" has been massive. Their impact on the international scene has been, if possible, even more tragic.

The Rockefeller Foundation in its 1946 Annual Report stated this goal:

The challenge of the future is to make this world one world — a world truly free to engage in common and constructive intellectual efforts that will serve the welfare of mankind everywhere.[17]

There was only one pitfall in the high-sounding program. Foundation executives, like other advocates of "one-world government" and "world peace through world law," choose to ignore the nature of world communism whenever it would be a roadblock to realization of their one-world dream. They have tried to make the world "one world" in line with their goal while it is not yet "truly free." Looking upon world government as the answer to the communist threat, they can't or won't see that the only world government the communists will embrace is one in which communism can eventually triumph.

On May 2, 1945, Raymond Fosdick, president of the Rockefeller Foundation, addressed the Woman's Action Committee for Victory and Lasting Peace in New York and voiced the sentiment on which foundation decisions and grants have been based since. He said:

The growing mistrust of Russia menaces the future of world peace.[18]

A more realistic observation is that if more Americans in high places, including those in foundations, had a *greater* mistrust of Russia, over 800-million human beings would not be in communist slavery today. Yet, Fosdick's naive attitude toward communism persists in foundation circles even today, as will be seen.

In some instances, the aid and assistance which foundations have given to world communism cannot be excused as naivete.

The 1947 Yearbook of the Carnegie Endowment for International Peace opens with *Recommendations of the President to the Trustees*. The program spelled out is in line with the goals of the Rockefeller Foundation's 1946 annual report. It is typical of the goals and efforts of most foundations in the international field. The recommendations included:

> . . . that the Endowment work for the establishment of United Nations headquarters in New York . . . that the Endowment construct its programs primarily for support of the United Nations . . . that the endowments program should be broadly educational in order to encourage public understanding and support of the United Nations at home and abroad . . . that Endowment supported organizations such as International Relations Clubs in colleges, the Foreign Policy Association, the Institute of Pacific Relations, the Council on Foreign Relations, and local community groups be utilized to achieve these goals of achieving broader understanding and support for the United Nations.[19]

This program, recommended and backed with foundation billions, throws some insight into the "halo" constructed around the United Nations in the 17 years following World War II. Was it done in good faith, with a belief that the United Nations was truly man's great hope for world peace? That program and those recommendations were written by the President of the Carnegie Endowment for World Peace, the infamous communist agent, Alger Hiss.[20]

They were a logical sequel to his State Department activities only 18 months before. Hiss' role as Roosevelt's adviser at Yalta was thoroughly aired in the months following his exposure as a communist agent. His part in the formation of the United Nations was largely ignored. The probable influence he exerted in creating the framework of the UN Charter in sessions with the communists at Yalta received no headlines. His assignment as Secretary General of the organizing conference of the United Nations at San Francisco in April 1945 was carefully kept in the background after his exposure.[21]

The Reece Committee found that foundations, headed by communists like Alger Hiss, and by innocents like Raymond Fosdick (against whom only bad judgment can be proved) contributed significantly to the spread of world communism. For example:

The Rockefeller and Carnegie foundations contributed over $3-million to the Institute of Pacific Relations,[22] branded by the Senate Internal Security Subcommittee as a transmission belt for communist and pro-communist propaganda. The

IPR also served as a "base" for Owen Lattimore, a "conscious articulate instrument of the Soviet conspiracy." Lattimore and his fellow agents, with foundation supplied funds, influenced American far-eastern policy against Chiang Kai-shek. Their actions, along with their foundation-financed propaganda efforts convinced the American people and press that the Chinese communists were simple "agrarian reformers." China was lost to communism, and the enslavement of 600-million Chinese followed. The foundations paid the bill. Years later, they were still justifying the "change" in China as "progress."[23] The Reece committee in its report stated:

> . . . the loss of China to the Communists may have been the most tragic event in our history, and one to which the foundation-supported Institute of Pacific Relations contributed heavily.[24]

The Carnegie Endowment for International Peace financed the Foreign Policy Association and underwrote distribution of its literature.[25] Research director of the FPA for over 20 years until her retirement in 1961 was the notorious, Russian-born, communist-fronter, Vera Michaels Dean. The FPA's dissemination of the works of pro-communist authors under the guise of objectivity through affiliated organizations across America has been thoroughly documented by a Fulton County, Georgia grand jury. Its report, with hundreds of exhibits, has been republished by the American Legion.[26]

With the almost total commitment of foundation funds in the international field to leftists causes, dozens of other examples can be cited.

Because of their widespread activities and the high esteem in which foundations are regarded they became a logical source of "experts" to staff military government organizations in Germany, Japan, and Italy at the conclusion of World War II. Efforts to sabotage the rebuilding of German and Japanese economies became evident. Doors were opened wide for communists to assume leading positions in postwar Germany and Japan. These actions became apparent to top military personnel and the plot was uncovered. Foundation executives had loaded their lists of recommended "expert" personnel with communists and fellow travelers.[27]

Propaganda efforts financed by the Foundations and actual pro-communist bias in materials prepared by Foundation staffs have played a leading role in the confusion and misguidance of the public and the intellectual community. The Foundation, because of its charitable "halo," connotes an air of "objectivity" and has great, if undeserved, influence. The

Ford Foundation Annual Report for 1951 is a prime example. It stated:

> Our policy in Asia has failed to lead us to the real objectives of the American people because its preoccupation with strategy and ideology has prevented our giving sufficient weight to the economic, social and political realities of Asia. There, as elsewhere, we have tended to label as communistic any movement that sought a radical change in the established order . . . It is surprising that we have not been able to understand the situation in Asia, because Americans should be peculiarly able to comprehend the meaning of revolution. Our own independence was achieved through a revolution, and we have traditionally sympathized with the determined efforts of other peoples to win national independence and higher standards of living. The current revolution in Asia is a similar movement, whatever its present association with Soviet Communism.[28]

Are the officers of a foundation who compare the Russian-armed and financed coup in China with our Revolutionary War qualified to spend millions in tax-free money to influence public and governmental opinion in the field of foreign affairs — or any field? This report was issued after Chinese communists had been killing American boys in Korea for 18 months! It was released three years after the communists completed their conquest of China and started on their well-publicized murder of 40-million Chinese.

The affinity of the tax-exempt, charitable foundations for left-wing causes continues today. The Rockefeller Brothers Fund financed and published a study entitled, *Prospects for America*. It reflects the personal work and participation of the Rockefeller Brothers and a sizeable group of leftist-oriented public figures, many of whom hold top spots in the Kennedy and Johnson administrations.[29] Of communism, the report says:

> It has been necessary to drum up support for United States foreign policy by stressing imminent threats and crises and *by harping on the less attractive features of communism.*[30]

What features of communism do the Rockefeller Brothers and their panel of "distinguished" Americans find attractive?

Without saying, "We must recognize Red China," the Rockefeller Brothers Panel Report tears down or ignores all arguments against recognition and presents the "reasons" for recognizing Red China.[31]

The Fund for the Republic, an off-shoot of the Ford Foundation, has become notorious for financing vicious and distorted attacks on the internal security program of the U. S.

government, Congressional committees which investigate communism and the FBI.[32]

The Reece Committee expressed the opinion that the Fund for the Republic had been founded for the specific purpose of attacking government security programs and anti-communists.[33] Paul Hoffman, first president of the Fund, denied the allegation. However, attacks by Fund officials on the FBI, Congressional investigating committees, and government security measures have continued.

W. H. Ferry, a vice president of the Fund for the Republic, for example, delivered a typical attack of ridicule and smear against J. Edgar Hoover and the FBI at a meeting of western Democrats in Seattle, Washington on August 6, 1962. Ferry described the FBI's attempts to fight communism as "ineffective spy swatting."[34]

The Ford Foundation has supplied continual grants, totaling over $1-million to the American Friends Service Committee to encourage pacifism, resistance to military service, conscientious objectors, and opposition to military preparedness.[35] The Friends Service Committee sponsored the World Youth Conference, a communist front and sent delegates to the communist-sponsored youth conferences behind the Iron Curtain.[36] The Friends Service Committee chairman, Henry J. Cadbury, and the executive secretary, Clarence Pickett, have lengthy records of affiliation with communist fronts and causes.[37] Yet, the Ford Foundation in its 1951 Annual Report justified its grants because the Friends Service Committee "had demonstrated over a long period its capacity to deal effectively with many of the economic, social, and educational conditions that lead to international tensions."[38]

The Reece Committee, in its evaluation of the impact of the tax-exempt foundations on education, public opinion, and foreign relations in the United States, charged in its final report:

It is the conclusion of this committee that the trustees of some of the major foundations have on numerous occasions been beguiled by truly subversive forces. Without many of the trustees having the remotest idea of what has happened, these foundations have frequently been put substantially to uses which have adversely affected the best interests of the United States . . . used to undermine many of our most precious institutions and to promote radical changes in the form of our government and our society.

It is difficult to realize that great funds established by such conservative individuals as Rockefeller, Carnegie, and Ford have turned strongly to the left. It appears to have happened largely through a process of administrative infiltration and through the influence of academic consultants of leftish tendencies. The trustees of these foundations with a few possible exceptions could not have intended this result. It seems to us that it must have happened through their lack of understanding or through negligence.[39]

In retrospect, viewing the reactions of most foundation executives to the Reece Committee's thorough study, it is difficult to accept the charitable attitude shown toward Foundation trustees by the Reece Committee. The committee efforts were met with ridicule, abuse, and scorn by the majority of trustees and executives of Foundations. Their leftist orientation continues today.

Chapter XII

Economics and Government

> *A people may want a free government, but if,*
> *from insolence, or carelessness, or cowardice,*
> *or want of public spirit, they are unequal to the*
> *exertions necessary for preserving it; if they*
> *will not fight for it when it is directly attacked;*
> *if they can be deluded by the artifices used to*
> *cheat them out of it; if by momentary discour-*
> *agement or temporary panic, or a fit of enthu-*
> *siasm for an individual they can be induced to*
> *lay their liberties at the feet of even a great*
> *man, or trust him with powers which enable*
> *him to subvert their institutions; in all these*
> *cases they are more or less unfit for liberty;*
> *and though it may be for their good to have*
> *had it even for a short time, they are unlikely*
> *long to enjoy it.*
>
> — *John Stuart Mill*[1]

GOVERNMENT has been the ultimate goal of the collectivist thinkers who have been infiltrating every segment of
American life for 60 years. In government, as in every other
field, the collectivists have first infiltrated quietly, and then
grabbed for control.

The seeds of Fabian socialism had already been sown in
Washington, in the multitude of government bureaus when
passage of the 16th Amendment in 1913 gave the federal
government and its managers unrestricted access to the wealth
of the American citizen.

Since then, bureaus have been piled on top of bureaus.
Two World Wars, the depression of the 1930's, a police action
in Korea and the Cold War have been used as excuses for
creating new offices and departments. Each one usurped, or
was given by Congress, some right or power once reserved to
the people, the states, or the peoples' representatives.

The offices were staffed, first with a trickle, then with a

flood of Fabian-indoctrinated theorists and professors from college campuses.

Seymour Harris of the Harvard Economics Department and a member of President Kennedy's "task force on economy" in an article in the September 18, 1961 issue of *New Republic* revealed their influence. He said:

> Economics is one thing; politics is another. No one has criticized the President for lack of political acumen. I have seen no evidence that Congress is prepared to go along with large deficits except for security reasons . . . But no administration has advanced as far as the Kennedy Administration in accepting Keynesian economics.[2]

What is Keynesian economics?

As collectivists have grabbed for control of the federal government they have skillfully used the "economic" theories of John Maynard Keynes, a British Fabian economist, as the vehicle for *buying* the votes and support of the masses *with their own money*.

Today's advocates of Keynes and his theories present him respectably as the "last hope for saving free enterprise,"[3] in the typical Fabian fashion of "never calling socialism by its true label."[4] However, no less an authority than Norman Thomas, six-time Socialist candidate for President of the United States, writing in *A Socialist's Faith,* said:

> . . . Keynes has had a great influence and his work is especially important in any re-appraisal of socialist theory. He represents a decisive break with laissez-faire capitalism.[5]

Keynes, with foresight, had himself predicted the use to which his theories might be put. Before publishing his major work, *The General Theory of Employment, Interest, and Money,* Keynes wrote these words to Fabian founder, George Bernard Shaw:

> To understand my state of mind, however, you have to know that I believe myself to be writing a book on economic theory which will largely revolutionize — not I suppose at once, but in the course of the next ten years — the way the world thinks about economic problems. When my new theory has been duly assimilated and mixed with politics and feelings and passions I can't predict what the upshot will be in its effect on action and affairs.[6]

As Keynes foresaw, his theories have been skillfully blended with propaganda of hate and fear to stir "feelings and passions" between rich and poor, white and negro, labor and management, Catholic and Protestant, Christian and Jew in Lenin's technique of "divide and conquer." Fear, insecurity and class hatred have dominated presidential campaigns and congressional elections in America for 30 years.

The Keynes brand of socialism differs from the Marxist variety in that it advocates strict *control* of the means of production and the supply of credit and money rather than government *ownership*. On the theory that when control is possible, ownership is not required, the Keynesian theories are particularly suited to the Fabian goal of "Change everything except the outward appearance." The national socialist movements headed by Hitler and Mussolini recognized the beauties of control rather than ownership and adopted Keynes theories in Germany and Italy.[7]

John Strachey, a one-time communist who entered the British Fabian Society in 1943 and became War Minister in the Labor Government of Great Britain in 1950, explains Keynes theories this way:

> The positive part of Keynes' work was a demand that capitalism should now be regulated and controlled by a central authority . . . The principal instruments of its policy should be variations in the rate of interest, budgetary deficits and surpluses, public works and a redistribution of personal incomes in equalitarian direction. This positive side of Keynes' work requires an authority to do the regulating, and that authority can be, in contemporary conditions, nothing else but the government of a nation state.[8]

Strachey hints to his socialist followers the ultimate possibilities in Keynes' theories. He says:

> Was it not apparent that Keynesism had only to be pushed a little further and a state of things might emerge in which the nominal owners of the means of production, although left in full possession of the legal title to their property, would in reality be working not for themselves, but for whatever hands grasped the central levers of social control? For Keynes had rashly shown that those levers had only to be pulled and pushed this way and that, in order to manipulate the system at will. And, in a democracy, would not those hands in the end almost certainly be those of the representatives of the wage-earning majority of the population? Might not the end of the story be that once proud possessors of the means of the the production would find themselves in effect but agents and managers on behalf of the community?[9]

Strachey cold-bloodedly admits the falsity of the "saving capitalism" mantle wrapped around Keynesian theories:

> . . . the capitalists have really good reasons for their reluctance to be saved by Keynesian policies.[10]

The vanguard of the Fabians who were to ultimately impose Keynes theories on the economy of the United States was led by Felix Frankfurter and Walter Lippman during World War I. Both came to government from Harvard University where they had been active in the Intercollegiate Socialist Society. As special assistants to the Secretary of the Navy, these two Fabians were to meet and develop a lasting, and world-shaping friendship with the young Assistant Secretary of the Navy, Franklin Delano Roosevelt.[11]

When the first war ended, Frankfurter went back to his Harvard teaching post. At least 300 of Frankfurter's students, including two very special pets, Alger Hiss and Dean Acheson, have found their way into strategic government posts. For 30 years, Frankfurter's disciples in government have hired, promoted, and covered up for each other and like-minded collectivists. A number of them were communists. Frankfurter, 25 years later as a Supreme Court Justice, appeared as a "character witness" at the perjury trial of his former pupil, Alger Hiss.[12]

The 1929 depression, the "temporary panic" John Stuart Mill warned about years before, gave the collectivists their opportunity. Franklin D. Roosevelt was the "great man" at the feet of whom the American people would lay their liberties, as Mill had also predicted.

In 1930, Franklin Roosevelt, as governor of New York, expressed the American tradition when he said:

> . . . the Constitution does not empower the Congress to deal with a great number of vital problems of government such as the conduct of public utilities, of banks, of insurance, of business, of agriculture, of education, of social welfare and a dozen other important features . . . and Washington must not be encouraged to interfere in these areas.[13]

Just two years later, however, the widely-heralded "liberal" brain trust presented the newly-elected FDR with a catchy slogan and the blueprint of the program through which in succeeding years they have nearly accomplished the collectivization of America. Roosevelt accepted the program, deserting the principles he enunciated so clearly two years before and the Democratic platform on which he was elected.

Stuart Chase, a longtime Fabian, in his book, *A New Deal*, written in 1931, outlined the ideal government. He said:

> Best of all, the new regime would have the clearest idea of what an economic system was for. The sixteen methods of becoming wealthy would be proscribed (punished) — by firing squad if necessary — ceasing to plague and disrupt the orderly processes of production and distribution. The whole vicious

pecuniary complex would collapse as it has in Russia. Money-making as a career would no more occur to a respectable young man than burglary, forgery or embezzlement.[14]

One year later, FDR used Chase's title as the rallying cry for his Administration. He named Chase to the National Resources Commission where he is credited with authoring FDR's order banning ownership of gold by U. S. citizens, the first step in the destruction of the citizen's independence and U. S. financial strength. Fabians, like Chase, advocate firing squads only when their gradual methods fail.

Chase moved steadily upward in the New Deal hierarchy. He served successively on the Securities and Exchange Commission, the Tennessee Valley Authority, and finally settled in UNESCO, the United Nations agency charged with the re-education of the United States to accept a one-world socialistic state.[15]

Thousands of others like Chase swarmed in to Washington to join holdovers strategically placed during World War I and the ensuing ten years. They played the ego of FDR and the economic plight of the nation like the strings on a violin. Congress was induced and coerced to transfer its Constitutional powers to the new bureaus, agencies, boards, and commissions which sprung up almost overnight. George N. Peek, appointed by FDR as the first head of the Agricultural Adjustment Administration, described it this way:

> A plague of young lawyers settled on Washington — in the legal division were formed the plans which eventually turned the AAA from a device to aid the farmers to a device to introduce the collectivist system of agriculture into this country.[16]

The "young lawyers" eventually drove Peek to resign from his position. He opposed their collectivist schemes for agriculture, the New Deal's first farm program, the successors to which still plague America today. Among the "young lawyers" were Alger Hiss, Adlai Stevenson, John Abt, Nathan Witt, Nathaniel Weyl, and Charles Kramer. All of them, except Stevenson, were to be identified 15 years later as secret communist agents.[17] Before they were exposed, they completed their dirty work in the Agriculture Department and spread out to capture other branches of government.

In 1952, the Senate Internal Security Subcommittee published results of hearings which showed the communist net of control, which started with this group in the Agriculture Department, had extended over the Labor, Treasury, State and Commerce Departments, the independent agencies and cabinet offices concerned with national defense, and later, the Central Intelligence Agency and United Nations agencies.[18]

This communist penetration and control of the United States government was the result of activities of two exposed communist cells. Two others known to have operated in the government at the same time have never been uncovered.[19]

Few in Congress, and even fewer Americans at the time, or even now realize, or will admit, what was happening. One lone voice spoke out and was quickly smashed, as nearly every vocal opponent of communism has been since. Dr. William Wirt, the superintendent of schools from Gary, Indiana, was invited to dinner at the home of a government employee while in Washington to attend a school administrators meeting in September 1933.

After dinner, the hostess, Alice Barrows, an employee of the Department of Education, and other guests disclosed that communists had infiltrated and taken control of the New Deal. Four of the dinner guests were government employees. The fifth was the Washington representative of *Tass*, the Soviet news agency.[20]

Wirt summarized what was said at the meeting and when government officials brushed him off, he mailed a statement to about 100 conservative leaders and newspapers across the United States. This provoked a Congressional investigation of his charges.

Wirt's statement was read into the record as the basis on which he would be interrogated. Because it deserves deep and detailed study much of it is reproduced here. The techniques Wirt was told would be used to discredit business, to entice labor, management, school officials, and farmers to "go along" are frighteningly similar to those *which have been used* in the ensuing 30 years. Wirt stated:

> "Brain Trusters" insist that the America of Washington, Jefferson, and Lincoln must first be destroyed so that on the ruins they will be able to construct an America after their own pattern. They do not know that the America of Washington, Jefferson, and Lincoln was the real New Deal for the common man. They wish to put the common man back into the feudal society of the Dark Ages.[21]

Wirt's statement as read into the record of the public hearing continued:

> I was told they believe that by thwarting our then evident economic recovery they would be able to prolong the country's destitution until they had demonstrated to the American people that the Government must operate business and commerce. By

propaganda they would destroy institutions making long-time capital loans — and then push Uncle Sam into making these loans. Once Uncle Sam becomes our financier he must also follow his money with control and management.[22]

Today, the Federal Government is very much in the business of making long term capital loans through the Area Redevelopment Administration, Small Business Administration, the Rural Electrification Administration, Export-Import Bank, Federal Land Banks, the various housing agencies, and dozens of other departments large and small.

Wirt stated that the "Brain Trusters" said, "We believe we have Roosevelt in the middle of a swift stream and that the current is so strong he cannot turn back or escape from it. We believe we can keep Mr. Roosevelt there until we are ready to supplant him with a Stalin. We all think Mr. Roosevelt is only the Kerensky of the Revolution."[23] Asked why the President would not see through the scheme, they replied:

We are on the inside, we control the avenues of influence. We can make the President believe he is making the decisions for himself . . . soon he will feel a superhuman flow of power from the flow of decisions themselves, good or bad.[24]

Wirt was told that most Americans under-estimate the power of propaganda, that since World War I propaganda had been developed into science. They said further:

. . . That they could make newspapers and magazines beg for mercy by threatening to take away much of their advertising by a measure to compel only the unvarnished truth in advertising.[25]

This is, of course, just exactly the power exercised over newspapers, magazines, radio and TV and their advertisers today by the Federal Trade Commission. Wirt went on to say in his statement before the Congressional committee:

They were sure that they could depend on the psychology of empty stomachs and they would keep them empty. The masses would soon agree that anything should be done rather than nothing. Any escape from present miseries would be welcomed even though it should turn out to be another misery.[26]

Wirt was told that leaders of business and labor would be silenced by offers of government contracts for materials and services, provided they were subservient; that colleges and schools would be kept in line by promises of Federal Aid, until the many "new dealers" in the schools and colleges gained control of them; they believed the farmers could be brought into line by letting them "get their hands in the public trough for once in the history of the country." To any opposition that developed, they would ask, "Well, what is your plan?"[27]

Wirt testified that the meeting at which he learned of these plans was held following a dinner party on September 1, 1933 at the home of Alice Barrows, an employee of the Department of Education. The home was located in a Virginia suburb of Washington, D. C. In attendance were:

> Robert Breuere, a member of the New Deal Textile Code Advisory Board and a World War I supporter of the revolutionary IWW movement; David Cushman Coyle, an employee of the Public Works Administration (PWA); Laurence Todd, Washington representative of the Soviet news agency, *TASS,* and a former official of the American Civil Liberties Union; Hildegarde Kneeland, an employee of the Department of Agriculture, member of the ACLU, and the person Dr. Wirt claimed did most of the talking about the communist plans to take over the New Deal; and Mary Taylor, also an employee of the Department of Agriculture.[28]

Wirt reported that the group indicated they looked for leadership to Dr. Rexford Guy Tugwell, a radical, who was assistant to Henry Wallace, and to Wallace himself. At the time, Henry Wallace was Secretary of Agriculture. He became vice president of the United States in Roosevelt's third term.

Of the six persons Wirt reported in attendance at the dinner, all testified. They admitted the dinner had been held, but denied Wirt's report of the after-dinner conversation. However, before the hearings began, A. A. Berle, Jr., a New Deal official, had been quoted by the Associated Press as admitting the conversations had taken place but that the government employees were just pulling Wirt's leg.[29]

During the hearing, to substantiate the charges that the economic recovery was being held down, Dr. Wirt cited figures to show that in the period April 19, 1933-August 1, 1933, that the country was recovering from the depression at a pace three times faster than ever before experienced in America. Business had reached 82% of normal, before the recovery mysteriously stopped. Wirt cited articles from *Collier's* magazine which said, "The farmer is whistling over the bettering times." At the same time the Department of Agriculture was saying, "This is an illusion, we must have controls." Controls were imposed and the recovery stopped.[30]

Republican members of the committee and Wirt's counsel, Senator James A. Reed (D-Mo) wanted the investigation continued, but the Democratic majority refused. Wirt's efforts were to no avail. He was ridiculed by *Time* magazine, the *New York Times,* and the far-left press. Wirt was "silenced" and within two years he died in a *mental institution.*

Eighteen years later in 1952, the Senate Internal Security Subcommittee in another investigation was to reveal that Alice Barrows, at whose home the meeting was held, had been a communist agent from the time she was employed in the U. S. Office of Education in 1919![31]

Even so, Wirt was not "cleared." The "trail" was "covered" in the Cumulative Summary Index 1918-1956, Congressional Investigations of Communism and Subversive Activities.[32] In this reference volume which lists all hearings into communist activities conducted by governmental agencies and all witnesses who have testified down through the years, Alice Barrows is listed in the cross reference for her first appearance in 1934 as "Alice P. Barrows" and as "Alice P. Borrows" on her second appearance in 1952.[33] This "mistake," in this official reference makes it unlikely that many students would encounter the second appearance which proves Wirt's case.

Wirt's charge that the "brain trusters" of the New Deal deliberately sabotaged the economic recovery which was well underway in the fourth and final year of the Hoover Administration is not without substantiation. Said the Democratic-oriented *New York Times* on June 16, 1934:

> The change for the better in the last half of 1932 is beyond dispute. That this evident revival of confidence was suddenly reversed in February 1933 is equally true.

Wilbur and Hyde, in their book, *The Hoover Policies,* said:

> In the months of August, September and October 1932, bank failures had almost ceased while banks reopened were more than suspensions. The great flow of gold the months previous to July reversed itself into an enormous inflow. The whole banking structure greatly strengthened. Wholesale commodity prices advanced during July, August and September. Cotton and wheat advanced over 20 per cent. U. S. cotton manufacturing advanced from 51.5 per cent of mill capacity in July to 97 per cent in October. Domestic wool consumption advanced from 16,500,000 pounds in May to 46,100,000 in September. The Federal Reserve Board's index of industrial production swept upward from 56 in July to 68 for both September and October.[34]

After the election of November 1932, President Hoover, the press, spokesmen of economic bodies all pleaded with Roosevelt to do a simple thing: merely assure the country that he intended to abide by his campaign promises.[35]

Roosevelt remained silent.

Rumors ran rampant that despite FDR's conservative campaign promises that the country was heading for alarming monetary, economic and social experiments.

Panic resulted.

Banks later found to be completely sound were stampeded into closing their doors. The recovery, well-advanced under Hoover, ground to a halt, and Roosevelt's supporters on the "far-left" were quoted as saying, "The worse the better."[36]

The senior editor of *The Reader's Digest,* Eugene Lyons, in his book, *The Herbert Hoover Story,* quotes Charles Michelson, chief of the Democratic Party Publicity Staff during the 1932 campaign as saying:

> The President-elect (FDR) told me on one occasion that the bank crisis was due to culminate just about inauguration day . . . Naturally he did not care to have the dramatic effect of his intended proposals spoiled by a premature discussion of them in advance of their delivery.[37]

Lyons says that if Roosevelt and his brain trust had planned to push the country over the brink in order to take over at the lowest possible point in history they would have behaved no differently. They did not merely refrain from doing or saying anything that would bolster confidence; they did and said precisely those things which shook confidence and confirmed fears.[38]

Press agentry built Roosevelt and the New Deal as saviors. Good hard statistics reveal that unemployment during the Hoover Administration averaged 6.2-millions annually, or just slightly higher than it has reached several times in the post-war era. In the first two Roosevelt Administrations, average annual unemployment was 9.9-million.[39] In other words, despite appropriation of billions for relief purposes, other billions for make-work schemes, and the transfer to the federal government of almost complete control over the nation's economy, things got worse, and not better, under Roosevelt. The advent of World War II, and not the New Deal and government intervention, ended the Depression.

By 1938, Garet Garrett, distinguished newspaperman, author and editorial writer for the *Saturday Evening Post,* published an essay, "The Revolution Was." In the opening paragraph, he said:

> There are those who still think they are holding the pass against a revolution that may be coming up the road. But they are gazing in the wrong direction. The revolution is behind them. It went by in the Night of Depression, singing songs to freedom.[40]

Garrett went on to show that every problem faced by the New Deal was solved in a way which transformed the traditional concept of limited self government into a system that could not fail to:[41]

Ramify the authority and power of executive government — its power, that is, to rule by decrees and rules and regulations of its own making.

Strengthen its hold on the economic life of the nation.

Extend its power over the individual.

Degrade Congress and the parliamentary principle.

Impair the great American tradition of an independent Constitutional judicial power.

Weaken all other powers — private enterprise, private finance, and the power of state and local governments.

In no instance was any action taken which did not contribute to the process which Garrett points out moved unerringly toward a redesign of the governmental structures into totalitarian *form*. With thousands of individual actions, decrees, and rules all meshing to accomplish this end, Garrett concluded that it was all according to a great master plan.

Checks and balances placed in the Constitution to prevent such centralization of power worked for a time. The Supreme Court declared early New Deal measures unconstitutional.

Roosevelt's heavily Democratic Congress facing the crisis of the Depression gave the President and the bureaucrats nearly everything they asked for. In rapid succession, the National Recovery Act (NRA), the Agricultural Adjustment Act (drafted by Hiss and his fellow communists), and the Bituminous Coal Act were all passed, giving the federal bureaucracy unprecedented power, and control of every phase of American life.

Citizens were subjected to varying degrees of federal harassment and red tape, all justified as being in the "public interest." A New York poultry dealer was arrested for letting a customer pick and buy a particular chicken from a cage, a violation of the NRA code.[42] Under the code, the customer was required to say, "I want a chicken," and take "potluck" on which one he got. The operator of a little tailor shop was jailed for charging 35c for pressing a pair of men's trousers.[43] This was five cents *below* the NRA minimum.

The Supreme Court found the NRA and its companion measures in violation of the Constitution — and every concept of American freedom.[44] Roosevelt, infuriated, retaliated with schemes to by-pass or replace the "Nine Old Men." All were rejected by even the New Deal controlled Congress.

However, several justices soon bowed to mounting pressure and several New Deal measures were upheld by 5 to 4 decisions of the high court.[45] Then, within two years of the defeat of the court-packing plans, deaths and retirement gave FDR his chance to control the Supreme Court. He appointed four new justices, Hugo Black, Felix Frankfurter, Stanley Reed, and William O. Douglas. None of the four had judicial experience prior to being named to the highest court in the land.[46]

In succeeding years, the four were to lead the Court in reversing dozens of previous Supreme Court decisions, making a mockery of American jurisprudence. Some actions stretched both the law and reality to the point of tragedy.

The Constitution, as written, distributed power between the three separate, but equal, branches of the federal government — the executive, legislative and judiciary. Authority was divided to prevent a concentration of power in any one part of the government, thus preventing the possibility of a dictatorship in the future.

A further safeguard was provided by spelling out specifically those areas in which the federal government could, *and could not,* function. These restrictions on government power were embodied in the Bill of Rights, the first ten amendments to the Constitution. The Ninth and Tenth Amendments reserved for the states and the people *all* powers not specifically given to the federal government.

One of the powers the federal government was logically given was the function of regulating *interstate* commerce, trade and businesses which operated across state lines. Regulation of *intrastate* commerce, business or trade conducted wholly within one state was left to the states. Thus, most of the owner-operated retail, commercial, and service business in the nation were free from interference in any way by the federal government.

In 1942, the Supreme Court, with Felix Frankfurter in the lead, changed this 150 year old concept. Without precedent in law or fact, the Court voted that because one of the tenants that rented space in a building in New Jersey sold its products in other states, that the building itself was in interstate commerce and thus subject to federal regulation.[47] Even more fantastic, the Court decided that the elevator operator who spent his days running the elevator up and down was also in interstate commerce.

Through such legal twisting and turning, the bureaucrats evaded constitutional limitations on their power and achieved control over nearly every segment of American business, large and small, *and their employees.*

In the same year, similar nimble "legal" footwork by the Supreme Court affirmed the federal government's complete control over American farmers. A farmer named Filburn planted 12 acres of wheat for which he did not have a federal allotment. He fed the wheat to animals raised on his own farm and slaughtered as food for his own family.

The government fined Filburn, who appealed the case to the Supreme Court. He argued that the government had no right to control his actions in producing food for the sole use of his own family. He claimed that under no conceivable stretch of the law could his actions be interpreted as "interstate commerce." Oh, yes, the Court said. If you had not used your own wheat for feed, you *might* have bought wheat from someone else, and that *might* have affected the price of other wheat which was transported in interstate commerce.[48] Therefore, the Court ruled, the federal government is perfectly justified under the interstate commerce clause of the Constitution in applying these controls.

The Supreme Court's role in the socialist-communist plan to transform the United States into part of a one-world socialistic society has been the subject of Congressional inquiries,[49] and several lengthy books.[50]

Criticism of the Supreme Court, which started early in the New Deal period, reached a peak on June 25, 1962 when the Court, by a 6 to 1 decision, denied New York school children the privilege of opening the school day with a non-sectarian prayer.[51] The same day, the Court decided that pornographic literature designed to appeal to homosexuals was not obscene and indecent and therefore could not be barred from the U. S. Mails.[52]

Twenty-five years after FDR appointed Justice Black to the Supreme Court in 1938, the leftist trio in black robes, Douglas, Frankfurter and Black still held sway. They contributed to the destruction of the rights of the separate states, permitted federal intervention into every phase of business and private life; and led the movement to destroy the security laws of the nation.

Justice Black, in his first 25 years on the bench, participated in 102 cases in which subversion and communists were involved. He compiled the astounding record of *reaching a decision favorable to the communists in all 102 cases.*[53] Justice Douglas participated in 100 such cases and *favored the communist position 97 times.*[54] Frankfurter, third man in the trio, went along with Douglas and Black until his final three years on the bench when he switched and rather consistently opposed the Communist position.[55]

In recent years, as recounted in Chapter III, Roosevelt's appointees have been joined by those of President Eisenhower, Earl Warren and William Brennan. Practically all legal restraints against communist subversion of our society have been destroyed by Court Action.

The communist infiltration of the New Deal was opposed at the time the Supreme Court controversies started, but to no avail. The Democratic Party's nominee for President in 1928, Alfred E. Smith, was one of those who spoke out. Al Smith watched the transformation of our government in silence until January 25, 1936, when in Washington, D. C. he said:

> It is not easy for me to stand up here tonight and talk to the American people against the Democratic Administration. This is not easy. It hurts me. But I can call upon innumerable witnesses to testify to the fact that during my whole public life I put patriotism above partisanship. And when I see danger . . . it is difficult for me to refrain from speaking out.[56]

Smith did speak out clearly and distinctly, but few listened. He said:

> What are these dangers I see? The first is the arraignment of class against class. It has been freely predicted that if we were ever to have civil strife again in this country it would come from the appeal to passion and prejudices that comes from demagogues that would incite one class of our people against another.
>
> In my time I have met some good and bad industrialists; I have met some good and bad financiers, but I have also met some good and bad laborers, and this I know, that permanent prosperity is dependent on capital and labor alike.[57]

After announcing that he had only one choice, his withdrawal of support from the New Deal, Smith concluded:

> Now in conclusion, let me give this solemn warning. There can only be one Capital, Washington or Moscow! There can be only one atmosphere of government, the clear, pure fresh air of free America, or the foul breath of Communistic Russia.
>
> There can be only one flag, the Stars and Stripes, or the Red Flag of the Godless Union of the Soviet.[58]

Al Smith was not the only Democrat to rebel. Former Congressman Martin Dies, head of the Special House Committee on Un-American Activities in the 1930's recalled later in a speech that his committee "compiled lists of thousands of Communists, agents, stooges, and sympathizers on the govern-

ment payroll."[59] He took the information to President Roosevelt personally. Roosevelt said, furiously:

> I have never seen a man who had such exaggerated ideas
> about this thing. I do not believe in communism anymore than
> you do but there is nothing wrong with the communists in this
> country; several of the best friends I've got are communists.[60]

Dies continued his fight against communist infiltration until
1944 when facing a "purge" by FDR he withdrew from the
1944 Democratic primary in Texas. Some of the actual communists and agents Dies tried to expose were rooted out of
the government years later. Many escaped exposure and even
today, FBI files are reported to contain evidence reflecting on
the loyalty of between 2,000 and 3,000 federal employees,
according to a statement entered in the Congressional Record
by Congressmen Paul Kitchin (D-NC) in 1962.[61]

For over 20 years, warning after warning has been ignored.
In 1946, for example, President Harry Truman promoted
Harry Dexter White, the assistant secretary of the Treasury,
to a high post on the International Monetary Fund, *after
J. Edgar Hoover* personally had White's complete record as a
long-time communist agent delivered to the White House.[62]

MODERN REPUBLICANISM

The collectivist-conceived bureaucratic empire grew and
thrived and was threatened only once — by the possible selection of Robert A. Taft as the Republican Presidential candidate in 1952.

The Fabians and internationalists in the Republican Party,
assisted by transfers from the normally Democratic-oriented
political arm of the Fabian movement, the Americans for
Democratic Action (ADA), succeeded in nominating Dwight
Eisenhower as the Republican standard bearer.

Just four years before, in 1948, Eisenhower and the open
ultra-liberal Supreme Court Justice William O. Douglas had
been the ADA's choices for the Democratic nomination.[63]
The late Philip Graham, publisher of the ultra-left-wing *Washington Post* was among the many "liberals" who moved into
the Republican Party briefly to stop Taft and nominate Eisenhower. Arthur Hays Sulzberger, publisher of the *New York
Times* was another.[64]

Eisenhower talked like an *economic conservative* but was
supported by liberals, avowed internationalists like Thomas
Dewey, and the "practical politicians." Their slogan was,
"I like Taft, but he can't win."

Taft was beaten in a convention where disputed delegations, charges of fraud, and whispers of huge sums changing hands marred the proceedings.[65]

During Eisenhower's eight years in office, he *talked* about balanced budgets and fiscal responsibility. His actions and programs increased the national debt by $25-billion.[66]

Republicans in Congress, who with a few conservative Democrats had blocked the most radical New Deal programs, bowed to party discipline and acceded to Eisenhower's requests. The establishment of the Health, Education and Welfare Department is an example.

Proposed and rejected regularly during the Truman Administration, the Health, Education and Welfare Department was established by Eisenhower in 1953 with a first year budget of less than a billion dollars. By 1960, HEW gathered in state and local programs and initiated its own new ones to control the powerful political weapon of disbursements to the states and people of over $15-billion annually[67] — this growth took place during an administration which publicly was "economy conscious."

Much of the increase financed Eisenhower's "matching grants-in-aid" which were supposed to "help" the states meet their "responsibilities" (as defined by the federal bureaucracy).

State legislatures accepted federal "guidance" and control of their unemployment compensation, highway construction, scientific education, and welfare programs to get the "free federal money" which had been collected in the states.

Over 400 cities accepted federal "guidance" on building codes, zoning laws, planning commissions, and land use plans to become "eligible" for federal urban renewal and public housing funds. At the same time, a direct line of authority was established between Washington and local governments, by-passing the state governments.[68]

The budget, the size of the federal government, and federal influence zoomed. For example, spending for purely *domestic* programs averaged $17.7-billion annually in Truman's last five years. In Eisenhower's last five years, it averaged $33.6-billion, an increase of 89%.[69]

It was this betrayal of the principles on which the Republican Party was elected in 1952 that prompted Senator Barry Goldwater (R-Ari) to rise in the Senate on April 8, 1957 to deliver the following speech, thus, breaking with the Eisenhower Administration:

It is, of course, with deepest sorrow that I must pass judgment upon my own party . . . Until quite recently I was personally satisfied that this administration was providing the reliable and realistic leadership so vital to the maintenance of a strong domestic economy, which, in turn, is a vital factor in maintaining world peace.

It is true that after 20 years of New Deal-Fair Deal experiments in socialism, Americans have been considerably softened to the doctrine of federal paternalism but what degree of slavish economic indigence has resulted should be treated with lessons in free enterprise and States Rights, not as the President recently suggested in a speech in Washington by educating people — to accept federal moneys for a project which they ought to be paying for themselves, directly through their State and local governments.

It is equally disillusioning to see the Republican Party plunging headlong into the same dismal state experienced by traditional Democrat principles of Jefferson and Jackson during the days of the New Deal and Fair Deal. As a result of those economic and political misadventures, that great party has lost its soul of freedom; its spokesmen are peddlers of the philosophy that the Constitution is outmoded, that States Rights are void, and that the only hope for the future of these United States is for our people to be federally clothed, federally supported in their occupations, and to be buried in a federal box in a federal cemetery.

In the Republican Party there are also vociferous exponents of this incredible philosophy. It may be, in fact, that they are among the "Modern Republicans" about whom there has been so much discussion in recent months. Certainly, the faulty tenets of Modern Republicans do not refute this big government concept.[70]

The next year, in 1958, the Eisenhower Administration ran up the biggest peace-time deficit in American history, a $12.5-billion endorsement of the Keynesian concept of "spend yourself to prosperity."[71] Goldwater won re-election into the U. S. Senate that year by a record majority — while Republicans in general were losing 12 seats in the U. S. Senate and about 40 seats in the lower House.

THE NEW FRONTIER

Fabian control of the Washington bureaucracy is now more openly acknowledged. Fewer Americans seem repelled by socialism. The attitudes of many have softened toward communism. Shocked and shaken by the subversion cases 15 years ago, Americans have become apathetic about high government officials with communist front records. Those who expose them are right wing radicals.

Even John Kennedy was affected. In 1953, as a Senator, Kennedy said:

> I'm not a liberal at all. I never joined the Americans for Democratic Action. I'm not comfortable with those people.[72]

Not many Americans are comfortable with the ideas of the political arm of the Fabian Society. But as president, John Kennedy appointed 40 members of this political underworld to high government posts. President Johnson continued them in their high posts.

For example, Arthur M. Schlesinger, Jr., a Harvard professor and ADA-founder, was Kennedy's special assistant. In 1947, Schlesinger wrote:

> If socialism (i.e., ownership by the state of all significant means of production) is to preserve democracy it must be brought about step by step in a way which will not disrupt the fabric of custom, law and mutual confidence upon which personal rights depend.
>
> That is, the transition must be piecemeal; it must be parliamentary; it must respect civil liberties and due process of law. Socialism by such means used to seem fantastic to the hard-eyed melodramatists of the Leninist persuasion; but even Stalin is reported to have told Harold Laski recently that it might be possible . . . There seems no inherent obstacle to the gradual advance of socialism in the United States through a series of New Deals.
>
> Socialism, then, appears quite practical within this frame of reference, as a longtime proposition. Its gradual advance might well preserve order and law . . . The active agents in effecting the transition will probably be, not the working classes, but some combination of lawyers, business and labor managers, politicians and intellectuals, in the manner of the first New Deal.[73]

In these three short paragraphs, Schlesinger confirms vividly what good Americans are called right wing extremists for saying: That the Fabians (gradualists) are socialists; that Keynesian economic policy is the path to socialism; that goals of communism and socialism are essentially the same; that New Deal welfare state proposals whether enacted by Democrats or Republicans are socialistic; that establishment of socialism will result in a curtailment of freedom; that socialism and communism appeal, not to the working class or the poverty stricken masses, but to the "liberal" intellectual, the college professor, and the turncoat businessman.

Chapter XIII

Internationalism

> *A real internationalist is one who brings his sympathy and recognition up to a point of practical and maximal help to the USSR in support and defense of the USSR by every means and in every possible form.*
>
> — *Andrei Vyshinsky*

FOR OVER 100 YEARS American Presidents and diplomats faithfully followed the advice left with them by George Washington when, in his farewell address, he said:

> The great rule of conduct for us, in regard to foreign nations, is in extending our commercial relations, to have as little political connections as possible . . . 'Tis our true policy to steer clear of permanent alliances, with any nation of the world.[1]

Since World War II, America has become so entangled in a web of treaties, executive agreements, and secret pacts that we have lost control of our political decisions, monetary system, and military forces. In 1954, a Congressional committee found that . . .

> . . . there is a definite tendency to sacrifice the national interest of our country in dealing with foreign affairs.[2]

By 1961, the sacrifice of the national interest became the rule rather than the exception. For example, the U. S. Army's crack 24th division was alerted in Germany in the spring of 1961. Part of it prepared to resist possible attacks from East Germany while other units stood by to be airlifted to the Congo to protect the communist-dominated Central Congolese government by fighting the pro-western, anti-communist forces of Moise Tshombe.[3] Major General Edwin A. Walker, who commanded the 24th at the time, told a Congressional committee . . .

> . . . under our national policy and by our own command, American sons were alerted in readiness to go to the Congo to fight the anti-communists and also to go to the East-West

Zone to fight communists. Those two boys, in my opinion, without any doubt are fighting each other.[4]

In 1963, the military forces of the United States were unleashed in the Caribbean area, not to protect Latin America from communist subversives spreading out from Cuba — but to protect Castro, Cuba, and Communism from attacks by liberty-loving Cubans. Meanwhile, halfway around the world, Americans were being killed in the guerilla warfare in South Viet Nam — by communists.

Traditional U. S. foreign policy was based on the concept that the primary function of American military forces and diplomats should be the protection of American lives, rights and property. This traditional concept has been replaced by a foreign policy which sacrifices national interests — and common sense — to something called "world opinion."

To fully understand how the transformation has been effected, it is necessary to examine several facets of national policy, including relations with the United Nations, the foreign aid program, the effect of treaties on the basic rights of Americans and the growth of the group which has engineered the basic changes in U. S. foreign policy.

THE UNITED NATIONS

In the 1930's, with each breach of the peace, in Manchuria in 1931, Ethiopia in 1935, China in 1936, Spain in 1937, and when Europe exploded in 1939, Americans were told that somehow it might not have happened if the U. S. Senate and "isolation minded" Americans had not rejected the League of Nations in 1919.

A national guilt complex was induced in America through reiteration of this theme in the press, textbooks, and through church publications and programs and government and other opinion-molding agencies.

After this pre-conditioning, when World War II ended, the United Nations treaty was ratified by the U. S. Senate with only two dissenting votes.[5] A majority of Americans grasped the UN as the "best hope for world peace."

The Communist Party, USA wholeheartedly supported the newly forming organization. *Political Affairs,* the party's official theoretical journal, in the April 1945 issue gave communists this order:

> Great popular support and enthusiasm for the United Nations policies should be built up, well organized and fully articulate. But it is also necessary to do more than that. The opposition must be rendered so impotent that it will be unable

to gather any significant support in the Senate against the UN Charter and the treaties which will follow.

The few voices in America which urged caution were rendered impotent, just as the communists planned. The opposition was assured that the UN could never act against American interests because the United States would have veto power. That other countries large enough to disrupt the peace also had the veto was ignored.

The communist leadership realized it. They knew in advance that the structure of the UN could be used to prevent it from ever acting against the communists. They knew what few Americans realize even today . . .

. . . that Alger Hiss was the principal American representative in discussions of plans for the UN and its Charter at the Yalta and Dumbarton Oaks conferences; that Hiss was to be the Secretary General of the United Nations Organizing Conference in San Francisco when the Charter was written and adopted; that in his dual role as Secretary General and top State Department official for UN affairs he could channel his choices into key positions in the newly forming UN Secretariat.[6]

In 1948, when Alger Hiss was exposed as a communist agent, the web of protective propaganda which guards the UN prevented most Americans from learning that he had been the UN's chief architect.

Disciplined members of the world-wide communist conspiracy were informed almost immediately that the UN was planned as the agency "which will smash the anti-Soviet intrigues of imperialist reactionaries." The entire Red scheme for the UN was revealed in a communist pamphlet, *The United Nations,* published in English in September 1945 by the People's Publishing House, Bombay, India.

According to this official communist pamphlet, the Soviet Union planned to . . .

. . . automatically veto any UN measure restrictive to or harmful to world communism while using the UN to promote friction between non-communist nations and frustrate their foreign policy.
. . . use the UN trusteeship council and the UN special agencies to detach all dependent and semi-dependent areas from any foreign influence except that of the Soviet Union — eventually bringing about a one-world Soviet system.[7]

In the ensuing years, the communists have followed the plan, using the veto 100 times. The U. S. has never used it.

As a result, the United Nations, established to prevent or stop wars, has watched ineffectively, or aided the aggressors, while wars have been waged in China, Malaya, Indo-China, Tibet, Laos, Hungary, Korea, the Middle East, Cuba, Indonesia, Algeria, the Congo, Goa, Angola, and on the Indian-Chinese border. The anti-western forces have won, or are winning them all.

There has been no major war, not because the UN has prevented it — but because the communists are winning the world without one. The plan "to detach all dependent and semi-dependent areas from any foreign influence except that of the Soviet Union," is being fulfilled as dozens of former colonies become "independent" and adopt the "neutralist" pro-communist position in the world struggle.

Despite 17 years of continual failures, in 1962 nearly 85% of the American people still placed faith and trust in the UN as the best hope for peace.[8] They fail to see the truth because emotion-provoking slogans have been substituted for factual, accurate information about the UN's founding, its structure, and its operation. UN failures in Hungary, Korea, and the Congo are frequently called victories.

Few Americans know that the UN Secretariat has become a haven for the communists and security risks who had been officials of the U. S. government in the 1940's. In 1952, the Senate Internal Security Subcommittee spent two months studying the activities of U. S. citizens employed by the UN.[9] Its report stated:

> American communists who had been officials of the United States Government penetrated the Secretariat of the United Nations after the United States Government had been apprised of security information regarding their conspiratorial activities.

In all, 21 Americans employed in key UN administrative posts took the Fifth Amendment during the SISS hearings when asked about their participation in the communist conspiracy. UN Secretary General Trygve Lie studied the Senate report and discharged the Fifth Amendment cases.

Lie's action was appealed and the UN Administrative Tribunal ruled that Lie had no right to fire employees who had permanent UN civil service status. Reinstatements with back pay and "damages" of up to $40,000 per employee were awarded.[10]

Dr. Robert Morris, who was chief counsel of the Senate committee which investigated the security risks in the UN, commented on the reinstatement of the Fifth Amendment cases and the large cash grants they received. In his book, *No Wonder We Are Losing*, he said:

Here was a Communist victory accomplished with the sanction of free delegations. The decision established, in effect, that even if UN authorities discovered secret Kremlin agents in their employ, they could do nothing about it. Let it be remembered that these were not Soviet-appointed officials, but part of the U. S. quota.[11]

Dr. Morris' comment points up a dilemma. Even if it were possible to eliminate all Americans of doubtful loyalty from the UN Administrative staff, many communists would still hold key UN positions. Under a quota system, each member nation, including the communist ones, names its own citizens to fill an allocated percentage of clerical, technical, and administrative jobs in the UN Secretariat. In theory, those appointed should function as unbiased "international civil servants" working for the best interests of the UN as a whole.

How it actually works in practice was described in the report of the Senate committee which studied the case of Povl Bang-Jensen in 1961. Bang-Jensen, a Danish civil servant, was fired in 1958 by Dag Hammarskjold for refusing to reveal the names of refugees who testified in the UN Hungarian inquiry to a high UN official from a communist country. Bang-Jensen feared communist reprisals against the relatives of the witnesses who were still in Hungary. As was discussed in Chapter IX, Bang-Jensen continued his fight to correct the serious lack of security in the UN Secretariat until his death by "suicide" two years after he was fired.

Quoting a study made by the International League for the Rights of Man, the Senate report on the Bang-Jensen case said:

> If the Secretary General retains on his staff Soviet nationals there is *prima facie* a possibility of leaks of information to the Soviet Union. Only those persons of extraordinary naivete would fail to recognize that, as between loyalty to the international civil service and the Soviet Union, the Soviet citizen is under extreme pressure to conform to the wishes of his government.[12]

The report cited cases of Soviet employees of the UN Secretariat caught while engaging in espionage activities against the U. S. and concluded:

> So long as Soviet nationals are members of the Secretary General's staff or serve directly under him, there is always a risk that confidential information in the office of the Secretary General which is desired by the Soviet government will find its way into their hands.[13]

The risk is not limited to information leaks. With some of the UN's highest staff offices held by communists, the manipulation of UN programs to benefit world communism is a distinct threat.

As an example, under a secret agreement made in 1945 by U. S. Secretary of State Edward Stettinius, a communist has always filled the second most important UN post, that of Under or Assistant Secretary for Political and Security Council Affairs. This committee implements Security Council police actions, oversees disarmament enforcement, etc. Under the terms of the secret agreement, the nine men who have held the post since the UN was organized in 1945 have all been from Iron Curtain countries.[14]

During the Korean War, for example, the chain of command from the UN Security Council to General MacArthur was through the Under-Secretary for Political and Security Council affairs, Constantine Zinchenko, a communist.[15] Is it any wonder that General George Stratemeyer, the Air Force commander in Korea, returned to tell a Senate committee:

We were required to lose the Korean War.[16]

The threat continues today. If U. S. proposals for arms control and disarmament are accepted, U. S. military forces will be transferred to the UN peace force, which is directed by the Under-Secretary for Political and Security Council Affairs, who has always been a communist.

There is still another danger in blind faith, trust, and respect in the UN. With communists filling administrative and technical positions in the Secretariat, the reports they write, the decisions they make carry the prestige of the United Nations. Unsuspecting Americans have no indication that the UN pamphlet they receive may have been written by an open communist.

The 1963 UNESCO bulletin on Colonialism is an example. Under the UN seal it said:

The unequal treatment of nationalistic colonialist oppression and discrimination on grounds of race or nationality, which still characterizes a number of capitalist countries today, are to be explained by the political and social systems prevailing in those countries.[17]

The UNESCO report completely ignored "oppression and discrimination" in the Soviet "colonies" of Hungary, Poland, Tibet, etc. and praised the Soviet Union for . . .

. . . successful establishment of full equality of rights between races and nationalities in the USSR.[18]

The United States pays 31% of the cost for the Soviet propaganda which is distributed into the under-developed nations of the world under the respectability of the United Nations emblem.

How many Americans look behind the blue UN "seal of approval" on the UNESCO literature and materials used in American schools to build "attitudes" for "world understanding" and "world citizenship" in their sons and daughters?

How secure would they feel in accepting this "seal of approval" if they knew that this program was directed for years by Mrs. A. Jegalova, chief of the UNESCO division of Secondary Education. Before becoming an "international civil servant" Mrs. Jegalova was chief inspector of the Ukrainian Branch of the Soviet Ministry of Education. Being a communist, Mrs. Jegalova is unlikely to approve any program originating in her department which is detrimental to world communism. If she did, the Kremlin would quickly call her home.

The UN Special Agencies, of which UNESCO is typical, have from their founding aided and assisted the world communist movement. For example, UNRRA, the United Nations Relief and Rehabilitation Agency, distributed billions of dollars in American aid following World War II.[19] In Yugoslavia, Poland, and China, where communist and anti-communist forces were maneuvering for control, UNRRA channeled its aid, 72% of which was supplied by the U. S., through communist groups.

Arthur Bliss Lane, American ambassador to Poland following the war, described in his book, *I Saw Poland Betrayed*, how UNRRA funds were used to solidify communist control of the country. He told how, in advance of the elections, official approval was given to the communist-dominated coalition government, and then:

> Over my personal protest . . . the agreement concluded in Warsaw provided that the Polish Government, and not UNRRA, should have complete jurisdiction over the distribution of UNRRA supplies in Poland . . . I learned of attempts to force the populace to join the two principal parties, the Workers (communist) and the Socialist. Those who joined were given preference ration cards entitling them to receive choice UNRRA supplies . . . as the agreement with the Polish government gave UNRRA no control over distribution of goods imported by UNRRA, Drury (local administrator-Auth.) could not prevent supplies being used for political purposes.[20]

The Polish people supported the communists or they didn't

eat. The story was the same in Yugoslavia and much of China.

How was such a faulty agreement made? David Weintraub, identified as a communist by Whittaker Chambers, left the U. S. government in 1944 to become chief adviser to UNRRA Governor General, Herbert Lehman. Later, he became chief of UNRRA supplies.[21] When UNRRA disbanded, Weintraub transferred into the UN Secretariat as Director of the Economic Stability and Development Division.

Similar records have been established by the UN Special Fund, the World Health Organization, and UNICEF. All have channeled American aid to Communist countries. In 1961-62, for example, the UN Special Fund, as discussed earlier, gave Castro $1.6-million.[22]

By 1963, the UN was headed by avowed Marxists. Following his election as Secretary General, U Thant was interviewed by *Newsweek*. He said:

> I believe in the philosophy of thesis, antithesis, and synthesis. From its present antithesis, I believe the world is moving towards a new synthesis.[23]

Newsweek did not tell its readers, but Thant's "philosophy" is a simple restatement of Hegel's dialectic, the basis or root of Karl Marx's dialectical materialism. Thant has also adopted another Marxist idea to finance the "synthesis" toward which he sees the world moving — the one-world socialistic government financed by the United States. Thant says:

> The concept of taxing the rich according to their capacity to pay, in order to cater to the poor according to their needs, is now well established as a simple canon of social justice in all democratic countries. It requires only a little imagination to lift this concept to a higher plane, namely the international plane, and to extend its scope from the country to the universe.[24]

How much of your income would the UN representative of Gabon, Algeria, Cuba or the Soviet Union vote to take away as simple "social justice?" The United States has no veto in the General Assembly.

In the maneuvering which followed the death of Dag Hammarskjold, the Soviet Union first demanded that UN administration be handled by a troika. This demand was withdrawn, *provided* that Ralph Bunche, American delegate to the UN, and a Soviet delegate, Georgi P. Arkadyev, be named as under-secretaries to "neutralist" U Thant.[25] This was done.

Did Russia get its troika? Thant's views have been examined. Arkadyev was a Russian communist. The record of Bunche, who supposedly represents America, was examined in detail on the floor of Congress in two speeches by Congressman James Utt (R-Cal). Utt said:

> Russia now has its troika: one an avowed Marxist, the second a dedicated communist; and the third with a pro-communist bias.[26]

Utt detailed Bunche's record as contributing editor of the openly communist magazine, *Science and Society,* in the 1930's; as founder of the National Negro Congress, cited as subversive by the Attorney General; as a high official of the Institute of Pacific Relations; and as an advocate of UN employment for a notorious communist agent.[27] Utt concluded his remarks, saying:

> It is my considered judgment that Dr. Bunche must be considered a security risk for our country The "troika" arrangement engineered by the communists is frightening and devastating when you consider that the United States of America has no foreign policy of its own except the United Nations.[28]

The implications of the Soviet use of the veto to block any effective anti-communist action; the use of UN headquarters as a base for Soviet espionage and propaganda activity within the United States; the UN's long record of aid to the world communist movement; the UN action in the Congo which destroyed the pro-western anti-communist government of Moise Tshombe, have impelled several distinguished world figures to speak out. Lord Beaverbrook, the noted British newspaper publisher, said:

> Here in New York city, you Americans have the biggest fifth column in the world — The United Nations.[29]

Before his death in 1953, the late Senator Robert A. Taft issued this warning:

> The UN has become a trap. Let's go it alone.[30]

In a speech at his birthplace in Iowa during the summer of 1962, former President Herbert A. Hoover, once a supporter of the United Nations, reluctantly announced:

> Unless the UN is completely reorganized without the Communist nations in it, we should get out of it.[31]

What force keeps the United States in the United Nations despite its consistent record of failures, financial bankruptcy, and pro-communist bias?

Why do so few Americans know of Alger Hiss' role as chief architect of the world organization; of the UN's refusal to fire American communists uncovered in key positions; of the Senate investigations which show that the UN is a base for Soviet espionage and propaganda activities in the United States; that official UN studies and records are actually the work of communists on the UN staff?

How can the murder of children, machine gunning of hospital invalids, rape, plunder and pillage committed by the UN Peace Force in Katanga be described as "peace-keeping operations" without the American people rebelling.

In 1954, a prominent U. S. Senator delivered a cryptic speech which might provide some answers. Senator William Jenner (R-Ind) said that there was a force operating to merge the United States into a one-world socialist system. He described it in this way:

> We have a well-organized political action group in this country, determined to destroy our Constitution, and establish a one-party state. This political action group has its own local politcal support organizations, its own pressure groups, its own vested interests, its foothold within our Government, and its own propaganda apparatus.
>
> The important thing to remember about this group is not its ideology but its organization. It is a dynamic, aggressive, elite corps forcing its way through every opening to make a breach for a collectivist one-party state . . . It cares nothing for party changes directed by the sovereign people . . . It has a strategy which is not derived from anything known to the two parties . . . Outwardly we have a constitutional government. We have operating within our Government and political system, another body representing another form of government, a bureaucratic elite, which believes our Constitution is outmoded and is sure it is on the winning side.[32]

What is this force? How does it operate? What are its goals? Is it the force which provides the protective web of propaganda and emotion-provoking slogans which safeguard the United Nations from rational evaluation?

THE ORGANIZED INTERNATIONALISTS

In May 1919, a group of young intellectuals who had helped draft the League of Nations Charter during World War 1 met at the Majestic Hotel in Paris. They were bitterly disappointed. The U. S. Senate and the American people had rejected the concept of a world governing body. In their discussions they conceived an organization which might study and promote a better "understanding" of international affairs. The group included Christian Herter and the brothers,

John Foster and Allen Dulles. They came home from Paris and incorporated the *Council on Foreign Relations*.

The influence achieved by Herter and John Foster Dulles 25 years later as Secretaries of State under Dwight Eisenhower, and Allen Dulles, as head of the powerful and controversial Central Intelligence Agency, is one indication of the power obtained by the group. This tells only part of the story.

Extremely selective in its membership, the Council has never been a "mass" organization. However, according to the CFR's 1960 membership roster,[33] its 1,400 members control the U. S. State Department, many top cabinet posts, the major newspapers, magazine, and radio and TV networks, most of the large tax-exempt foundations, a host of other opinion molding groups and organizations, and the nation's largest companies including U. S. Steel, AT&T, General Motors, du Pont, IBM and others.

Despite its influence, the CFR is relatively unknown. It has been the subject of one official, although brief, pronouncement by Congress. In 1954, the Special House Committee to Investigate Tax-Exempt Foundations headed by Congressman Reece said that the CFR's "productions are not objective but are directed overwhelmingly at promoting the globalistic concept."[34] The committee's final report expressed concern that the CFR had become . . .

> . . . in essence an agency of the United States Government . . . carrying its internationalist bias with it.[35]

How the Council on Foreign Relations functions as "an agency of government" became clear in an eight part examination of the organization published in 1961. The author, Dan Smoot, a former FBI man and Administrative Assistant to J. Edgar Hoover, found that . . .

> . . . since 1944, all candidates for President, both Republican and Democrat, have been CFR members, except Truman who became President by "accident." Every Secretary of State since Cordell Hull (except James Byrnes) has been a CFR member. Over 40 CFR members comprised the American delegation to the UN Organizing Conference in San Francisco including Alger Hiss, Nelson Rockefeller, Adlai Stevenson, Ralph Bunche, John Foster Dulles, and the Secretary of State Edward Stettinius. CFR affiliates have controlled an unusual number of cabinet posts and top Presidential advisory positions.[36]

The influence is so great that Smoot labeled the group, *The Invisible Government,* and published a book by that name on its membership, activities, and philosophy.

CFR members continue in key government posts under

both Democratic and Republican Administrations. The Dulles Brothers, Herter, Arthur Dean, Douglas Dillon, Charles Bohlen, John McCloy, John McCone, Henry Cabot Lodge, and Ralph Bunche hold high positions no matter which party is in power. Except for Bohlen, and possibly Bunche, all are regarded as Republicans.

The Kennedy-Johnson Administrations appear to be totally controlled by CFR members and former members. They include:

President John F. Kennedy, Secretary of State Dean Rusk, Secretary of Treasury Douglas Dillon, Secretary of Labor and Supreme Court Justice Arthur Goldberg, UN Ambassador Adlai Stevenson, Presidential assistants Arthur Schlesinger, Jr. and McGeorge Bundy, State Department Adviser Dean Acheson, Federal Reserve chairman William McC. Martin, Assistant and Under-Secretaries of State Chester Bowles, Averell Harriman, George McGhee, George Ball, Harlan Cleveland, and Brooks Hays, Assistant Secretaries of Defense Roswell Gilpatric and Paul Nitze, State Department Policy Planner Walt Whitman Rostow, Presidential Disarmament Adviser John McCloy, Chief Disarmament Negotiator Arthur Dean, Presidential Assistant for Science and Technology Jerome Wiesner, and USIA Director Edward R. Murrow.[37]

These are just a few of the more than 60 CFR members who have held top advisory posts, ambassadorial appointments, etc. in the Kennedy-Johnson Administrations — a remarkable achievement for a group with only 1,400 members.

Even when CFR members retired or are replaced, another CFR man gets the job. When General L. L. Lemnitzer (CFR) retired as Chairman of the Joint Chiefs of Staff, he was replaced by General Maxwell Taylor (CFR). When Allen Dulles (CFR) became a center of public controversy over the failure of his CIA-directed Cuban invasion, he was replaced by John McCone (CFR).

How can so much power be concentrated in the membership of such a small organization without public attention? As Senator Jenner pointed out, this group has its own propaganda apparatus. Among the 1,400 CFR members are:

Henry Luce, editor-in-chief of *Time, Life* and *Fortune;* David Lawrence, *U. S. News & World Report;* the late Philip Graham, publisher of *Newsweek* and the *Washington Post;* Gardner and John Cowles, who publish *Look* and own several influential newspapers and broadcasting companies; Arthur Hays Sulzberger, chairman of the board, *New York Times;* Mark Ethridge, publisher, *Louisville Courier Journal;* syndicated columnists Marquis Childs. James Reston, Ernest K. Lindley,

Walter Lippmann and Hanson Baldwin; plus dozens of other lesser known writers, editors and publishers.

Other key editors and publishers belong to local affiliated CFR "chapters" in 30 key cities in the United States. Other CFR members who hold important posts in other opinion-making media are:

William S. Paley, chairman of the board, CBS; David Sarnoff, chairman of the board, Radio Corporation of America (operators of NBC); broadcasters Edward R. Murrow, Charles Collingwood, William L. Shirer, and Irving R. Levine; Harry Scherman, founder and board chairman of the Book-of-the-Month Club; Joseph Barnes, editor-in-chief, Simon & Schuster, John Gunther, best-selling author of the "Inside" series; public opinion pollsters George Gallup and Elmo Roper and others.

CFR member William Benton is a principal owner of the Encyclopedia Brittanica, which may account for the omission of Alger Hiss' role in the founding of the United Nations in this standard reference work.[38]

Senator Jenner described a "political action group" with its own pressure groups, political support organizations, etc. CFR members hold controlling influence in the American Association for the United Nations, The Foreign Policy Association, World Affairs Council, U. S. Committee for the United Nations, United World Federalists, Atlantic Union, NATO Citizens Council, and other one-world propaganda organizations. The Council for Economic Development, Business Advisory Council, and the Advertising Council are similarly controlled.[39]

ACCORDING TO PLAN

What are the goals of this small organization whose members exert such influence on the United States and the world?

Since 1945, CFR members have largely controlled the United States government and its foreign policy. In that time, world communism has increased the number of its slaves by 520% to over one-billion. Communism has received no serious setback in its drive toward world domination, despite military and foreign aid expenditures of over $500-billion by the U. S. government to "fight" communism. That record, in itself, is an indictment.

The writings and speeches of CFR members reveal that the failures of the West have not been accidents. Events since World War II have developed largely according to plan.

Arthur Schlesinger, Jr., member of the CFR and special assistant to Presidents Kennedy and Johnson, spelled out the "no-win" policy which the CFR-dominated State Department has been following since 1945. Writing in the May-June 1947 issue of *Partisan Review,* Schlesinger said:

> Reduced to its fundamentals, the American problem is to arrange the equilibrium of forces in the world so that, at every given moment of decision, the Soviet General Staff will decide against aggressions that might provoke a general war on the ground that they present too great a risk. At the same time, the U. S. must not succumb to demands for an anti-Soviet crusade nor permit reactionaries in the buffer states to precipitate conflicts in defense of their own obsolete perogatives.[40]

The United States, according to Schlesinger, should *not* try to "win" over communism, free the captive peoples, *or even permit them to free themselves*. The "obsolete perogatives" which Schlesinger would deny to the Eastern Europeans, Tibetans, Laotians, Koreans and others in the satellites are national sovereignty, and freedom — the right to choose their own governments. Is this one man's view? Schlesinger said:

> Can the United States conceive and initiate so subtle a policy? Though the secret has been kept pretty much from the readers of the liberal press, the State Department has been proceeding for some time along these lines. Both Byrnes and Marshall have perceived the essential need to be firm without being rancorous, to check Soviet expansion without making unlimited commitments to the anti-Soviet crusade, to invoke power to counter power without engaging in senseless intimidation, to encourage the growth of the democratic left. The performance has often fallen below the conception, but the direction has been correct. Men like Ben Cohen, Dean Acheson, and Charles Bohlen (all CFR members-Auth.) have tried to work out the details and whip up support for this admittedly risky program.[41]

The "risky" policy of containment-rather-than-victory which Schlesinger outlined, and which the State Department still follows, has resulted in nearly 800-million people going behind the Iron and Bamboo Curtains. The leaders of the "democratic left" which the policy was to encourage — Mao Tsetung, Ben Bella, Sukarno, Nkrumah, Adoula, Lumumba, Fidel Castro, Juan Bosch, Romulo Betancourt, and Cheddi Jagan — inevitably turn out to be communists, or complete tools of the world communist movement.

John Foster Dulles was perhaps the most successful practitioner of the "admittedly risky program" which Schlesinger outlined. A founder of the CFR, Dulles served in the State Department as an assistant and adviser to Dean Acheson and later as Secretary of State under President Eisenhower. Dulles was widely acclaimed for slowing down the Soviet offensive from the pace it maintained under Acheson. Few realize, however, that he promoted no aggressive steps to topple their empire.

Under his direction, the State Department initiated aid to communist countries and cultural exchanges, agreed to permanent partitions of Korea and Viet Nam, tolerated and encouraged the rise of "neutralism" and implemented the rule laid down eight years before by Schlesinger in denying the Hungarians their right to win their revolt.

To understand Dulles' actions, it is necessary to ignore his vigorous anti-communist statements and well-publicized policy of "brinkmanship" and learn his true beliefs and goals from his early writings.

In 1942, Dulles was chairman of the Federal Council of Churches Commission to Study the Bases of a Just and Durable Peace. The report he prepared recommended:

> . . . a world government, strong immediate limitation on national sovereignty, international control of all armies and navies, a universal system of money, world-wide freedom of immigration, progressive elimination of all tariff and quota restrictions on world trade and a democratically-controlled world bank.[42]

The report also called for world-wide redistribution of wealth. It held that a "new order of economic life is both imminent and imperative." It accepted Marxian concepts by denouncing various defects in the profit system as being responsible for breeding war, demagogues, and dictators.

Four years later, Dulles authored another statement for the Federal Council of Churches. Entitled, *Soviet-American Relations,* it was published in the Council's 1946 Biennial Report. It is one of the earliest published speculations that "changes" in both Russia and the United States will make possible a merger of the two systems into a world government. Dulles said:

> Moreover, Communism as an economic program for social reconstruction has points of contact with the social message of Christianity as in its avowed concern for the underprivileged and its insistence on racial equality . . . neither state socialism nor free enterprise provides a perfect economic system; each can learn from the experience of the other . . . the free enterprise system has yet to prove it can assure steady production and employment . . . Soviet socialism has changed much particularly in placing greater dependence upon the incentive of personal gain.[43]

In finding similarities between Communism and Christianity, Dulles chose to ignore the mass murder of 20-million human beings in the first 25 years of Communist control of Russia and the 15-million persons in Soviet slave labor camps as he spoke. In the 17 years after Dulles saw signs of "mellowing" the communists have exterminated another 40-million people in Russia, China, Hungary, Cuba, Poland, Tibet and Korea.

When Methodist Bishop G. Bromley Oxnam revealed in testimony before the House Committee on Un-American Activities in 1953 that Dulles was the author of the statement, the *Chicago Tribune* suggested editorially that Scott McLeod, State Department Security Chief, might do some checking on his boss.[44]

The thesis that communism is mellowing, first stated by Dulles in 1946, is the underlying theme of most CFR-influenced projects. It is the basis for the overall State Department policy plan prepared by Walt Whitman Rostow (CFR) which was discussed in Chapter IV.[45]

In accepting the theory that communism is "mellowing," these CFR members reject the concept that communism is total evil. Dulles' comparison of communism with the "social message of Christianity" is indicative of this viewpoint. There are other examples. Arthur Schlesinger, Jr., in the article previously quoted, "condemned" communism in this way:

> The crime of the USSR against the world is its determination to make experiments in libertarian socialism impossible.[46]

Was not the extermination of millions of human beings a crime, Mr. Schlesinger? A similar attitude was expressed by a panel assembled by the Rockefeller Brothers in 1956 to study the major problems facing the world. Of the 14 citizens serving on the Foreign Policy panel, nine were CFR members, including Philip Moseley, director of studies for the CFR, John Nason, president of the CFR "subsidiary," the Foreign Policy Association, Dean Rusk, and Adolf Berle, Jr. About communism and the Soviet threat and U. S. reactions to it, their final report states:

> It has been necessary to drum up support for United States policy by stressing the imminent threats and crisis and *by harping on the less attractive features of communism,* including the brutalities of the regime and the persistent exploitation of its own and other peoples.[47]

What features of communism does this CFR-dominated panel find attractive? Perhaps, they share the attitude expressed by Arthur Schlesinger, Jr. who on his return from the Soviet Union stated:

> The answer to the Soviet success is as plain as day. It lies in the power of the Soviet Union to focus its national energies. The visitor to Soviet Russia finds it frightening to see what energy a great nation can generate when it allocates its talent and resources according to an intelligent system of priorities.[48]

If this communist dictatorship is the success that Schlesinger envies, why was it necessary for the United States to ship the Soviet Union $11-billion in lend-lease aid during World War II? Why can't the Soviets produce sufficient food for their people? Why must the United States pump billions of dollars in aid into the Soviet satellites and supply Russia itself with machine tools, industrial plants, and technical know-how?

WHY?

As Americans awaken to examine the U. S. State Department's long and consistent record of aid and comfort to the communist enemy, and read the statements of those who formulate the policies, they logically ask, "Are these people communists or communist sympathizers? If they aren't communists why do they protect communism at every opportunity, send aid to communist countries, help install Castro in power knowing that he was a communist and now protect him from anti-communist harassment?

The answer was provided by another CFR-member, Dr. Lincoln P. Bloomfield, in an official study entitled, *A World Effectively Controlled by the United Nations*. It was prepared on a contract with the State and Defense Departments in 1962. In it, Dr. Bloomfield discloses, perhaps unwittingly, why U. S. planners consistently aid world communism. He says:

> . . . if the communist dynamic was greatly abated, the west might lose whatever incentive it has for world government.[49]

That is the answer. *If American aid were stopped, the communist empire would likely collapse*. The internationalists would lose their principal arguments for turning American weapons over to a UN peace force, instituting world-wide redistribution of American wealth, and the socialization of America, all of which are advocated as necessary to meet the "threat of communism."

Of course, the communists are working for world government also. That is why Alger Hiss, Harry Dexter White, Lauchlin Currie and other agents, sympathizers, and dupes have worked within the CFR. The communists need a world government to achieve world domination. They are confident that once a world governing body is established in coalition with American socialists, internationalists, and idealists that they, the communists, can control it, just as they have controlled every other coalition government into which they have entered.

Naturally, all 1,400 members of the Council on Foreign Relations do not advocate a socialized economy and one world government. They do, however, support individual "pieces" of the overall program. Senator Jenner, in the speech quoted earlier, explained with a story how patriotic Americans help the movement bent on destroying America without comprehending the ultimate results of their actions. He said:

> Under the Nazi regime in Germany, a man worked making baby carriages. His wife was going to have a baby, but the Nazi government would not let anybody buy a baby carriage. The man decided he would secretly collect one part from each department and assemble the carriage himself.
>
> When the time came he and his wife gathered up the pieces and assembled them. When they finished they did not have a baby carriage. They had a machine gun.[50]

That story, Senator Jenner said, explains what has been happening to our form of government. He continued:

> Someone, somewhere, conceived the brilliant strategy of revolution by assembly line. The pattern for total revolution was divided into separate parts, each of them as innocent, safe and familiar looking as possible. But . . . when the parts of a design are carefully cut to exact size, to fit other parts with a perfect fit in final assembly, the parts must be made according to a blueprint drawn up in exact detail.
>
> The men who make the blueprints know exactly what the final product is to be . . . This assembly line revolution is like a time-bomb . . . It is ready to go off, but it is not going to be set off until the time is ripe, until a switch is pulled. The switch is not to be pulled until the American people are conditioned, or convinced that resistance is hopeless.[51]

Thus loyal Americans — businessmen, editors, Congressmen, civic leaders — are entrapped into producing the pieces and supporting the programs which when assembled can destroy the United States.

What are these pieces? Some of them have been discussed separately: Disarmament, foreign aid, and assistance to keep the communist empire from disintegrating, the socialization of the American economy to permit easy merger into a one-world socialist system, the power treaties have to over-ride or supersede the Constitution. How do they all fit together?

FOREIGN AID

Each year, as protests against foreign aid spending develop, Americans are told that because they are the richest people on earth they must help the poorer countries to keep them from going communist.

As a result, in the years 1945-63, the United States added $106-billion to its national debt,[52] borrowing this money to give $107-billion in foreign aid to 80 countries.[53] The recipients of this American aid have a combined national debt substantially less than that of the "rich" United States.

By 1963, the drain on the American economy and credit had reached a point where national bankruptcy was entirely possible. American gold reserves available to meet foreign obligations dropped to below $4-billion while the U. S. owed other countries $22-billion, payable in gold.[54] If these creditors demanded payment, bankruptcy would result.

This risk might be worth taking if the slogan a Missouri senator uses to justify his foreign aid votes were valid. He regularly tells constituents, "I'd rather vote dollars to fight communism than send American boys to die."
No one can dispute the sentiment, but unfortunately, most American foreign aid dollars *help* rather than *harm* communism.

As has been discussed, since the early foreign aid grants which helped Europe to rebuild after World War II, manipulation of U. S. aid has been a key factor in the communization of Poland, Yugoslavia, China, Laos, Indonesia, British Guiana, Ghana, and Algeria. Over $6-billion has been given directly to the communist enemy.

Foreign aid has been used to socialize the economies of once friendly nations. Established patterns of life have been disrupted. The turmoil and chaos necessary for eventual communization have been created with foreign aid money. For example:

> Multi-million dollar public housing developments were built on the outskirts of five Lebanese cities. Natives of mountain villages were enticed to occupy the housing projects. When these villagers left their farms, they lost their livelihood, and the drop in food production caused a national crisis.[55]

Bolivia is a prime example of how U. S. foreign aid has been used, not to raise living standards of the poor, but to socialize an economy:

> In 1952, a new revolutionary government siezed Bolivia's tin mines, the country's principal industry. The railroads were also nationalized. Under government operation, the number of

miners has doubled, even though tin output has dropped by 50%. The mines and the railroads, once operated at a profit, have been losing $20-million a year, subsidized by annual American foreign aid grants of this amount. The aid has simply paid for the bureaucratic inefficiency which socialism always produces — while inflation and higher taxes have actually lowered the living standard of the people.[56]

Most Americans, in believing that foreign aid stops communism, do not realize that Joseph Stalin was one of the earliest proponents of American aid to under-developed nations. In 1944, in his book, *Marxism and the National Colonial Question,* Stalin said:

It is essential that the advanced countries should render aid — real and prolonged aid — to the backward countries in their cultural and economic development. Otherwise, it will be impossible to bring about peaceful coexistence of the various nations and peoples — within a single economic system, which is so essential for the final triumph of socialism.[57]

That Stalin advocated foreign aid is not, in itself, a condemnation. However, the results of over $100-billion grants given by the U. S. speak for themselves. Nations have been socialized, friends have been antagonized and destroyed, and the drain on the U. S. economy, public and private, could bring an economic collapse and the socialization of America "which is so essential for the final triumph of Socialism." If foreign aid were limited to small grants for technical assistance to show people how to help themselves, it might do a good job. That was not the role Stalin foresaw for foreign aid — and that is not how it has been administered by American "planners."

GOLD OUTFLOW AND INFLATION

Between 1950 and 1963, the gold bullion owned by the U. S. Treasury which was available to meet foreign obligations dropped by 75%. The overall stock of gold dropped from $24-billion to $15.8-billion.[58]

Theoretically, loss of gold results when foreign nations sell more in America than we sell overseas. The difference, or balance of payment, is settled in gold. Actually, American exports have regularly exceeded imports — but not by enough to cover the cost of foreign aid grants overseas, the sale of agricultural products for "soft" currencies which are not redeemable in gold, and the cost of maintaining our military bases and personnel in foreign lands. The problem has been accentuated because foreign banks and investors are no longer willing to accept U. S. currency in payment. For years, the American dollar was "as good as gold" but inflation produced by unbalanced budgets in 27 of the last 33 years has eroded the value of the dollar. Payments in gold rather than dollars are demanded.

Our gold stock has dwindled steadily. Of the $15.8-billion remaining, almost $12-billion must, by law, be reserved as "backing" for the paper money in circulation. Therefore, by 1963, just under $4-billion was available to meet foreign obligations, *which totaled over $22-billion*.[59] At anytime, the investors, bankers and governments of Western Europe could force America into bankruptcy by demanding payment of American debts in gold — which is not available.

Treasury Secretary Dillon (CFR), economists and bankers like David Rockefeller (CFR) have recommended repeal of the requirement that gold backing equal to 25% of the paper money in circulation be maintained. Such a bill was introduced in the 87th Congress.[60] It would free $12-billion in gold to meet foreign obligations, postponing the crisis *temporarily*.

Without the restraint imposed on the issuance of paper money by the gold reserve requirement, future national deficits could be financed with printing press dollars. Printing press inflation, as contrasted with the gradual, long-term debasement of currency, could reduce the value of the dollar to 10 cents or even one cent within months.

Such runaway inflation would destroy confidence in free enterprise and representative government. The insurance and savings of millions of individuals, rich and poor, would be wiped out.

The resulting "national emergency" could be used as justification for abolishing the constitutional processes and establishing a totalitarian, socialistic government. The Americans who might be expected to oppose such a takeover would have no resources to finance opposition. Their savings would have been confiscated by runaway inflation.

Fantastic? Part of a plan? Do the pieces fit the "blueprint" Senator Jenner discussed? Whether part of a plan or not, the events are developing, the trend is established.

It has happened in several nations. Reporting on his experience in Hungary in 1946, *Saturday Evening Post* writer Demaree Bess said:

> . . . the Russians had unleashed the wildest currency inflation on record . . . that wild inflation was aimed at certain groups of Hungarians as deliberately as guns aimed in battles.

It wiped out the savings of the country's most solid citizens, the thrifty, and hard-working middle class.[61]

In the same article, Demaree Bess described how inflation was a key weapon in the communization of China. He said:

> When Red Armies entered Shanghai, they were openly greeted by the Shanghai American Chamber of Commerce in the belief that they could not possibly be more dangerous to business interests than Chiang's inflation had been. Those Americans, like their Chinese counterparts, soon discovered how wrong they were. But then it was too late.[62]

The inflation which discredited Chiang Kai-shek's government was planned in Washington by Assistant Secretary of the Treasury Harry Dexter White (CFR) and implemented in China by the Treasury Department's representative, Solomon Adler, who was also a communist agent.[63]

A similar pattern was established in Bolivia. When the revolutionary MNR group siezed power in 1952, a systematic program of runaway inflation was implemented. The free market rate of exchange on the Bolivian peso for the dollar stood at 190 on the day of the revolution. Four years later, the exchange rate was 15,000 pesos for one dollar.[64] The Bolivian citizen who had pesos worth $10,000 on the day of the revolution had buying power of only $125 four years later. The Minister of Foreign Affairs of the revolutionary MNR government as much as admitted that the inflation was planned to destroy political opposition. In commenting on the failure of other revolutions, he said:

> Liberalism liquidated conservatism politically but not economically . . . It let the conservatives keep economic power in their hands. This was a great mistake: those who retain economic power will one day recover political power.[65]

The lesson of Bolivia should stand as a warning. It could happen here. It will happen here unless more Americans awaken to reverse the trend which has taken the nation to the brink of fiscal disaster.

TREATIES VS. THE CONSTITUTION

A key "piece" in the blueprint for revolution described by Senator Jenner is an interpretation of the U. S. Constitution which permits the Constitution to be changed — *or even abolished* — by a treaty. Article VI provides:

> This Constitution, and the Laws of the United States which shall be made in Pursuance thereof; and all Treaties made, or which shall be made, under the Authority of the United States, shall be the supreme Law of the Land; and the Judges in every

State shall be bound thereby, any Thing in the Constitution or Laws of any State to the Contrary, notwithstanding.[66]

As interpreted by the U. S. Supreme Court, this means that treaties supersede the Constitution. American rights of freedom of speech, religion, press, assembly, etc. can be changed or abolished by a treaty.

The first such Supreme Court ruling was in the case, *Ware vs. Hylton,*[67] in 1796. The taking of Hylton's property to fulfill a treaty with Great Britain, in violation of the "due process" clause of the Fifth Amendment, was upheld.

In a more recent case, *Missouri vs. Holland,*[68] the Supreme Court decided in 1920 that powers reserved to the States by the Tenth Amendment to the Constitution could be given to the national government by a treaty.

In 1942, the doctrine that treaties supersede or over-ride the Constitution was extended to apply to executive agreements negotiated by the President, or in the name of the President by members of the bureaucracy. In this case, *United States vs. Pink,*[69] the Court held that a personal agreement between President Roosevelt and the Russian Foreign Minister, Litvinov, nullified provisions of the laws of New York state, and of the American Constitution, which forbid confiscation of private property.

The implications are frightening. The founding fathers envisioned that the Constitution could be changed only with the approval of three-fourths of the states. Today, an executive agreement, perhaps made in secret without Congress and the States being aware of it, much less approving, can at some future date be judged to have changed the Constitution.

In 1954, during debate on a Constitutional Amendment which would have corrected this "loophole" in the Constitution, Senator William Jenner reviewed the situation. He said:

Since 1920, we have had the most insidious development of this new principle by one little extension after another. The doctrine that treaties were outside the limits of the Constitution meant that they were above the laws of the States. The doctrine that treaties were above the Constitution was soon extended to executive agreements.

If we note that today executive agreements mean personal arrangements, like that between Roosevelt and Litvinov, or administrative decisions by a minor foreign policy official like John Stewart Service; if we add that these agreements on foreign affairs now spread into areas formerly considered purely domestic, we come closer to the full measure of our danger.[70]

The danger is great. Over 10,000 executive agreements

have been negotiated with reference to the North Atlantic Treaty Organization alone.[71] Many of these are secret, yet, all have the power to over-ride the Constitution. The tragic Yalta Pact, part of which has never been revealed, has the power to supersede the Constitution.

Other agreements and treaties are proposed or made nearly every day. Any one could have the power to destroy the United States, the Constitution, and the rights of American citizens. For example:

A proposed United Nations Treaty Against Genocide provides penalties for causing "mental harm" to a member of a minority group. Such an offender, under the terms of the treaty, could be arrested, transported abroad, and tried without a jury and punished by the proposed International Criminal Court.[72]

Refusing to give a Negro, Catholic, or Jew a job for any reason, or describing such minorities in derogatory terms could be construed by the International Court as causing "mental harm." Even though these actions are deplorable, the "remedies" proposed by the Treaty would violate an American citizen's rights of freedom of speech, to trial by jury, and to trial in the State and District where the crime is alleged to have been committed.[73] The Congress would be prevented by Article I and Amendments IX and X of the Constitution from defining such actions as crimes — but a treaty would do so. Even so, the Treaty was endorsed by the State Department. It is, however, still awaiting the action by the Senate which would make it the law of the land. Other UN Treaties on Human Rights, against discrimination in education, etc. have similar rights-destroying "hooks."

During debate on the Bricker Amendment which would have closed this Constitutional loophole, Senator Pat McCarran (D-Nev) showed that obligations assumed by the United States in Articles 55 and 56 of the UN Charter gives Congress absolute powers prohibited to it by the Constitution. He said:

The Congress of the United States today, because of power granted to it by treaty, could enact laws . . . taking over all private and parochial schools, destroying all local school boards . . . and substituting a federal system. If Congress should find that international cultural cooperation required international control of all radio communications . . . Congress could by law provide for censoring all radio programs . . . it could provide for censoring of all press telegrams.

Congress could utilize this power to put into effect a complete system of socialized medicine, from cradle to grave . . . Congress could even legislate *compulsory* labor, if it found that the (UN Charter's) goal of full employment required such legislation or would be served by it.[74]

The Bricker Amendment would have safeguarded American rights and the Constitution from destruction by treaties. It would have prevented world government through a "backdoor approach." It provided:

> A provision of a treaty or other international agreement which conflicts with this Constitution, or which is not made in pursuance thereof, shall not be the supreme law of the land nor be of any force or effect.[75]

The Bricker Amendment received a favorable 60-31 majority in the U. S. Senate, but was one vote shy of the two-thirds majority needed for passage. President Eisenhower and Secretary of State John Foster Dulles used the full prestige of their offices to defeat the measure. Both claimed the amendment would hamper the President in conducting American foreign policy.

Concerned Americans might ask how the Bricker Amendment would have hampered the conduct of *legitimate* American foreign policy. Were those who opposed it planning treaties and agreements which would conflict with the Constitution? Were they protecting such agreements already in existence?

An agreement which could be enforced to limit the right of Americans to speak out against communism or advocate the defense of Laos, Berlin or Cuba or even the United States, may already be in effect.

When Soviet Foreign Minister Andrei Gromyko proposed an agreement to outlaw "war propaganda" at the Geneva disarmament talks early in 1962, American Secretary of State Dean Rusk rightly termed such a ban "impossible." Rusk said that enforcement would infringe on the Constitutional rights of private citizens and the press to criticize communists or advocate firm action against communism.

Yet, six weeks later on May 25, 1962, the United States and the Soviet Union agreed on a *Joint Declaration Against War Propaganda*.[76] Under its terms . . .

> . . . an American who suggests blockade or invasion of Cuba, or engages in other "war propaganda" activities may be risking "condemnations" or "punishment by appropriate practical measures, including measures in legislative form."[77]

Decoded, the legal double-talk means that offenders may be jailed or have other punitive action taken against them.

The communists withdrew their approval of the joint

declaration within four days so whether it is still binding on the United States is not clear.

It could be a "ticking timebomb" waiting for some nation to ask the International Court of Justice (World Court) to order the United States to enforce a "gag" on its citizens and press.

In such an event, the U. S. citizen would have one protection, if the U. S. State Department used it. Before ratifying the United Nations Charter in 1945, the U. S. Senate amended the agreement on the International Court of Justice Statute to bar the Court from jurisdiction over matters which were essentially domestic "as determined by the United States."

Without that six word reservation authored by Senator Tom Connally (D-Tex) the World Court might interfere in American internal affairs on the pretext that our tariffs, immigration policies, racial conflicts, or school curriculums affect U. S. relations with other countries and are therefore "foreign" and not "domestic."

Advocates of repealing the Connally Reservation and removing this safeguard for the American people include Presidents Eisenhower and Kennedy and leading members of Congress. They attack the reservations as a "roadblock" to achieving "world peace through world law." This is an idealistic slogan which is, unfortunately, meaningless. There is no significant body of international law except maritime regulations. The Statute of the Court specifically prohibits building up an acceptable body of international law by forbidding the use of prior decisions as precedents in future cases. Article 59 of the Statute provides:

> The decision of the Court has no binding force except between the parties and in respect of that particular case.[78]

Therefore, the judges can make a decision favoring a communist nation using one set of standards and refuse to grant the United States the same consideration under the same circumstances. This places the judges in the unique position of deciding what the "law" shall be for each case they hear. There is no appeal from their decisions, no matter how unjust,[79] and the decisions can be enforced with the military power of the United Nations "peace force."[80]

THE UN PEACE FORCE

As has been discussed, what is widely labeled as "disarmament" is in reality a transfer of the weapons of the world — and therefore the power to rule the world — to the United

Nations. If this should be accomplished, and the official policy of the U. S. Government is to work for this end, then a decision of the Court could be enforced on the United States. If, for example, the Court should decide that the wealth of America is a source of irritation to less well-to-do nations, it could order that America's wealth be redistributed throughout the world.

The UN Peace Force would be charged with enforcing that edict. If all American weapons had already been transferred to the UN, the U. S. could not resist the Court order. Such a set of circumstances seem fantastic — but they follow exactly the reasoning and justification given by the UN for using armed force to prohibit self-determination for the people of Katanga in Africa.[81]

IS THERE A PLAN?

Is there a conspiratorial plan to destroy the United States into which foreign aid, planned inflation, distortion of treaty-making powers and disarmament all fit?

This question divides many knowledgeable and dedicated conservatives. They waste time and effort and split their ranks with senseless debate. It doesn't really matter whether the "parts" have been planned for an "assembly line revolution" as Senator Jenner charged, or if they are the work of well-meaning but misguided idealists.

The fact is that the "pieces" exist. They fit the pattern whether they were planned by the communists or some other secret and msyterious revolutionary group or not. They can be used by the communists or other power seekers.

To some, the implications of foreign aid, the gold outflow situation, the aid and comfort to communists by elected and appointed officials, the abuse of treaty-making, etc. are over-powering. A key factor in the plan is to make the "trend" look "inevitable" — to convince Americans that resistance is hopeless.

Those who have constructed the "pieces" are few in number, but they exert fantastic control in government, financial circles, the press, unions, schools, etc.

The power of an informed people can be greater. People still have the right to vote, the freedom to educate and alert. These are difficult, time-consuming, costly, and often discouraging jobs. They can be done. They must be done. There is still time to reverse the trend in 1964 by putting patriots in Washington, in state capitals, and in county court houses and on city councils and school boards.

Senator Jenner sounded the call in 1954 — but he was not heard. His message must be taken across our nation if America is to survive. He said:

The American people may be confused about minor issues. They may accept for a time so-called remedies for very real difficulties, which eat away at the foundation of their liberties. But once they recognize any act of government or party or faction as a threat to their Constitution they will rise up in determined anger. . . .

In times of danger to the Constitution there can be no partisan differences between the historic political parties which work under the Constitution. . . . The line of division today is between real Democrats and real Republicans on one side in defense of the Constitution, and on the other the secret revolutionaries and those they have brainwashed in their ruthless pursuit of power.

That is the task — to educate and alert the great mass of apathetic Americans to the danger and to show them what to do.

Chapter XIV

What Can You Do?

> *It is natural to man to indulge in the illusions of hope. We are apt to shut our eyes against a painful truth . . . Is this the part of wise men, engaged in a great and arduous struggle for liberty? Are we disposed to be of the number of those who, having eyes, see not. and having ears, hear not, the things which so nearly concern their temporal salvation? For my part, whatever anguish of spirit it may cost, I am willing to know the whole truth; to know the worst and to provide for it.*
>
> — *Patrick Henry*[1]

DO WE FACE A HOPELESS BATTLE? Has time run out for America? The answer is up to *you*.

The end will not come when the commissars finally haul 60-million hopelessly diseased, capitalistic "animals" off to liquidation centers or when Communist Party Chief, Gus Hall, gets his wish to see the "last Congressman strangled to death with the guts of the last preacher."

If the battle is lost, the real end will come long before. It will come when those who oppose collectivism have been so discredited by smears, discouraged by disasters, or divided by dissenters that they can no longer continue to fight.

The end will come when businessmen accept "You can't fight city hall" as their philsophy and settle down to "exist" within the framework of a completely-controlled, federally-dominated economy. When fear of a lost government contract, an income tax audit, or the disfavor of a vocal customer is more important for most Americans than standing up for principle, the fight will be over.

The battle will be lost, not when freedom of speech is finally taken away, but when Americans become so "adjusted" or "conditioned" to "getting along with the group" that when they finally see the threat, they say, "I can't afford to be controversial." Time will run out for free men, when individuals read facts like those in this book, shrug their shoulders, and say, "What can one person do? It's too big to fight."

How far down that path are we? Look around and see for yourself. We are losing rapidly. A cold analysis of the world situation and of the degree of control exercised by the collectivists can only produce the realization that the odds against our survival are great.

The communists are extremely close to total victory. But it is not inevitable. Their one fear is that Americans will awake in time to the danger and do something about it.

That is our hope and our challenge.

What should you do?

Before his death, the late Congressman Francis Walter (D-Pa) who served for eight years as Chairman of the House Committee on Un-American Activities gave Americans a brief, but concise guide to follow. His statement, *How to Fight Communism,* said:

> Get the facts . . . get the help of others . . . organize . . . act.[2]

The words of J. Edgar Hoover quoted in the first chapter of this book tell how to get the facts. Mr. Hoover said of communism and its threat:

> The way to fight it is to study it, understand it, and discover what can be done about it. This cannot be accomplished by dawdling at the spring of knowledge; it can only be achieved by dipping deeply into thoughtful, reliable, and authoritative sources of information.[3]

Two years earlier, Mr. Hoover issued a similar statement, and added:

> This program must encompass, not only a penetrating study of Communism, but also a thorough grounding in the basic principles of our individual freedom under law.[4]

Within those two statements can be found the basic guidelines for intelligent action against communism. Congressman Walter gave more detailed advice, saying:

> Get the facts. Study communism. You can't fight an enemy you don't know. This is a fundamental rule of warfare. Learn communism's basic doctrines, its strategy, its tactics; its line on current national and international affairs; the names of major communist fronts and leading communists and fellow travellers. This is minimum knowledge required for effective anti-communism.[5]

ENLIST OTHERS

Once you have informed yourself, the next most important

job is awakening others. Congressman Walter gave this advice:

> Get the help of others. Two heads are better than one —
> and ten men are more powerful than two.[6]

Before you can convince others you must gain their attention and build respect for your knowledge. The communists recognize this fact. In the official communist *Manual on Organization,* party members are given these instructions:

> In order to win the confidence of the workers, the unit must
> be able to give a correct answer to every question which bothers
> the workers. The units must follow very carefully every step
> that is taken by the capitalist class in the city and county
> councils, state legislatures, and Congress and expose all their
> moves.[7]

Can you do less? Communists use "facts" slanted to tell the communist story. They present them in person or in the propaganda they spread through the communications media they control. You can only combat the false propaganda with the truth.

To stay informed, once you get a basic knowledge, try to read at least two daily newspapers with opposite editorial viewpoints. In addition, subscribe to at least one weekly newspaper or magazine which specializes in depth coverage of conservative activities. There are many of varying format, quality, price, etc. Several are:

HUMAN EVENTS	THE WANDERER	DAN SMOOT REPORT
410 First St., S.E.	128 E. 10th St.	P. O. Box 9538, Lakewood
Washington 3, D. C.	St. Paul, Minn.	Dallas 14, Texas
$9 per year	$5 per year	$10 per year

All three publications are factual in their news presentation. In the *opinions* presented they do not always agree. They are, however, among the very few publications which documented the communist background of Fidel Castro while most news media pictured him as an idealistic liberal. The *Wanderer,* listed above, is a Catholic publication. Several Protestant publications are: *Christian Beacon,* Box 190, Collingswood, N. J., $2 per year and *Christian Economics,* 250 W. 57th Street, New York 19, N. Y.

TAKE ACTION

Once you are informed — and have started to inform others — you must start acting. Knowledge without action produces demoralization. Congressman Walter gave this admonition:

Knowledge that is not put to use is wasted. No matter how much you learn about communism, you will contribute nothing to the fight against it unless you . . . translate your learning into deeds that weaken communism.

Uncoordinated action has little effect. Too many concerned people jump from project to project, never completing any. Congressman Walter warned:

Organize your helpers and plan your action. Mere numbers are not enough. Any project you undertake should have at least as much planning and organization as the communists normally put into their schemes. And that's plenty.

It is not necessary to form your own organization. Thousands have already been formed by concerned Americans, including this author. Many have been ineffective because of lack of resources, inability of part-time leadership to plan and supervise activities, and lack of coordinated effort between small groups.

There are a number of well established national organizations. Some, like the American Legion and the Daughters of the American Revolution oppose communism as part of their overall program. Others, like the John Birch Society, are primarily anti-communist organizations. Still others are formed for a single purpose, such as opposing Red China's admission to the UN. Well established, national conservative anti-communist groups likely to have a local branch near you include: The John Birch Society, Belmont 78, Mass.; The Cardinal Mindszenty Foundation, P. O. Box 321, St. Louis 5, Mo.; and the Christian Anti-Communism Crusade, P. O. Box 890, Long Beach 1, Calif.

The John Birch Society is a non-sectarian organization directed by a full-time staff of over 120 people who coordinate the group's program of education and action against communism. The society operates 100 anti-communist book stores, a speakers bureau, a monthly magazine, and two publishing companies. The Cardinal Mindszenty Foundation is a Catholic-oriented group directed by a council of bishops and priests who have lived and suffered under communism. It offers a study program on communism and distributes radio programs and newspaper columns on communism nationally. The Christian Anti-Communism Crusade is fundamentally Protestant. It conducts anti-communism schools and seminars in the U. S. and supports an extensive Christian missionary program overseas. All three groups are supported by persons of all religious faiths.

MISCELLANEOUS GROUPS

Christian Crusade, Tulsa 2, Okla. and the Twentieth Century Reformation Hour, Collingswood, N. J. are fundamental Christian organizations which sponsor anti-communist broadcasts on hundreds of radio stations daily. Check the radio guide or write to the group for the station nearest you.

There are dozens of other organizations which specialize in exposing the communist attack against certain segments of American society, including: America's Future, 542 Main St., New Rochelle, N. Y. (schools); Church League of America, Wheaton, Ill. and Circuit Riders, Inc., 110 Government Place, Cincinnati 2, Ohio (churches); Americans for Constitutional Action, 20 E. St., N.W., Washington 1, D. C. (politics); Young Americans for Freedom, 514 C Street, N.E., Washington 2, D. C. (youth); The Foundation for Economic Education, Irvington-on-Hudson, N. Y. (economics); plus many, many others.

Concerned Americans should carefully investigate the goals, programs, policy, personnel, and leadership of these or other anti-communism organizations to decide for themselves how effective they are. Rather than judge solely on word of mouth or the sometimes slanted newspaper accounts, write to any or all for their literature.

GET INTO POLITICS

A program for victory over communism cannot be achieved until Americans elect a President and a Congress with the will to win *and* the courage to "cleanse" the policy-making agencies of government of those who, for one reason or another, have aided the communists down through the years. To accomplish this, conservative Americans must make their voices heard in the political parties.

The Communist Party General Secretary, Gus Hall, sees this danger to communism and is working to prevent it. In June 1963 he ordered communists to join with the "non-communist left" within the Democratic Party to elect candidates of the "people's political movements" (i.e., Red favored movements) and to . . .

    . . . single out for defeat such individuals as Keating and Dodd, as well as a number of others.[8]

Hall specifically called for the purging from the Republican Party of the ultra-right (anti-communist) forces. Hall admitted that while "moderates" of the Eisenhower-Kuechel wing of the Republican Party had not lost out completely . . .

. . . as can be seen from the speech of Senator Keuchel of California . . . the alliance of the ultra-right and Conservative aggressive imperialist elements has pushed the Republican Party to the right.[9]

Within two weeks after Hall's demand for defeat of the ultra-right in the Republican Party, a massive smear campaign was launched in major news media, with a lengthy article, *Rampant Right Invades the GOP,* in *Look* magazine's July 16, 1963 issue. Nelson Rockefeller called upon Senator Barry Goldwater to repudiate his ultra-right support.[10] Drew Pearson and other prominent columnists, wittingly or unwittingly fell into line with the Gus Hall directive. Pearson accused Young Republicans of "fascist tactics" in electing a Goldwater supporter as their national chairman.[11]

Within six weeks after Gus Hall issued his order against the ultra-right, the "purge" reached all the way down to the local level as "modern Republican" officials fired conservative precinct captains and workers.

Whether the American people, in general, and rank-and-file Republicans, in particular, will fall for the communist-led attack to drive the anti-communists out of key positions in the Republican Party will probably be a major factor in determining whether the battle against communism is won or lost. If the communists and the "liberal internationalists" control the presidential nominations in both parties in 1964, as they have for 30 years, the hope for victory over communism will receive a massive setback. Work in the party organizations by informed conservatives can prevent this.

Cries of "We are being sold out to the communists" or decrying the strength and success of the AFL-CIO machine will not win the 1964 elections. COPE has devised no secret formula for winning elections. It puts into practice the instructions an obscure county chairman of the Whig Party gave his workers in 1840. His name was Abraham Lincoln, and he said:

. . . the following is the plan of organization . . . divide (your) county into small districts, and . . . appoint in each a subcommittee, whose duty it shall be to make a perfect list of all the voters in their respective districts, and to ascertain with certainty for whom they will vote . . . keep a constant watch on the doubtful voters, and from time to time have them talked to by those in whom they shall have the most confidence . . . on election days see that every Whig is brought to the polls.[12]

Lincoln knew that elections are not necessarily won by the party or candidate which is right — but by the organization which gets its voters to the polls. Issues and beliefs of a candidate are important — but they cannot win unless they are backed by a functioning organization geared to locate friendly voters, register them, and get them to the polls on election day . . . then, keep the election honest.

Issues, properly used, can motivate average, apathetic citizens to become doorbell ringers for candidates with principles. Several thousand informed, motivated workers in a congressional district of several hundred thousand voters can turn the tide, *if they are properly trained, organized and directed*.

In 1962, for example, 29-year old William Brock of Lookout Mountain, Tennessee ran for Congress in a district where Democrats outnumbered Republicans 8 to 1. Brock was a Republican, yet he was elected to Congress because his presentation of the issues attracted workers who put Lincoln's plan into action.

Half of the American people cannot be educated about communism overnight. However, if one out of every hundred citizens is alerted, educated and mobilized into a functioning political organization, they can nominate and elect good Americans in 1964.

A SPIRITUAL COMMITMENT

Conservatives can win the political battles necessary to insure America's survival — and still lose the long term war against communism.

J. Edgar Hoover gave the ultimate answer in accepting an award from the Freedom Foundation at Valley Forge on February 22, 1962. He said:

> The basic answer to communism is moral. The fight is economic, social, psychological, diplomatic, strategic — but above all it is spiritual.

Another anonymous writer said the same thing in a slightly different way. His advice:

> Pray to God with the knowledge that everything depends on him — and work as if everything depended on you.

Without God, man can accomplish nothing. Yet, today, unfortunately, millions of Americans attend churches which are "man-centered" rather than "God-centered." Millions of persons who call themselves Christians attend church regularly and have never heard the Bible message of personal and individual salvation.

The answer to man's problems, the solution to the peril

facing America is found in the Holy Scriptures. In II Chronicles 7:14, God tells us:

> If my people, which are called by my name, shall humble themselves and pray and seek my face, and turn from their wicked ways; then will I hear from heaven, and will forgive their sin, and will heal their land.

CONCLUSION

There is much to be done if America is to block communist domination of the world. Much of the work is up to *you*.

First, you must educate yourself. Determine that the facts in this book are true. Then, alert and educate others. Stay informed — and start to act. Join with others who are already well-organized for the battle against communism.

Recognize that those who refuse to work politically to protect their freedom may someday face a choice between fighting with guns or becoming slaves. Avoid being sidetracked into ineffective, defensive actions. Most of all, avoid demoralization. Examine your own personal religious beliefs. Is God a meaningful, consuming force in your life?

The books, literature and other aids you'll need all cost money. Political activity, even on the precinct level, involves expenses. Political campaigns, anti-communist organizations all need financial support. As you evaluate costs, remember that if rampant inflation comes to America your savings will be worthless. If Communism comes to America you will lose not only your money, but your freedom, your children, your home, and possibly your life.

The costs cannot be measured in money alone. Educating and alerting others will not make you popular. Many dedicated Americans have already suffered smears, economic sanctions, and personal attacks for standing up for what they knew was right. J. Edgar Hoover commented on this tragic fact in a speech to the Daughters of the American Revolution in 1954. Mr. Hoover said:

> In taking a stand for preservation of the American way of life, your organization became the target of vile and vicious attacks. So have all other patriotic organizations and, for that matter, every other person who has dared to raise his voice against communism. It is an established fact that whenever one has dared to expose the communist threat he has invited upon himself the adroit and skilled talents of experts of character assassination. The Federal Bureau of Investigation has stood year after year as taunts, insults and destructive criticism have been thrown its way.
>
> To me, one of the most unbelievable and unexplainable

phenomena in the fight on Communism is the manner in which otherwise respectable, seemingly intelligent persons, perhaps unknowingly, aid the Communist cause more effectively than the Communists themselves. The pseudo liberal can be more destructive than the known communist because of the esteem which his cloak of respectability invites.[13]

Six years later, Mr. Hoover repeated much the same message, when in a letter to law enforcement officials, he said:

It is indeed appalling that some members of our society continue to deplore and criticize those who stress the communist danger. What these "misguided" authorities fail to realize is that the Communist Party, USA, is an integral part of international communism. As the world-wide menace becomes more powerful, the various Communist parties assume a more dangerous and sinister role in the countries in which they are entrenched. Public indifference to this threat is tantamount to national suicide.

Lethargy leads only to disaster. . . . Only the intelligent efforts of all Americans can prevent the decay of public apathy from laying open our Nation to the Red Menace.[14]

Because the repeated warnings of J. Edgar Hoover and other great Americans have been suppressed, ignored, and ridiculed, only great sacrifices in time, energy and money will turn the tide.

The choice is yours. You can throw out your chest with pride and say, "It can't happen here." But nearly every one of the 800-million people captured by the communists since 1945 doubtless said the same thing.

The alternative is to begin immediately to educate yourself; to embark on a program of action. If you delay, your motivation will pass, your concern will recede, but the danger will increase.

The choice you must make was enunciated by Winston Churchill when he told the people of England:

If you will not fight for right when you can easily win without bloodshed; if you will not fight when your victory will be sure and not too costly; you may come to the moment when you will have to fight with all the odds against you and only a precarious chance of survival.

Because we have ignored warning after warning, we are now at that place in history. Unless you do your part now, you will face a further choice, also described by Mr. Churchill. He said:

There may be even a worse case. You may have to fight when there is no hope of victory, because it is better to perish than live as slaves.

What will you do?

REFERENCES

Chapter I

1 Lenin, Selected Works, Vol. VII, pg. 298
2 Report, U. S. Foreign Assistance, U. S. Agency for Int. Dev., Mar. 21, 1962
3 Dallas Morning News, Oct. 13, 1961
4 Cong. R. H. Poff, Human Events, Jul. 14, 1961, pg. 443; Nov. 10, 1961, pg. 748; Cong. Pelly, Cong. Record, Aug. 14, 1961
5 N. Y. Times News Service, Dallas Morning News, Jul. 13, 1961
6 Cong. D. L. Latta, Human Events, Aug. 4, 1961, pg. 506
7 Letter, SF/131/1 Cuba, Jun. 8, 1961, Paul Hoffman, Managing Director, United Nations Special Fund
8 Sen. Thomas Dodd, Southern Calif. School of Anti-Communism, Los Angeles, Aug. 28, 1961
9 Ibid.
10 Ibid.
11 Arens, Dangers To U. S. Internal Security, National Education Program, Jun. 22, 1959, pg. 6
12 Ibid.
13 Ibid.
14 House Document 227, 85th Congress, 1st Session, Vol. II, pg. 892
15 Hearings, Communist Threat To The U. S. Through The Caribbean, Senate Internal Security Subcommittee, 86th-87th Congress, Parts 1-12
16 Ibid., pg. 798
17 Ibid., pg. 799
18 National Review, Jan. 16, 1962
19 Report, American Bar Association Committee on Communist Strategy and Tactics, Congressional Record, Aug. 22, 1958
20 Hearings, Communist Threat To The U. S., SISS, pg. 726
21 Senate Report 2050, 82nd Congress, 2nd Session, pg. 224
22 Human Events, Jul. 14, 1961, pg. 437
23 Report, Interlocking Subversion In Government Departments, SISS, 83rd Congress, 1st Session, pg. 6, 8-10
24 Ibid., pg. 29-32
25 Ibid., pg. 5, 40-43
26 Ibid., pg. 5
27 Ibid., pg. 5
28 Ibid., pg. 2
29 Ibid., pg. 1 fn.
30 Donovan, Eisenhower, The Inside Story, pg. 253-4; Adams, First Hand Report, pg. 142-3
31 Hoover, FBI Law Enforcement Bulletin, Apr. 1, 1961

Chapter II

1 Weyl, Red Star Over Cuba, pg. 104-05
2 Skousen, The Naked Communist, pg. 103-04

3 Dodd, Freedom and Foreign Policy, pg. 197-200
4 Burnham, Web Of Subversion, pg. 80
5 The Communist Party, USA, What It Is, How It Works: A Handbook For Americans, Senate Document No. 117, 84th Congress, pg. 43
6 Ibid., pg. 45
7 Ibid., pg. 8
8 Hearing, Communist Espionage in the U. S., Testimony of Frantisek Tisler, HCUA, May 10, 1960, pg. 1726
9 Report, The Communist Mind, HCUA, 85th Congress, May 29, 1957
10 Ibid.
11 Lenin, Selected Works, Vol. IX, pg. 475-8
12 Report, The Communist Mind, HCUA, May 29, 1957
13 Ibid.
14 Ibid.
15 Ibid.
16 St. Louis Globe Democrat, May 12, 1963
17 Skousen, The Naked Communist, pg. 7-30
18 A Manifesto, Fabian Tract No. 2, 1884, quoted: Shaw, Man Of The Century
19 Henderson, George Bernard Shaw, Man Of The Century, An Authorized Biography, pg. 343
20 Ibid., pg. 219
21 Ibid., pg. 240
22 Shaw, Intelligent Woman's Guide To Socialism, pg. 470
23 Webb, Socialism In England, pg. 27, quoted: Keynes At Harvard, pg. 19
24 Henderson, GBS, Man of the Century, pg. 284
25 Keynes At Harvard, pg. 33
26 Hubbard, Political and Economic Structures, pg. 111
27 Ibid., pg. 112
28 Lenin, Selected Works, Vol. II, pg. 155
29 Ibid., Vol. X, pg. 140
30 Lenin, Left-wing Communism, An Infantile Disorder, pg. 38
31 Lenin, Selected Works, Vol. VIII, pg. 284
32 Quoted by J. Edgar Hoover, Struggle On A New Plane, House Doc. 227, pg. 4
33 Hoover, Communist Target Youth, HCUA, Jul. 1960
34 Declaration of 81 Communist Parties, Moscow, Dec. 5, 1960
35 Report, New Drive Against The Anti-Communist Program, SISS, Jul. 11, 1961
36 Moorhead, The Russian Revolution, pg. 81
37 Lansbury, My Life, quoted: Keynes At Harvard, pg. 22
38 Henderson, GBS, Man of the Century, pg. 316
39 Ibid., pg. 310

Chapter III

1 Congressional Record, Sep. 22, 1950, pg. A6832
2 Syndicated Column, Ralph McGill, Miami News, Dec. 5, 1962
3 See page 25
4 World Communist Movement, Selective Chronology, HCUA, 1960, pg. 18
5 Lyons, The Herbert Hoover Story, pg. 190-1
6 Hearing, Export of Strategic Materiel To USSR, SISS, Oct. 23, 1961, Pt. 1, pg. 5
7 Wittmer, The Yalta Betrayal, pg. 14
8 Report, Interlocking Subversion In Government Dept., SISS, Jul. 30, 1952
9 Skousen, The Naked Communist, pg. 164-5
10 Hearings, Shipment of Atomic Material to USSR, HCUA, 81st Cong., pg. 1156
11 Report, Interlocking Subversion In Gov. Dept., SISS, Jul. 30, 1952, pg. 29
12 Hearings, Occupation Currency Transactions, Senate Appropriations, Armed Services and Banking Committees, 1947, pg. 8, 27, 175-9
13 Sherwood, Roosevelt and Hopkins, pg. 590
14 Foreign Relations of the U. S., Diplomatic Papers, The Conferences at Cairo and Teheran, 1943, Dept. of State, 1961
15 Protocol of Proceedings, The Crimea (Yalta) Conference, Feb. 11, 1945, Sec. III, VII, VIII, X, XI
16 Ibid., Agreement Regarding Japan, Sec. 1, 3
17 Welles, Seven Decisions That Shaped History, pg. 217
18 Hearings, Institute of Pacific Relations, SISS, 82nd Congress, pg. 81
19 Senate Report No. 2050, 82nd Congress, 2nd Session
20 Report, Interlocking Subversion In Gov. Depts., SISS, Jul. 30, 1952, pg 32
21 Senate Report 2050, 82nd Congress, 2nd Session, pg. 225
22 Ibid., pg. 224
23 Flynn, While You Slept, Chapter 9
24 Ibid., Chapter 10-11
25 Speech, Acheson, National Press Club, Washington, D. C., Jan. 12, 1950
26 Higgins, Korea and the Fall of MacArthur, pg. 48
27 Ibid., pg. 53, 68
28 Ibid., pg. 91
29 Ibid., pg. 112
30 Hearings, Interlocking Subversion in Gov. Depts., SISS, 1954, pg. 1653-1708; 1711-33; 2019-46; Committee on Armed Forces, Military Situation In The Far East, 1951, pg. 3-320
31 Adams, First Hand Report, The

Story Of The Eisenhower Administration, pg. 28
32 Donovan, Eisenhower, The Inside Story, pg. 126
33 Ibid.
34 Ibid., pg. 125-6
35 Ibid., pg. 126
36 Ibid., pg. 247
37 Ibid., pg. 249
38 Adams, First Hand Report, pg. 381-93
39 Donovan, Eisenhower, The Inside Story, pg. 400
40 Report, U. S. Foreign Assistance, Jul. 1, 1945-Jun. 30, 1961, Revised, Statistics and Reports Div., U. S. Agency for Int. Dev., Mar. 21, 1962, pg. 25
41 Speeches, Tito, Jun. 7-12, 1956
42 Yugoslav Communism, A Critical Study, SISS, Oct. 18, 1961, pg. 258-9, 282
43 Ibid., pg. 283
44 Ibid.
45 Ibid., pg. 266
46 Ibid., pg. 257
47 Morris, No Wonder We Are Losing, pg. 207
48 Report, U. S. Foreign Assistance, Agency For International Dev., Mar. 21, 1961, pg. 33
49 Ibid., pg. 89
50 Judd, Speech, The Basic Themes of Survival, Reserve Officers Association of the United States, Part IV
51 Ibid.
52 Consultations: Soviet Justice; Showplaces Prisons vs. Real Slave Labor Camps, HCUA, Apr. 4, 1960; How The Chinese Reds Hoodwink Visiting Foreigners, HCUA, Apr. 21, 1960
53 Charts, Congressional Record, May 2, 1962, pg. 7028-31
54 Ibid.
55 Ibid.
56 Pennsylvania vs. Nelson, 350 US 497 (1956)
57 Cole vs. Young 351 US 536 (1956)
58 Slochower vs. Board of Education of New York 350 US 551 (1956)
59 Watkins vs. United States 354 US 178 (1957)
60 Consul General For Yugoslavia vs. Artukovic
61 Service vs. Dulles 354 US 363 (1957)
62 Report, Committee on Federal-State Relationships, The Conference of Chief Justices, August 1958
63 Congressional Record, Aug. 22, 1958
64 Hearings On Dept. of Justice, House Appropriations Comm., Jan. 16, 1958, pg. 173-4
65 News Record of 1957, Information Please Almanac, 1958, pg. 11
66 Donovan, Eisenhower, The Inside Story, pg. 253-54
67 Adams, First Hand Report, pg. 142-43

68 Hearings, Institute of Pacific Relations, SISS, pg. 4777-8
69 Ibid., pg. 4776
70 Report, Interlocking Subversion In Gov. Depts., SISS, Jul. 30, 1953, pg. 43-4
71 Hearings, Scope of Soviet Activity In The U. S., SISS, Part 49, Nov. 21, 1956
72 Donovan, Eisenhower, The Inside Story, pg. 246
73 Hearings, Army Personnel Actions Relating To Irving Peress, Senate Comm. on Gov. Operations, Part 3, Mar. 17, 1955, pg. 189; Part 5, Mar. 23, 1955, pg. 389, 424
74 Congressional Record, Nov. 15, 1954, pg. 16039
75 Hearings, Communist Infiltration In The Army, Senate Committee on Gov. Operations, Part 3, Feb. 18, 1954, pg. 152-3
76 Lokos, Who Promoted Peress?, pg. 37
77 For a detailed study of the conflicting Zwicker testimony and Senate correspondence with the Justice Department over perjury action, see Who Promoted Peress?, pg. 44-58
78 See Lokos, Who Promoted Peress?, Chap. VI, pg. 148-56
79 Hearings, Doctor Draft Amendments, Sen. Armed Serv. Comm. Apr. 1, 1954, pg. 12
80 Pg. 247
81 Adams, First-Hand Report, pg. 137, 141, 148, 151
82 Congressional Record, Mar 30, 1950, pg. 4402
83 Senate Report 2050, 82nd Congress, pg. 225
84 Hearings, Institute of Pacific Relations, SISS, pg. 122-3, 4938
85 Ibid., pg. 4938
86 Ibid.
87 Ibid., pg. 122-3; Report, pg. 147-8
88 Congressional Record, Jun. 2, 1950, pg. 8000; Hearings, SISS, pg. 81
89 Congressional Record, Mar. 30, 1950, pg. 4403-4
90 Hearings, State Dept. Employee Loyalty Investigation, Senate Foreign Relations Comm., pg. 226, 263, 269-70
91 Ibid., pg. 267
92 Ibid., pg. 247
93 Ibid., Report, pg. 43
94 Buckley, McCarthy and His Enemies, pg. 97
95 Christopher News Notes, No. 119, April 1962
96 Congressional Record, Aug. 31, 1960, pg. 17407
97 Dodd, Freedom and Foreign Policy, pg. 39
98 Ibid.
99 Crimes Of Khrushchev, HCUA, Part I, pg. 3
100 Ibid., Part II, pg. 2
101 Ibid., Part I, pg. 7
102 Ibid., pg. 1
103 Ibid.
104 Illinois State Journal, Springfield, Illinois, Sep. 29, 1959
105 Cushing, Questions and Answers About Communism, 4th Edition, pg. 230
106 Page numbers refer to Hearings, Communist Threat To The U. S. Through The Caribbean, SISS, 1960-61, 12 Parts
107 Hearings, Communist Threat To The U. S., SISS, pg. 761
108 Ibid., Part 10
109 Time, Jul. 27, 1959
110 Dubois, Fidel Castro, pg. 145
111 Weyl, Red Star Over Cuba, pg. 195
112 Ibid., pg. 17
113 Ibid.
114 Hearings, Communist Threat To The U. S. Through The Caribbean, SISS, pg. 737

Chapter IV

1 Ware, The Sayings of Confucius, pg. 26
2 New York Times, Jan. 25, 1962
3 Kennedy, Foreword, To Turn The Tide, pg. xiv
4 Dallas Times Herald, Mar. 26, 1961
5 The New York Times, Jan. 3, 1962
6 Dallas Morning News, Mar. 5, 1962
7 Human Events, Jun. 23, 1962, pg. 455
8 The New York Times, Jun. 14, 1962
9 The Baltimore Sun, Jun. 18, 1962
10 Reprinted, Congressional Record, Aug. 23, 1961, pg. A6656
11 St. Louis Globe Democrat, Feb. 16, 1961
12 Report, Special Committee to Investigate Tax-Exempt Foundations, 83rd Congress, Dec. 16, 1954, pg. 180-1
13 Rusk, Speech, World Affairs Council, Univ. Of Pa., Jun. 14, 1951
14 Baltimore Sun, Jun. 18, 1962
15 New York Daily News, May 15, 1962
16 Human Events, Dec. 6, 1961, pg. 826
17 Ibid., Jul. 21, 1962, pg. 544
18 Hearings, Communist Threat To U. S. Through Caribbean, SISS, Part 13, pg. 873-9
19 Columnist Edith Roosevelt, Speech, St. Louis, Mo. May 22, 1963
20 Edith Roosevelt, Column, Shreveport Journal, Sep. 15, 1962
21 St. Louis Post Dispatch, Apr. 22, 1961
22 Rickenbacker, National Review, Aug. 13, 1963, pg. 106
23 Hearings, Communist Threat To U. S. Through Caribbean, SISS, Part 13
24 Ibid., pg. 874-5
25 Ibid., pg. 875-8
26 Ibid., pg. 877-8

27 Letter to Gen. Delmar T. Spivey, USA (Ret) as quoted on The Manion Forum broadcast, No. 353, Jul. 2, 1961

28 Letter, SF/131/1 Cuba, Jun. 8, 1961, Paul Hoffman, Managing Director, United Nations Special Fund

29 Congressional Record, May 11, 1961

30 Ibid., Aug. 18, 1961

31 Human Events, Sep. 15, 1962, pg. 691

32 Ibid.

33 Dallas Times Herald, Oct. 6, 1962

34 St. Louis Globe Democrat, Oct. 23, 1962

35 The New York Times, Oct. 6, 1962

36 News & Courier, Charleston, S. C., Dec. 10, 1962; St. Louis Globe Democrat, Dec. 13, 1962; St. Louis Post-Dispatch, Apr. 3, 1963

37 St. Louis Globe Democrat, Jul. 27, 1963

38 Bulletin, Cuban Information Service, Dec. 1, 1962

39 St. Louis Globe Democrat, Jul. 27, 1963

40 St. Louis Post-Dispatch, Mar. 28, 1963

41 Russell, Interview WSB-TV, Atlanta, Ga., St. Louis Globe Democrat, Dec. 12, 1962

42 Kennedy, TV Report To Nation, Jun. 5, 1961, To Turn The Tide, pg. 170-2

43 Kennedy, TV Report To Nation, Jul. 25, 1961, To Turn The Tide, pg. 184

44 Ibid., pg. 183

45 Human Events, Aug. 11, 1961, pg. 510

46 Cong. Thomas Pelly, Human Events, Aug. 25, 1961, pg. 550

47 Dallas Morning News, Jul. 13, 1961

48 Report, Visa Procedures, The Struelens Case, SISS, Aug. 6, 1962, pg. 1

49 Ibid., pg. 1-2; Dodd, Cong. Rec., Aug. 3, 1962, pg. 14528-46; Schuyler, Who Killed The Congo?, Human Events, Aug. 4, 1962, pg. 579; Barron's, Tragedy In The Congo, Human Events, Dec. 22, 1961, pg. 877

50 Report, Visa Procedures, The Struelens Case, SISS, pg. 2

51 New York Times, Sep. 6, 1961

52 Dodd, Congressional Record, Sep. 8, 1961

53 Human Events, Sep. 22, 1961, pg. 622-3

54 Dodd, Congressional Record, Aug. 3, 1962

55 Report, Visa Procedures, The Struelens Case, SISS, pg. 28

56 Dodd, Congressional Record, Sep. 8, 1961

57 Bruce, Congressional Record, Sep. 12, 1961

58 New York Times, Dec. 14, 1961

59 Dr. E. Van den Haag, Report, War In Katanga, American Comm. To Aid Katanga Freedom Fighters

60 Dodd, Congressional Record, Jan. 25, 1962

61 St. Louis Post Dispatch, Dec. 31, 1962

62 Ibid., Dec. 19, 1961

63 Ibid., Apr. 18, 1963

64 Report, The Struelens Case, SISS, 87th Congress, Aug. 6, 1962

65 Ibid., pg. 69-70

66 Ibid., pg. 71

67 Ibid., pg. 50-2

68 Ibid., pg. 48-50

69 Ibid., pg. 65-9

70 Ibid., pg. 69

71 Ibid.

72 Human Events, Sep. 15, 1961, pg. 608

73 St. Louis Post Dispatch, Oct. 16, 1962

74 Kennedy, Inaugural Address, Jan. 20, 1961

75 Johnson, Message to Congress, Nov. 27, 1963

76 Human Events, May 12, 1961, pg. 290

77 Ibid., Jun. 30, 1961, pg. 405-6

78 Ibid., Dec. 1, 1961, pg. 806

79 St. Louis Globe Democrat, Nov. 6-19, 1963

80 Ibid., Jun. 30, 1961, pg. 405

81 Ibid., Apr. 7, 1961, pg. 210

82 Ibid., Mar. 31, 1961, pg. 195

83 Chicago Tribune, as reprinted, Human Events, Sep. 15, 1961, pg. 619

84 Ibid.

85 St. Louis Globe Democrat, Jul. 4, 1963

86 Ibid.

87 Ibid.

88 Editorial, St. Louis Post Dispatch, Aug. 25, 1961

89 St. Louis Post Dispatch, Oct. 7, 1962

90 Human Events, Mar. 24, 1961, pg. 180

91 Report, Proposed Shipment of Ball Bearing Machines To USSR, SISS, Feb. 28, 1961; Hearings Export of Strategic Materials, SISS, Part 1, pg. 26-9

92 Letter, Luther Hodges to Cong. John Moss, Jun. 28, 1961

93 Statement, Gen. Counsel, P. O. Dept. Concerning Foreign Propaganda, Undated

94 Congressional Record, Mar. 1, 1962, pg. 2828

95 Human Events, Oct. 13, 1961, pg. 671

96 Hearings on SR 191, Senate Armed Services Committee, 1961

97 Ibid.

98 Ibid.

99 Human Events, Aug. 11, 1961, pg. 510

100 Ibid.

101 Ibid.

102 Report, Military Cold War Education and Speech Review Policies, Sen. Armed Services Comm., Oct. 19, 1962, 203 pages

103 Ibid., Part VII
104 Hearings on SR 191, Sen. Armed Services Comm., 1961, pg. 53, 123
105 National Review, Nov. 18, 1961
106 NBC News, Three Star Extra, Sep. 14, 1961, 6:45 PM EDT
107 Letter, J. Herbert Stone, Regional Forester to Forest Supervisor, Okanogan National Forest, Jul. 12, 1961
108 Letter, Leo D. Caron, Forester, to J. Herbert Stone, Regional Forester, Jul. 26, 1961
109 Kennedy, State of the Union message, Jan. 29, 1961
110 Report, New Drive Against The Anti-Communist Program, SISS, Jul. 11, 1961, pg. 3
111 Ibid., pg. 32
112 The Worker, Jul. 14, 1961
113 Hearings, New Drive Against The Anti-Communist Program, SISS, pg. 44-5
114 Ibid., pg. 33-7, 38-44, 51-6, 63, 65-7, 69-70
115 Ibid., pg. 75
116 New York Times, Nov. 19, 1961
117 Hoover, Speech, The Faith To Be Free, NBC-TV, Dec. 7, 1961
118 Document 7277, U. S. Department of State, Sep. 1961, pg. 5-8
119 Ibid., pg. 19
120 Sports Afield, August 1963
121 Tower, Congressional Record, Jan. 29, 1962
122 Ibid.
123 Clark, Congressional Record, Mar. 1, 1962, pg. 2936
124 1962 Annual Report, Arms Control & Disarmament Agency, pg. 57-83
125 Ibid.
126 Arms Control and Disarmament Act, Sep. 26, 1961, Sec. 2a, b, c, d
127 1962 Annual Report, Arms Control & Disarmament Agency, pg. 46-8
128 St. Louis Globe Democrat, Mar. 27, 1963
129 1962 Annual Report, Arms Control & Disarmament Agency pg. 58
130 St. Louis Post Dispatch, Mar. 2, 1963
131 St. Louis Globe Democrat, Dec. 18-19, 1962
132 Ibid., Mar. 3, 1963
133 St. Louis Post Dispatch, Mar. 28, 1963
134 Newsweek, Feb. 11, 1963
135 St. Louis Globe Democrat, Dec. 5, 1962
136 New York Times, Nov. 16, 1961
137 Saturday Evening Post, Jun. 23, 1963
138 Human Events, Aug. 10, 1963, pg. 9
139 St. Louis Post Dispatch, Sep. 10, 1962
140 St. Louis Globe Democrat, Dec. 10, 1963
141 Dodd, Congressional Record, Feb. 21, 1963, pg. 2662
142 Ibid., pg. 2663-4
143 Ibid.
144 Ibid., pg. 2661
145 St. Louis Globe Democrat, Aug. 7, 1963
146 Ibid., Jul. 6, 1963
147 Ibid., Mar. 8, 1963
148 Congressional Record, Aug. 10, 1962, pg. 15093-4
149 St. Louis Post Dispatch, Aug. 5, 1963
150 Kennedy, Message To Senate On Test Ban Treaty, St. Louis Post Dispatch, Aug. 8, 1963
151 St. Louis Post Dispatch, Nov. 28, 1961
152 Ibid.
153 Ibid.
154 Ibid., Aug. 12, 1963
155 Ibid., Jan. 12, 1961
156 Washington Star, Jul. 12, 1963
157 Kennedy, Message To Senate On Test Ban Treaty, St. Louis Post Dispatch, Aug. 8, 1963
158 Congressional Record, May 31, 1955, pg. A3764
159 Chicago Tribune, Jun. 18, 1962
160 Ibid.
161 Hearings, Military Cold War Education and Speech Review Policies, Senate Armed Services Comm., Jun. 4, 1962, Part 6, pg. 2805
162 Lenin, Selected Works, Vol. VIII, pg. 298
163 St. Louis Post Dispatch, Sep. 18, 1955
164 Goldwater, Why Not Victory? pg. 150 and jacket
165 Chicago Tribune, Jun. 17-18, 1962
166 Ibid.
167 Ibid.
168 Human Events, Sep. 22, 1961, pg. 623
169 Morton, Congressional Record, Feb. 22, 1963
170 Congressional Record, Feb. 6, 1962, pg. A882
171 Harlan Cleveland, WRC-TV, Dec. 22, 1962, 6-6:30 PM EST

Chapter V

1 Report, Communist Indoctrination — Its Significance To Americans, Major Wm. E. Mayer, U. S. Army Psychiatrist, pg. 14-5
2 Ibid., pg. 11-12
3 J. Edgar Hoover, Communist Illusion and Democratic Reality, Dec. 1959, pg. 10-1
4 Report, Communist Indoctrination, Major Wm. Mayer, pg. 7, 29-31
5 Ibid., pg. 30
6 Ibid., pg. 33-4
7 Ibid., pg. 39-41
8 Ibid., pg. 22
9 Ibid., pg. 18-9
10 Ibid., pg. 12
11 Ibid., pg. 28
12 Ibid.
13 Ibid., pg. 6
14 Ibid., pg. 38
15 J. Edgar Hoover, Congressional Record, Oct. 10, 1962, pg. A7547

16 Illegitimacy, U. S. Dept. of Health, Education and Welfare, Apr. 1960, Table 2, pg. 10

Chapter VI

1 The Tablet, Aug. 11, 1959
2 Dworkin, Dewey On Education, pg. 19-32
3 Ibid., pg. 22
4 Ibid., pg. 25
5 America's Future, 1956
6 Gordon, What's Happened To Our Schools?, pg. 16
7 Ibid.
8 Schlesinger, The Age Of Roosevelt, pg. 156, 176, 563
9 British Fabian Society, 49th Annual Report, 1932
10 Report, Special House Committee To Investigate Tax Exempt Foundations, 83rd Congress, 1954, pg. 137, 153
11 Ibid., pg. 137
12 The New Republic, Jul. 29, 1936, pg. 343
13 Progressive Education, April 1932, pg. 261-2
14 Ibid.
15 Ibid.
16 Counts, The Soviet Challenge To America, pg. 324
17 Counts, Foreword to translation of New Russia's Primer, Ilin, Houghton, 1931
18 Ibid.
19 Counts, Dare The Schools Build A New Social Order, pg. 28-9
20 Hearings, Special House Committee To Investigate Tax-Exempt Foundations, 83rd Congress, 1954, pg. 482
21 Rugg, The Great Technology, pg. 32
22 Ibid., pg. 271
23 Ibid., pg. 258
24 Report, Spec. Comm. To Investigate Tax-Exempt Foundations, 83rd Cong. pg. 150
25 Ibid.
26 Frontiers of Democracy, Dec. 15, 1942, pg. 75-81
27 Report, Spec. Comm. To Investigate Tax Exempt Foundations, 83rd Cong. pg. 154
28 Ibid.
29 Ibid., pg. 155
30 Ibid., pg. 156
31 See pages
32 The Social Frontier, Feb. 1936, pg. 134-5
33 Ginn and Company, 1950
34 Harcourt, Brace and Company, 1950
35 Harper & Brothers, 1951
36 Allyn and Bacon, 1951
37 D. C. Heath & Company, 1948
38 D. C. Heath & Company, 1951
39 The New Our New Friends, Scott, Foresman & Co., pg. 156-9
40 Ibid., pg. 159
41 Report, President's Commission on High Education, 1947, Vol. III, pg. 48
42 UNESCO, Towards World Understanding, Vol. I, pg. 6

43 Harper and Company, 1955
44 NEA Journal, April 1946, pg. 175
45 Hoover, Speech, Freedoms Foundation Awards Ceremony, Valley Forge, Pa., Feb. 22, 1962, reprinted, Congressional Record, Mar. 1, 1962, pg. 2906
46 Henry Holt and Co., 1951
47 McGraw-Hill Book Co., 1952
48 See page 29
49 Morris, No Wonder We Are Losing, pg. 3-19
50 Ibid., pg. 17
51 Congressional Record, Oct. 10, 1962, pg. 21831-2
52 Sweezy vs. New Hampshire, 354 US 234 (1957)
53 Slochower vs. Board of Education of New York, 350 US 551 (1956)
54 The Pasadena Story, NEA Commission For Defense Of Democracy Through Education, Jun. 1951, pg. 23
55 See page 104
56 Editorial, Tulsa World, Mar. 27, 1962
57 Editorial, Tulsa Tribune, Apr. 26, 1962

Chapter VII

1 Oxnam, Personalities In Social Reform, pg. 99
2 Bundy, Collectivism In The Churches, pg. 97-8
3 Oxnam, Personalities In Social Reform, pg. 76-7
4 Bundy, Collectivism In The Churches, pg. 101
5 Oxnam, Personalities in Social Reform, pg. 73-4
6 Investigation of Communist Activities In New York City Areas, Part VI, HCUA, Jul. 7, 1953, pg. 2075-7
7 Guide To Subversive Organizations, HCUA, Dec. 1, 1961, pg. 107
8 St. Louis Post Dispatch, Sep. 25, 1961
9 Investigation of Communist Activities In N. Y., HCUA, Part VI, Jul. 7, 1953, pg. 2075-7
10 Ibid., Part VII, pg. 2169
11 Ibid., pg. 2177
12 A Yearbook of the Church and Social Service In The U. S., 1916, Federal Council of Churches, pg. 23
13 Investigation of Communist Activities In The New York Area, HCUA, Jul. 7, 1953, Part VI, 2092
14 Testimony of Bishop G. Bromley Oxnam, HCUA, Jul. 21, 1952, pg. 3725
15 Issues Presented By The Air Reserve Training Manual, Hearings, HCUA, Feb. 25, 1960, pg. 1303
16 Ibid., pg. 1288
17 The Communist Party Line, J. Edgar Hoover, SISS, 1961
18 Study Conference on Churches and World Order, National Council of Churches, Cleveland, Ohio, Oct. 30, 1953

19 Fifth World Order Study Conference, Cleveland, Ohio, Nov. 18-21, 1958

20 Statement, General Board, National Council of Churches, Feb. 22, 1961

21 Ibid.

22 Presbyterian Life, Apr. 1, 1963

23 110 Government Place, Cincinnati 2, Ohio

24 Hearings, Issues Presented By the ARTM, HCUA, Feb. 25, 1960, pg. 1303-4

25 Congressional Record, March 3, 1960, pg. 3981

26 Holy Bible, R.S.V., Isaiah 7:14

27 Christian Century, Mar. 15, 1961

28 Ibid.

29 Ibid., Mar. 7, 1962, pg. 286

30 Adult Student, Sept. 1962, pg. 14-38

31 Adult Student, General Board of Education, The Methodist Church, Sept. 1962, pg. 15

32 Ibid., pg. 20

33 Ibid., pg. 20-21

34 Ibid., pg. 23

35 Surprising Beliefs of Our Young Ministers, Redbook, August 1961

36 Workers With Youth, Gen. Board of Educ., The Methodist Church, Sep. 1962, pg. 5

37 Ibid.

38 Morrell, Of Bread And Circuses, Facts Forum, Feb. 1956

39 The Rightist Crisis In Our Churches, Look, Apr. 24, 1962

40 Speech, Communism and Religion in the U. S., Wm. Sullivan, Asst. Dir., FBI, Dallas, Texas, Oct. 19, 1961

41 Communist Propaganda and the Christian Pulpit, J. Edgar Hoover, Christianity Today, Oct. 24, 1960

42 Ibid.

Chapter VIII

1 Trohan, Human Events, Dec. 5, 1961; Oct. 20, 1961, pg. 705

2 See pages 11-12, 50-53

3 N. Y. Times News Service, St. Louis Post Dispatch, Jan. 25, 1962

4 Ibid.

5 Ibid.

6 Ibid.

7 See pages 50-53

8 The Wanderer, Sept. 27, 1962, pg. 4

9 Guide to Subversive Organizations, HCUA, Dec. 1, 1961, pg. 121

10 Ibid., pg. 61

11 Select Committee to Investigate Tax-Exempt Foundations, 82nd Congress, Dec. 23, 1952, pg. 725

12 Hearings, Military Cold War Education and Speech Review Policies, Senate Armed Services Committee, 87th Congress, Part IV, pg. 1491

13 See page 179

14 Who's Who In America, 1961

15 Ibid.
    Your Child, pg. 98

16 Romerstein, Communism and

17 Petition of Clemency to President Kennedy for Carl Braden and Frank Wilkinson, Christmas 1961

18 New York Times, Jan. 2, 1962

19 Ibid., Feb. 22, 1962

20 Romerstein, Communism and Your Child, pg. 99

21 See page 30-31

22 See page 43-44

23 National Review, Nov. 4, 1961

24 Donovan, Eisenhower, The Inside Story, pg. 247-49

25 Chicago Tribune, Oct. 10, 1947 quoted by Hughes, Prejudice and The Press, pg. 86

26 Hughes, Prejudice and the Press, pg. 14-15

27 Ibid., pg. 285

28 Ibid., pg. 33

29 Buckley, McCarthy And His Enemies, pg. 141; Congressional Record, Nov. 14, 1951

30 Monthly Bulletin, John Birch Society, Apr. 1, 1961, pg. 6

31 Ibid., pg. 10-11

32 Church News, official publication of the Mormon Church, Mar. 16, 1963

33 Report, Senate Factfinding Subcommittee on Un-American Activities, California State Legislature, Jun. 1963, pg. 37

34 Ibid., pg. 42-3

35 Ibid., pg. 61-2

36 Pourade, New Disturbing Journalistic Era Opens, Human Events, Oct. 13, 1961, pg. 673-78

37 Ibid., pg. 673

38 Human Events, Apr. 7, 1961, pg. 213

39 Fabian News, Oct. 1909, pg. 78, quoted in Keynes at Harvard, pg. 46

40 Shafer, The Turning Of The Tides, pg. 2

41 Congressional Record, Jan. 11, 1962, pg. A76

42 Ibid., pg. A76, A81, A82

43 Ibid., pg. A70

44 Ibid.

45 Ibid.

46 Ibid.

47 NEA Journal, Mar. 1935, quoted, Bending The Twig, pg. 55-6

48 Lattimore, Ordeal By Slander, quoted, Human Events, Feb. 17, 1961, pg. 111

49 Human Events, Feb. 17, 1961, pg. 111

50 Ibid.

51 Ibid., pg. 110

52 See page 72

53 Human Events, Oct. 20, 1961, pg. 692

54 Smith, The State Of Europe, quoted, National Review, Dec. 31, 1962

55 Smith, The State Of Europe, pg. 393

56 Ibid., pg. 395-6

57 Smith, Last Train From Berlin, quoted, National Review, Dec. 31, 1962

58 National Review, Dec. 31, 1962, pg. 511

59 Human Events, Feb. 10, 1962, pg. 109
60 National Review, Jul. 3, 1962, pg. 473
61 Human Events, Jul. 14, 1961, pg. 446
62 St. Louis Globe Democrat, Jan. 13, 1962
63 See page 144-45
64 Reprinted by Human Events, Aug. 11, 1961, pg. 525
65 St. Louis Globe Democrat, Feb. 22, 1961
66 St. Louis Post Dispatch, Oct. 3, 1962
67 United Press International News Wire, Sep. 30, 1962, 11:23 PM CDT
68 Speech, Brig. Gen. Clyde Watts, USA (Ret), Alton, Ill., Apr. 28, 1963
69 See pages 30, 43-44, 50-53
70 Hunter, An Analysis of the Editorial Policies of The St. Louis Post Dispatch, Dec. 3, 1961
71 Ibid., Appendix I, pg. 21-42
72 Ibid., pg. 42-51

Chapter IX

1 Chisholm, Psychiatry, February 1946
2 Ibid.
3 Chisholm, Speech, Conference on Education, Asilomar, Calif., Sep. 11, 1954
4 Psychiatry, Feb. 1946
5 Ibid.
6 Mental Health and World Citizenship, Int. Cong. On Mental Health, London, 1948, pg. 8
7 Psychiatry, February 1946
8 Overstreet, The Great Enterprise, pg. 110
9 Ibid., pg. 115
10 Psychiatry, February 1946
11 Ibid.
12 See page 157
13 A Draft Act Covering Hospitalization Of The Mentally Ill, Section 6a
14 Ibid., Sec. 9b, Sec. 9f
15 Ibid., Sec. 9f
16 Maisel, Reader's Digest, Feb. 1962, pg. 98
17 Ibid.
18 DeToledano, Seeds Of Treason, pg. 272
19 Telegram Tribune, San Luis Obispo, Calif., Mar. 14, 1957
20 Report, The Bang-Jensen Case, Senate Internal Security Subcommittee, Sept. 14, 1961, pg. 1, 3, 8-17
21 Ibid., pg. 3, 27-39
22 Ibid., pg. 43
23 Ibid., pg. 17
24 Congressional Record, May 17, 1962, pg. 8065-8071
25 Ibid.
26 See page 152-53
27 Washington (D. C.) Star, Oct. 7, 1962
28 Ibid.
29 Hearing, Court of Federal Judge Chas. Clayton, Nov. 20-21, 1962

30 Yearbook of Neurology-Psychiatry for 1958-59, pg. 369
31 Ibid.
32 Preface, International Conciliations, Mar. 1948
33 Law Enforcement Looks At Mental Health, Law And Order, March 1961, page 25-6
34 Boroff, Coronet, August 1961
35 Ibid., pg.
36 Ibid.
37 Life, Sept. 21, 1962
38 Congressional Record, Oct. 10, 1962, pg. 21835
39 Ibid.
40 Congressional Record, Oct. 10, 1962, pg. 21837-38
41 Life, Sept. 21, 1962
42 Ibid.

Chapter X

1 Lenin, Leftwing Communism, An Infantile Disorder, pg. 38
2 Hearings, Special Committee on Un-American Activities, 75th Congress, 3rd Session, Vol. II, pg. 1659
3 Ibid.
4 Ibid., Vol. I, pg. 248-251
5 Congressional Record, Sept. 22, 1950, pg. A6831
6 Report, Interlocking Subversion, SISS, Jul. 30, 1953, pg. 5
7 Congressional Record, Sept. 22, 1950, pg. A6831
8 Hearings, Communism In Labor Unions, HCUA, 80th Congress, 1st Session, page 51-52
9 The Worker, June 3, 1962
10 Ibid.
11 Foreword, The Naked Communist, Skousen
12 Gompers Statement, Jan. 22, 1917, Human Events, Mar. 10, 1961
13 Shafer, The Turning Of The Tides, pg. 2
14 Gompers, Speech, 1903, Human Events, Dec. 22, 1961, pg. 874
15 Partisan Review, May-June 1947, Cong. Record, Feb. 6, 1962, pg. A881
16 Ibid., pg. A883
17 Hearings, Special Committee On Un-American Activities, 78th Cong., Appendix, Part IX, pg. 261-6
18 Congressional Record, Feb. 6, 1962, pg. A883
19 COPE Manual, How To Win
20 See page 40-41
21 Morris, No Wonder We Are Losing, pg. 196-9
22 Ibid.
23 Report, 100 Things You Should Know About Communism, HCUA, pg. 81
24 Ibid.
25 Hearings, Communist Infiltration in the U. S. Government, 1953, HCUA, pg. 1649-84
26 Burnham, The Web Of Subversion, pg. 66
27 Report, Interlocking Subversion In Government Departments, SISS, Jul. 30, 1953, pg. 40-3

Chapter XI

1 Spec. Comm. To Investigate Tax-Exempt Foundations, 82nd Cong. (Cox Comm.)
2 Spec. Comm. To Investigate Tax-Exempt Foundations, 83rd Cong. (Reece Comm.)
3 Report, Reece Committee, Dec. 16, 1954, pg. 1-4
4 Fosdick, The Story of the Rockefeller Foundations, pg. 29
5 See page 177
6 Keppel, The Foundation: Its Place In American Life, pg. 107
7 Hearings, Reece Committee, 1954, pg. 475
8 Report, Reece Committee, pg. 85-7
9 Hearings, Reece Committee, pg. 945
10 Report, Reece Committee, pg. 117
11 Ibid., pg. 118
12 Ibid., pg. 120, 135-41, 149
13 Ibid., pg. 137
14 Ibid., pg. 154-6
15 Ibid.
16 Ibid., pg. 156-7
17 Hearings, Reece Committee, pg. 934
18 Report, Reece Committee, pg. 32
19 Ibid., pg. 185
20 Ibid.
21 Report, Interlocking Subversion, SISS, Jul. 30, 1953, pg. 6
22 Report, Reece Committee, pg. 41, pg. 179-80
23 See page 179
24 Report, Reece Committee, pg. 180
25 Ibid., pg. 175
26 American Legion Post 140, 3905 Powers Ferry Road, Atlanta, Ga., $1 per copy
27 Report, Reece Committee, pg. 200-1
28 Ibid., pg. 186
29 Prospects For America, Rockefeller Bros. Panel Reports, pg. XXIV, 466-7
30 Ibid., pg. 39
31 Ibid., pg. 46
32 Report, Reece Committee, pg. 111-4
33 Ibid.
34 Daily News, Philadelphia, Pa., Aug. 7, 1962
35 Report, Reece Committee, pg. 186-7
36 Ibid., pg. 186
37 Ibid., pg. 137
38 Ibid., pg. 136
39 Ibid., pg. 41

Chapter XII

1 Mill, Essay On Representative Government
2 Congressional Record, Oct. 10, 1961
3 Harris, Saving American Capitalism
4 Shaw, Intelligent Woman's Guide To Socialism and Capitalism, pg. 94
5 Thomas, A Socialist's Faith, pg. 117

6 Harrod, Life Of John Maynard Keynes, pg. 462
7 Veritas, Keynes At Harvard, pg. 86-87
8 Strachey, Contemporary Capitalism, pg. 310
9 Ibid., pg. 287-288
10 Ibid., pg. 284
11 Keynes At Harvard, pg. 34-35
12 Toledano and Lasky, Seeds of Treason, pg. 236
13 Goldwater, Conscience of a Conservative, pg. 25
14 Chase, A New Deal, pg. 163
15 Who's Who In America, 1961
16 Report, Interlocking Subversion, SISS, Jul. 30, 1953, pg. 44
17 Ibid.
18 Ibid.
19 Ibid., pg. 4
20 Hearings, House Select Committee To Investigate Certain Statements of Dr. William Wirt, 73rd Congress, 2nd Session, April 10 and 17, 1934
21 Ibid.
22 Ibid.
23 Ibid.
24 Ibid.
25 Ibid.
26 Ibid.
27 Ibid.
28 Ibid.
29 Ibid.
30 Ibid.
31 Hearings, Interlocking Subversion, SISS, Jun. 23, 1953, pg. 823-40
32 Committee On Government Operations, U. S. Senate, Jul. 23, 1956
33 Ibid., pg. 43, 160, 343, 345
34 Wilbur and Hyde, The Hoover Policies, quoted by Lyons in The Herbert Hoover Story, pg. 305-06
35 Lyons, The Herbert Hoover Story, Chapters 19-21
36 Ibid., pg. 307
37 Ibid.
38 Ibid., pg. 308
39 Ibid., pg. 292
40 Garrett, The People's Pottage, pg. 7
41 Ibid., pg. 11
42 A. L. A. Schechter vs. U. S., 295 US 495 (1935)
43 Gordon, Nine Men Against America, pg. 14
44 Schechter vs. U. S., Carter vs. Carter Coal Co., 298 US 495 (1936) U. S. vs. Butler, 297 US1 (1936)
45 Gordon, Nine Men Against America, pg. 15
46 Ibid., pg. 16-25
47 A. B. Kirschbaum vs. Walling, 316 US 517 (1942)
48 Wickard vs. Filburn, 317 US 131 (1942)
49 Hearing, Limitation Of Apellate Jurisdiction of The U. S. Supreme Court, SISS, Feb. 19-21, 25-28, 1958, Appendix IV, Part II
50 Gordon, Nine Men Against America

51 Congressional Record, Jun. 26, 1962
52 Manuel Enterprises Case, Congressional Record, Jun. 26, 1962, pg. 10944
53 Chart, Congressional Record, May 2, 1962, pg. 7028-31
54 Ibid.
55 Ibid.
56 Speech, reprinted in Root's Brainwashing In The High Schools, pg. 205-07
57 Ibid.
58 Ibid.
59 Congressional Record, Sep. 22, 1950, pg. A6832
60 Ibid.
61 Ibid., Jan. 16, 1962, pg. A192
62 Morris, No Wonder We Are Losing, pg. 174-6
63 Aims of the ADA, Part II, Los Angeles Times, Sep. 4, 1961
64 Adams, First Hand Report, pg. 31-2
65 Taft, How I Lost The Nomination, Human Events, Dec. 2, 1959
66 Public Debt of the U. S., 1870-1962, Treasury Dept., The World Almanac, 1963
67 The New York Times, Jan. 18, 1960
68 Congressional Record, Oct. 5, 1962
69 Goldwater, Conscience of a Conservative, pg. 66
70 Congressional Record, Apr. 8, 1957
71 Public Debt of the U. S., 1870-1962, Treasury Dept., The World Almanac, 1963
72 The ADA: Its Impact on The New Frontier, Part I, Los Angeles Times, Sep. 3, 1961
73 Congressional Record, Feb. 6, 1962, pg. A881

Chapter XIII

1 Washington, Farewell Address, 1796
2 Report, Spec. Comm. To Investigate Tax-Exempt Foundations, Dec. 16, 1954, pg. 169
3 Hearings, Military Cold War Education, Sen. Armed Service Comm., Apr. 4, 1962, pg. 1474
4 Ibid.
5 Congressional Record, Jul. 28, 1945
6 Report, Interlocking Subversion, SISS, Jul. 30, 1953, pg. 6-10; Foreign Relations of the U. S., The Conferences at Malta and Yalta, 1945, Dept. of State, pg. 44, 58, 794
7 As quoted, Widener, Behind the UN Front, pg. 57
8 Congressional Record, Mar. 1, 1962, pg. 2937
9 Hearings, Activities of U. S. Citizens Employed By The UN, SISS, Dec. 1952
10 Document AT/DEC/32, UN Administrative Tribunal, Sep. 1, 1953
11 Morris, No Wonder We Are Losing, pg. 154
12 Report, The Bang-Jensen Case, SISS, Sep. 14, 1961, pg. 16
13 Ibid., pg. 17
14 Ibid., pg. 21
15 Ibid.
16 See page 32
17 St. Louis Globe Democrat, Feb. 22, 1963
18 Ibid.
19 Report, U. S. Foreign Assistance, Jul. 1945-Jun. 1961, Agency for International Development, Mar. 21, 1962, pg. 9, 12, 13, 17, 20, 24, 25, 31
20 Lane, I Saw Poland Betrayed, pg. 67, 68, 102
21 Report, Interlocking Subversion, SISS, Jul. 30, 1953, pg. 10-12
22 See page 60
23 Newsweek, Nov. 13, 1961
24 Speech, Upsala, Sweden, May 1962
25 New York Times, Oct. 5, 1961
26 Congressional Record, Jan. 15, 1962, pg. 198
27 Ibid., Jan. 15, 1962; Apr. 11, 1962
28 Ibid., Jan. 15, 1962
29 Ibid.
30 Ibid.
31 Ibid.
32 Ibid.
33 Annual Report of the Council on Foreign Relations, 1960, pg. 57-70
34 Report, Spec. House Comm. To Investigate Tax-Exempt Foundations, 1954, pg. 176
35 Ibid., pg. 177
36 Smoot, The Invisible Government. Dan Smoot Report, Vol. 7, Nos. 24-31
37 References to CFR membership in this chapter, except as noted, are based on membership rosters published in the CFR Annual Reports for 1960 and 1961.
38 Encyclopedia Brittanica, 1959, Vol. 22, pg. 705-12
39 Smoot, The Invisible Government, pg. 168-71
40 Congressional Record, Feb. 6, 1962, pg. A883
41 Ibid.
42 Time, Mar. 16, 1942
43 Fed. Council of Churches, 1946 Report, pg. 240-6, as quoted, Bundy, Collectivism in the Churches, pg. 174-7
44 Ibid., pg. 175
45 See page 89-91
46 Congressional Record, Feb. 6, 1962, pg. A883
47 Prospects For America, Rockefeller Bros. Panel Reports, pg. 39
48 Schlesinger, The Big Decision — Private Indulgence or National Power, pg. 13
49 Bloomfield, A World Effectively Controlled By The UN, ARPA-IDA Study Memo No. 7, Mar. 10, 1962, Dept. of State Contract SCC 28270, Feb. 24, 1961
50 Congressional Record, Feb. 23, 1954, pg. 2014ff

51 Ibid.
52 Public Debt of the U. S. 1870-1962, U. S. Treasury, The World Almanac, 1963
53 Report, U. S. Foreign Assistance, Agency for Inter. Dev., Mar. 21, 1962
54 See pages 219-220
55 Campaigne, American Might and Soviet Myth, pg. 27-8
56 Ibid., pg. 31-2, and Gutierrez, The Tragedy of Bolivia, pg. 57-74
57 Stalin, Marxism and the National Colonial Question, pg. 114-5
58 St. Louis Globe Democrat, Jul. 6, 1963
59 Ibid.
60 Cong. Abraham Multer, (D-NY), HR 6900, 87th Congress
61 Bess, Silent Weapon of the Cold War, Saturday Evening Post, Oct. 18, 1958
62 Ibid.
63 See page 30
64 Gutierrez, The Tragedy of Bolivia, pg. 71
65 Ibid., pg. 75
66 Constitution of the United States, Article VI, Par. 2
67 3 Dall 199, as quoted, MacBride, Treaties vs. the Constitution, pg. 41
68 252 US 416 (1920)
69 315 US 203 (1942)
70 Congressional Record, Feb. 23, 1954, pg. 2014ff
71 Ibid.
72 Treaty Against Genocide, quoted, MacBride, Treaties vs. the Constitution, pg. 22
73 U. S. Constitution, Amendments I, VI
74 Congressional Record, Jan. 28, 1954, pg. 899
75 The 1954 Bricker Amendment, Section One

76 St. Louis Post Dispatch, May 26, 1962
77 Joint Declaration Against War Propaganda, Par. 1, 2, 5
78 Statute of the International Court of Justice, Article 59
79 Ibid., Article 60
80 Charter of the United Nations, Article 94
81 See pages 65-68

Chapter XIV

1 Patrick Henry, Liberty or Death Speech, Virginia House of Burgesses, 1775
2 Walter, How To Fight Communism, HCUA, 88th Congress
3 Hoover, Letter To Law Enforcement Officials, Apr. 1, 1961
4 Hoover, Communist Illusion and Democratic Reality, Dept. of Justice, Dec. 1959
5 Walter, How To Fight Communism, HCUA
6 Ibid.
7 Peters, Manual on Organization, Communist Party, USA, pg. 57
8 Hall, Political Parties and the 1964 Elections, The Worker, Jun. 23, 1963
9 Ibid.
10 St. Louis Globe Democrat, Jul. 15, 1963
11 St. Louis Post Dispatch, Jul. 19, 1963
12 Basler, Collected Works of Abraham Lincoln, Vol. 1, pg. 201-3
13 Hoover, Speech to DAR, Apr. 22, 1954, as quoted: Report, Spec. Comm. To Investigate Tax-Exempt Foundations, 83rd Congress, Dec. 16, 1954, pg. 114
14 Hoover, Letter to Law Enforcement Officials, Mar. 1, 1960

INDEX